ROSIE LEWIS

Broken

A traumatised girl.
Her troubled brother.
Their shocking secret.

HARPER
element

Certain details in this story, including names, places and dates, have been changed to protect the family's privacy.

HarperElement
An imprint of HarperCollins*Publishers*
1 London Bridge Street
London SE1 9GF

www.harpercollins.co.uk

First published by HarperElement 2018

1 3 5 7 9 10 8 6 4 2

© Rosie Lewis 2018

Rosie Lewis asserts the moral right to be
identified as the author of this work

A catalogue record of this book is
available from the British Library

ISBN 978-0-00-824280-0

Printed and bound in Great Britain by
CPI Group (UK) Ltd, Croydon

MIX
Paper from
responsible sources
FSC
www.fsc.org
FSC™ C007454

This book is produced from independently certified FSC paper
to ensure responsible forest management

For more information visit: www.harpercollins.co.uk/green

Broken

By the same author

Helpless (e-short)

Trapped

A Small Boy's Cry (e-short)

Two More Sleeps (e-short)

Betrayed

Unexpected (e-short)

Torn

Taken

Prologue

July 2014

Archie opens his eyes and blinks. For a second he wonders where he is, then he realises and his tummy flips over. Something hard is digging in his side. It feels cold and pointy, like one of his Transformers. There's something wrong with his back as well. Not an ache exactly, but it feels funny and wrong.

Cold, that's what it is. He tries rolling over but a pain shoots down his shoulder and his head begins to hurt. It feels as if his skin is stuck to the wooden floor. Where's his top? He can't remember taking it off but his brain is fuzzy. He shakes his head and tries to think. If he can just get back to his room, maybe he can work it out. There's a clinking noise as he tries to roll again. He freezes and holds his breath. As his eyes adjust to the half-light he realises there's a pile of empty glass bottles wedged between his body and the bed.

He begins to ease himself away but stops suddenly and cocks his head. Someone is snoring, someone close by, and there are other sounds as well. Softer sounds. Like people breathing in and out. How many, he can't tell. He tries to keep track but all the sounds keep tripping over each other and mixing him up.

If there are just two or three of them he might risk creeping back to his room – he wants to check that Bobbi's okay – but if there are more and one of them wakes up … no, he can't chance it. Not after what happened before.

If only he could decide what to do.

And then it starts. A stirring. A swishing noise, then a thud. A wire of fear flashes through his tummy. Strange scary shadows rise above him and he holds his breath, shrinking back into the cold floor.

The shapes move over one another, two, then three, then more. All making a tangled, groaning mess. There's a strange smell as well. Sweat and booze and something musty that makes his throat burn. Then he hears a woman's voice. She sounds sad, frightened. His stomach lurches and there's a vile taste in his mouth. All he wants to do is run back to his room and to Bobbi. With a stab of shame, he realises that he's too frightened to move.

The shadows and the noises, they make him feel sick, make his tummy roll. Somehow, though, he can't tear his eyes away. Biting down on his lower lip, silent tears roll down his cheeks.

Chapter One

'You can't miss it, love,' the elderly gentleman assured me, pointing towards the complicated one-way system I'd just escaped from. It was New Year's Day 2015 and I was on my way to meet a nine-year-old boy named Archie Brady and his five-year-old sister, Bobbi. The siblings had been temporarily accommodated by Joan Oakley, a foster carer who had accepted the referral four days earlier. 'Follow the road round as far as the greengrocer's then take an immediate left. Straight over the next roundabout, under the railway bridge and Bob's your uncle.'

I thanked him distractedly, trying to get my bearings. I performed a U-turn on the icy road, hoping that this time I wouldn't get tangled up in the endless maze of side streets around the town centre. It was already 10 a.m. and I wanted to have a quick handover chat with Joan and make it back home before lunchtime. One thing I've learned over the last twelve years of fostering is that car journeys and fretful children are a toxic mix. Adding hunger to the equation would be a bit like tossing a stick of dynamite into the interior of my Fiat and hoping for the best.

The children were bound to feel uncertain about another move so quickly after the last and I wanted to do everything I could to lessen their anxiety. It's generally acknowledged that any change in carer should take place as early in the day as possible. That way the child has a chance to acclimatise to their new surroundings before climbing into an unfamiliar bed.

Joan was keen to bring an end to the unexpected placement as well, by all accounts. 'She's tearing her hair out' were the actual words the social worker from the placements team used when I spoke to her the day before. Apparently Joan already had her hands full caring for a baby with neonatal abstinence syndrome (NAS). She had agreed to take the siblings as a favour after the out-of-hours team had been unable to get hold of the foster carer on their emergency rota.

Like me, Joan was a short-term or task-based foster carer. Our 'job' is a temporary one but placements can last anything from one night to four years. Short-term foster carers support the child from the moment they're removed from home and through the uncertain stage when their birth family is being assessed by the local authority. Once a final judgment has been made by the courts, foster carers help to manage the child's transition either back to their birth family or onto permanency with long-term foster or kinship carers or an adoptive family.

At least, being a bank holiday, the roads were free of the usual weekday traffic, and I arrived at Joan's house a little over ten minutes later. As I walked across her driveway, where a Ford Focus full of child car seats was parked, my eye was drawn by the flicker of a curtain at one of the windows on the second floor. I looked up as I rang the doorbell and caught a glimpse of blonde hair.

'Rosie, you're just how I pictured you,' Joan said warmly, holding the door open with one hand, the other cradled around the small bump strapped to her chest. Around sixty or so, Joan wore a cheery expression, despite the dark circles under her eyes. We had never met before, but knew of each other through a social worker who worked at Bright Heights, the fostering agency I was registered with. I had heard that Joan was a well-respected carer and rarely had a vacancy.

'Sounds ominous,' I joked as I wiped my feet on the doormat. Joan smiled and bobbed her way along the hall to the sitting room. It was a routine I'd been through several times before with newborns who were withdrawing from drugs. Babies with substance addiction – known as neonatal abstinence syndrome – often need the constant comfort of a cuddle during their first few weeks of life because the pain of withdrawal, the jitters, stomach cramps and fever can be intense.

The sitting room was cosy, the lights woven around the mantelpiece casting a cheery glow on the peach-coloured walls. There was no sign of the siblings, but distant chatter and a thump overhead suggested they were upstairs. I nodded towards her middle. 'You've got a tiny one there.'

She eased the sling down an inch. I caught a glimpse of dark hair and the tiny curve of a delicate ear before the baby began to squall and Joan was on the move again. 'Two weeks old and still only five pounds,' she said, swinging her shoulders from side to side. 'I heard you'd adopted recently. Megan, isn't it? How's she doing?'

News travelled with surprising speed around fostering circles. When Megan's adoption was finalised in June 2014, I had been touched to receive congratulatory cards from lots of foster carers, some of whom I had only met once or twice. Like Joan's new charge, Megan, now three and a half, had been born addicted to drugs. She suffered painful withdrawal symptoms and was barely out of my arms during her first few weeks of life.

Like me, my birth children, Emily and Jamie, then sixteen and thirteen, had grown increasingly attached to her, and vice versa. When Megan's social worker suggested that I throw my hat into the ring for assessment as her adopter, I had jumped at the chance. 'She's a right little pickle,' I said, remembering this morning's meltdown over a major misdemeanour of mine – cutting her toast into triangles instead of squares. 'But she's *our* little pickle. We wouldn't be without her now.'

The pouches beneath Joan's eyes creased as she smiled. 'I heard it was touch-and-go for a while.'

I blew out some air and nodded. It was true. After being turned down as an adopter for Megan because of safety concerns (her birth family knew where I lived), we went through the difficult process of moving her onto adoptive parents. The placement broke down and she returned to us a few weeks later, but the move had left its mark. Megan was still fearful of separation, even for short periods. Getting her settled at nursery in September had been a challenge. For the first few weeks she became so distressed at drop-off time that I decided to stay with her.

By the end of the winter term she was managing four mornings and one longer day a week on her own, but still clung to me before she went in. Fortunately the staff were amazing. They grew teary when I explained Megan's background and always made an extra special effort to welcome her. 'To be honest I forget she's adopted most of the time.'

Joan smiled. 'Make yourself comfortable, if you can find a space. You won't mind if I don't join you?'

'Knock yourself out,' I said with a chuckle, and then, 'Oh dear, Joan, your poor back.' I couldn't actually find a space to sit down. Strewn across the sofa were several half-opened packets of wet wipes, a few unused nappies, a cellular blanket, a couple of children's magazines and various other toys. 'I'll perch here, shall I?' I gestured to the arm of the sofa.

She grimaced. 'Sorry, Rosie. But you know how tough it is.'

I waved her apology away. 'Joan, you're dressed. That's a miracle in itself.'

She came to a stop a few feet in front of me and gave me a grateful smile. 'Talking of tough … you're looking for a new challenge, are you?'

'Ha, well … how much of a challenge are we talking about?'

She blew out some air. 'Have you ever seen *Armageddon*?'

I laughed. 'Oh, Joan, don't.' She didn't laugh back, just half-cocked an eyebrow. 'What? That bad?'

'Put it this way,' she said, glancing at the door and lowering her voice. 'I've only had them a few days and I've been distracted, so it's difficult to tell how much is boredom, how much is down to the shock of the move and – well, you'll see for yourself soon enough. I mean, Archie's been fairly quiet ...'

She stopped at the sound of footsteps. Moments later a young girl burst into the room. As soon as she caught sight of me she came straight over and laid her head on my lap. My stomach clenched with pity. I glanced at Joan. She gave me a meaningful look and said something inaudible out of the corner of her mouth.

Being overfamiliar with strangers isn't unusual behaviour for children from chaotic backgrounds. While some children with a history of trauma and neglect withdraw into themselves, others trust no one to keep them safe and take matters into their own hands. Bobbi was probably trying to minimise any threat I posed by making herself appear both appealing and vulnerable. It was the reptilian part of her brain at work; her own little fight for survival. 'Hello. You must be Archie?'

She lifted her head. 'Huh?'

I gave her a teasing smile. 'Pleased to meet you, Archie.'

She giggled. 'I'm not a boy! I'm Bobbi!' She was a pretty girl with deep-set brown eyes and pale, barely-there eyebrows. Her complexion was pallid though, and she looked far too thin.

'Oh, of course you are,' I said, smiling. 'Silly me.' There was a flicker of movement across the room. I half-registered a boy standing in the doorway. 'This must be your sister then?'

As I turned towards him I was struck by a flash of recognition. I ran my eyes over his wavy brown hair and the pale skin of his thin face and then I remembered where I'd seen him before. I had helped out on a domestic violence workshop for children a few months earlier and Archie had been one of the attendees. He had stuck in my mind because when the social worker asked the children at the end of the session what they had enjoyed most about the course, Archie had answered, 'The biscuits.'

Already classed as 'children in need' by the local authority following episodes of domestic violence between their mother and her partner, the comment had heightened professionals' concerns over the siblings' welfare, particularly as both were very small for their respective ages. As many as three children die each week in the UK through maltreatment and the biscuits comment, while far from definitive proof of neglect, was certainly something to jangle already twitching nerves.

I decided not to say anything about recognising him. He certainly didn't need reminding of his past – *'Coo-ee! I was there when you were at one of the lowest points in your life. Remember me?'*

'Archie,' Joan said. 'This is Rosie, love.'

He took a few steps into the room, his sister giggling a high-pitched cackle in front of me. 'I think I know you. Weren't you on that course I went to?'

'Yes, that's right. Lovely to see you again, Archie. You're both coming to stay with me, then?' They nodded in unison, Bobbi beginning to spin around on one leg. 'That's good. My children can't wait to meet you.'

'How many have you got?' Archie asked as Bobbi lowered her head back to my thigh. Singing loudly, she grabbed the arm of the sofa and began running on the spot, head-butting me in the process. I put a hand on each of her shoulders and gently eased her away. She frowned at me

7

then threw herself backwards onto a nearby footstool and made loud panting noises.

'I have two daughters,' I said, ignoring the sideshow and focussing my attention on Archie. For a brief second I pictured myself through his eyes; a woman in her mid-forties with shoulder-length, wavy blonde hair and hazel, slightly tired eyes, ones that hopefully displayed the promise of kindness. 'Emily is twenty and studying to be a nurse, Megan's going to be four in July, and then there's Jamie. He's seventeen.'

'I want to be a nurse, Joanie!' Bobbi shouted from the footstool. 'Joanie, Joanie, I'm going to be a nurse one day!'

I decided now was as good a time as any to mention the new love in our lives and the latest addition to our family – a six-month-old pup whom Megan had named Mungo. A mongrel pup with some Spaniel and, I suspected from all the holes he'd dug in the garden, some Terrier as well, he was almost as effusive in his affection as little Megan. Although we all loved animals, I had resisted getting a pet because Jamie suffered from asthma. His symptoms had lessened over the years though, and so a few months ago we decided to take the plunge. 'We also have a dog who'll be very pleased to meet you,' I said, aware that Joan was trying to calm Bobbi, who didn't seem open to the idea at all. Alternately barking and lapping open-mouthed at the air, it was as if Joan wasn't even there.

Archie smiled when I told him Mungo's name, though his eyes kept an expressionless quality, as if they weren't quite plugged in with the rest of him. 'Does your son like football?'

'Yes. He loves cricket and rugby as well. How about you?'

He nodded sombrely. 'I support Man U.'

Before I could respond, Bobbi bolted off the foot stool and charged at him. Head down, she rammed him in the groin with such ferocity that he staggered backwards and clonked his head on the wall. He yelped, arms flailing as he struggled to regain his balance. Then, in a display of what I considered to be remarkable self-constraint, he gave her a mild push in the chest and then cradled his head, his other hand clamped to his groin.

I winced. Joan marched forwards. 'What have I told you, Bobbi?' she said crossly. 'You mustn't keep lashing out like that!'

Bobbi looked vacant, as if nobody had said a word. Joan took another step towards her and leaned close. 'Bobbi! Did you hear me?' she demanded. From her middle came the tiniest mewing sound. Joan straightened, shifting once again from one foot to the other. 'Poor Archie, look, you've hurt him. Say sorry. NOW please!'

'S'alright, Joan,' Archie said, still rubbing the back of his head. 'She didn't mean it.'

'Hmm, I'm not so sure about that.' Joan puffed out some air. 'Bobbi, upstairs. Fetch your things.'

After a resentful glance at her brother, Bobbi turned and stalked from the room. Archie rolled his eyes and limped after her. Joan gaped at me, her hand flapping towards the door. 'Did you see that?! I don't believe it!'

'What? The head-butt?'

She snorted. 'No, I can believe that alright. I can't believe she actually did what I asked.'

I looked at her. 'The placing social worker said you're thinking ADHD.'

'Yes, wouldn't surprise me,' Joan said. Attention deficit hyperactivity disorder is a prevalent condition in fostered children. Latest research suggests that there may be a genetic link and one emerging theory is that undiagnosed sufferers turn to drugs in an unconscious attempt at self-medication. It's one of the reasons I feel sorry for birth parents who lose their children through substance addiction, although my sympathy never extends to those who have been deliberately cruel or abusive. 'She's all over the place from morning till night,' Joan continued. 'Can't keep still for a second. Can't stop fretting about food either, poor little lamb. She can't sleep. And when she blows, well, you'll need to dive for cover. She never stops making a noise. I mean, literally never. She's a little tea leaf as well.'

'Oh?'

Joan nodded. 'Yep. Pinches anything that's not screwed down. And she bites.'

I nodded slowly, absorbing her words. This placement was certainly going to be lively. 'And Archie?'

She thought for a moment. 'I haven't quite worked him out yet. He's polite enough, I'll give you that. And on the whole he's been quiet.'

'Yes, you've said.'

She nodded, glancing down at the baby.

'What is it, Joan?'

She frowned. 'I'm not sure,' she said, giving me a long steady look. 'Be careful is what I'm saying, I suppose, with your little one around.'

I stared at her for a moment and then glanced away. My eyes were drawn to a lopsided Christmas tree draped with cracked baubles and balding tinsel. It was leaning cheerlessly against a side table, as if all the socialising of the festive season had literally drained the life out of it. Joan noticed my interest. 'One of Bobbi's recent victims,' she said soberly. I laughed, but she shook her head woefully. 'I'm not joking, Rosie. Be ready to hit the ground running. You're in for a bumpy ride.'

If I'm honest her words did worry me a little, but perhaps not as much as they should have.

Chapter Two

'You got food at your house, miss, have you? Have you got food?'

'It's Rosie. And yes, don't worry, we have plenty of food.'

'Cos I like bread and chocolate spread and crisps, have you got some? Have you, Rosie? Have you?'

'Yes, Bobbi, we –'

'I like jam as well but not peanut butter, I hate that. Have you got jam, Rosie? Have you got any jam?'

And so it continued all the way home. She was a nervous passenger, startling every time I applied the brake, craning her head and strumming the window as we stopped at each red light. When we went over a sleeping policeman she clutched at the headrest in front of her and held on for dear life. My heart went out to her. She really was an anxious little girl. I glanced at her brother in the rear-view mirror. He sat gazing out of the window, quietly self-contained. I should have been grateful for his calm, but there was something unsettling about the glazed look in his eyes. I felt relieved when he finally spoke. 'Shut it, Bobbi,' he said, but mildly. I don't think she heard him. She certainly didn't react, or listen when I tried to get a response in.

I suspected that her constant chatter was another sign that her reptilian brain stem was in control of her thinking, trying to ensure her survival by reminding me that she needed attention. I felt sad to think that a little girl had been so poorly treated that she feared for her life. That said, I also wondered how my three were going to react to her constant chatter.

The roads narrowed as we neared home; a typical Edwardian semi-detached house of red brick in the north of England, with a windswept garden and a river beyond. Our surrounding towns are lively enough to keep the youngsters interested once they hit their teens, but small enough to retain some of their old-world charm.

'Here we are,' I said cheerfully over the top of Bobbi's monologue. I pulled up outside our house and peered through the windscreen. Emily was holding Megan up at the living-room window. I waved as I got out of the car and Megan jumped up and down in Emily's arms. 'Looks like we have a welcoming committee,' I said as I opened one of the rear doors and helped Bobbi release her seatbelt. Archie climbed out the other side, threw his rucksack over his shoulder and came to stand beside me.

'I can do it,' Bobbi said, refusing my proffered hand and slinking out of the seat herself. As soon as her feet touched the driveway, Megan appeared in front of her, a big beaming smile on her face. Mungo skidded over as well and, just over Bobbi's hip-height, sniffed excitedly at her armpits and then at her feet.

Bobbi grinned and screamed excitedly. Mungo turned tail and shot off back to the house. A bit taken aback, Megan stared at her for a second, but then reached for her hand. 'Come and play!' she chirped, her breath misting the cold air. Bobbi, who was over a year older but only about two inches taller, scowled and shrank away. Megan gave me a bewildered look and my heart lurched. She had been so excited yesterday when I told her that two new children were coming to stay.

Archie leaned over and rested his hands on his knees. 'Hello, what's your name?' he asked engagingly, his whole demeanour softening.

'Meggie,' she said with a smile, noticing him properly for the first time.

'Nice to meet you, Meggie. I'm Archie.'

'Arty,' Megan repeated as best she could, a big grin on her face.

'Hi, Archie,' Emily said with casual friendliness. She had been welcoming little strangers into our home since she was around eight years old and seemed to have a natural ability for making them feel at ease. Archie flushed and leaned down to stroke Mungo's floppy brown ears.

Megan made another attempt at grabbing Bobbi's hand. With her effusive spirit and tactile nature, it was hard for her to comprehend anyone turning down the offer of instant friendship.

'I know!' Emily said, eyeing me over the top of the girls' heads. 'Let's go back inside and find some toys for Bobbi.' She swept Megan up and headed back towards the door.

'Yay!' Megan shouted over her shoulder. I felt a swell of gratitude for Emily's quick thinking. Since Megan's adoption I had been more careful when considering referrals, only accepting those I was confident would allow me to give her plenty of individual attention. Being born with a cleft palate had left her hard of hearing so she needed more support than other children her age, though she managed well with the use of a hearing aid. Besides struggling with transitions, her exposure to drugs and alcohol in utero had left its mark developmentally. She struggled to learn at nursery, partly because of her hearing difficulties but also because she was easily distracted – a common legacy of exposure to dangerous substances in the womb.

She was a confident girl though, with an awe-inspiring zest for life. She loved the company of other children and was used to fostering – she had grown up with it – but still, she was a vulnerable child with her own set of challenges. I had to bear that in mind.

'I want fooooood!' Bobbi whined as I carried their suitcases into the hall. Still wearing her hat, coat and gloves, she charged off up the hall. 'Where's the fridge, Rosie? Is it in here? Rosie, is it here?'

'Come in, love,' I said to Archie, who was hovering at the open door. I smiled at him. 'I'll just see to your sister and then I'll give you a tour.'

'Thank you,' he said politely as I stowed their belongings in front of the stairs. 'You have a nice house,' he added as I straightened. I did a double take. Compliments from a child of his age were unexpected, and even more so from someone with a background of domestic abuse. Whenever I accepted a placement I braced myself for verbal insults and even physical abuse. Charming behaviour wasn't something I'd prepared myself for.

I smiled at him then draped my coat over the banister and went through to the kitchen, where Bobbi had already opened several cupboard doors. 'Here you are, Bobbi, you can have this for now,' I said, planting a banana in her hand. I shepherded her out of the kitchen and pulled out one of our dining chairs. She threw herself onto it and immediately began kicking the legs. I bent down and slipped off her shoes. The kicking stopped but almost instantly she began banging her free hand on the table and shouting at the top of her voice.

Her brother appeared at the doorway. 'Would you like some fruit, Archie? Or do you want to wait for lunch? It won't be long.'

'I can wait,' he said quietly. 'I need the toilet though.' At that moment Megan scooted in, carrying a box of Duplo, closely followed by Emily and Jamie.

'Rosie, Rosie, Rosie!' Bobbi shouted with a mouth full of banana. She pulled on my top. When I didn't turn around she picked up one of the placemats from the table and jabbed me in the back with it.

'Just a minute, Bobbi,' I said firmly, stepping out of her reach. 'The bathroom's straight ahead at the top of the stairs, Archie. This is Jamie, by the way.'

'Hi, Archie,' Jamie said easily, as if he were already part of the furniture. And then to me, 'I'm off to band practice, Mum. See you later.'

Archie, still wearing his rucksack on top of his coat, studied Jamie with interest then followed him up the hall. Emily planted a kiss on my cheek. 'Sorry to run out on you so quickly, Mum, but I said I'd meet Holly at the library.' In her middle year of nurse training, Emily spent much of her time off duty from the local university teaching hospital either at the library or bent over the desk in her room.

'We'll be fine,' I said chirpily. I was a big fan of subliminal messages and I was talking as much to the children as to her. I usually muddle through the first few days after children arrive, doing my best to keep a calm environment while everyone adjusts to the changing family dynamics.

Employing foster carers is a snip for local authorities, who have to pay upwards of £5,000 a week if a child is placed in a residential unit or care home. Apart from financial considerations, a care home is usually the last resort for any child. Establishing them in a safe, family environment is the best way for them to build self-esteem as well as a sense of belonging and fair play.

It's much cheaper for local authorities to place children with their own in-house carers than with those registered with private fostering agencies like Bright Heights, but recruitment challenges mean that it often isn't possible.

While the allowances I receive as an agency foster carer are on a par with the amounts paid to carers registered with the local authority, the heavy fees charged by the agencies make fostering a profitable business; one of the reasons that hedge-fund investors have been so keen to get involved. It's a fact I'm uncomfortable with and I'm often tempted to jump ship and transfer to my local authority.

'Would you two like to do some colouring while I rustle up some lunch?' I said as Emily and Jamie left.

The suggestion was not to Bobbi's liking. 'No, I want food now!' she shouted, underlining the sentiment by flinging one of the placemats across the room.

It isn't unusual for fostered children to have issues with food. The digestive discomfort caused by a surge in stress hormones can be difficult to distinguish from hunger pangs, and lots of children seek to cure their 'funny tummy' by feeding it. Megan's exposure to drugs and alcohol had left her with her own digestive difficulties and she suffered with frequent tummy aches, as well as bouts of unexplained sickness. 'It's coming very soon, Bobbi. You don't need to worry; they'll always be enough food for you here.' I quickly set out some paper and colouring pens on the table and Megan climbed up onto the chair next to Bobbi.

Thanks to a knock-through by the previous owner our house is open-plan downstairs, so I could see the girls from the kitchen as I prepared some sandwiches. Bobbi chattered continuously as she drew, the noise rising as she washed her hands at the kitchen sink. 'Rosie, it is ready now? Is it? Is it ready?'

'Yes, my sweet, it's here.' There was still no sign of Archie so as the girls sat next to each other at the table I called up to him.

'Coming!' he called back. 'This looks nice,' he said when he eventually came down. I smiled at him as he sat next to me but he kept his gaze averted. I noticed a few dark blotches that looked suspiciously like chocolate sticking to his chin and, poking out through the zipped opening of the rucksack at his feet, a shred of clear cellophane wrapping.

'Rosie, have you got more food in the kitchen?' Bobbi asked, her faint eyebrows furrowed with anxiety.

I laughed. 'I have, but we have enough here for now.' I had placed a platter of nibbles at the centre of the table and sandwiches with a variety of fillings, giving everyone a plate so that they could help themselves. Bobbi already had eight triangles piled high on her plate, as well as some crisps and about ten cherry tomatoes.

She glugged down a cupful of water and picked up two more triangles, squashing them together and ramming them into her mouth. 'Slow down, sweetie, there's no rush!' I said. I preferred not to worry too much about table manners early on in a placement – I usually had plenty of other fish to fry – but Bobbi was almost gagging on her food. I was worried that she might actually choke.

'We have plenty of food for everyone here,' I repeated. Her eyes flicked in my direction. She slowed her chewing, but within a few seconds later she had renewed her mission with gusto. Archie ate with less abandon, but had probably already partaken of a starter in the loo.

I remembered reading something about babies and young children who have experienced real hunger internalising the idea that no one will keep them safe. Once hard-wired into their brain, it can take years to overwrite such a deeply ingrained belief. A pat on my arm from Megan interrupted my thoughts. 'Did you see my cloptiker, Mummy?' she said, pointing to the picture at the top of a pile of drawings at the side of the table.

'Wow, that's great, Meggie!' Already showing a flair for art, she would sit for hours drawing and colouring. She looked at me, her eyes shining with pride.

'It's horse shite,' Bobbi piped up, her voice thick with food. I gave her a sharp glance and looked back at Megan, who, thankfully, seemed not to have heard. Though her hearing difficulties were only mild and her hearing aid helped, she still struggled to make out words when they were muffled.

'I think it's cool, Megan,' Archie chipped in kindly. She beamed.

I gave him a grateful smile then looked at Bobbi. 'We don't use rude words like that, Bobbi.'

'Huh?' She folded another triangle of bread in half and rammed it into her mouth.

'I said, you mustn't use rude words. Say "fiddlesticks" if you can't think of anything nice to say.'

She swallowed hard and then giggled. Megan laughed too. The pair of them grinned at each other and shouted 'Fiddlesticks!' at the tops of their voices. It was the first positive interaction between them and I couldn't help but smile.

Ten minutes later as I piled the plates together, Bobbi asked for more sandwiches. 'You've had enough for now, sweetie,' I said gently. 'But next time you feel hungry, I promise there will be food for you. There's always fruit, whenever you want it. And we'll be having dinner in a few hours, okay?'

She scowled at me and went red in the face. I thought she might protest further but, with every last crumb consumed, she agreed to join us for a tour of the house.

Megan led the way upstairs. Mungo waited obediently at the bottom, head cocked with interest. 'This is *my* room,' Megan announced proudly at her open door. 'None of you are definitely not allowed in here.'

'Alright, Meggie,' I said, dropping a hand to her shoulder. Every foster carer is obliged to draw up a Safer Caring policy detailing a set of house rules that every house member must comply with. Designed to keep everyone safe, one of the universal rules is that everyone must stay covered up at all times, whether in pyjamas and dressing gown or fully clothed. Every member of the house must also stay out of every bedroom but their own. Even as the children's foster carer, I was supposed to knock before entering their room, and should never, under any circumstances, sit on their beds.

Strictly speaking, only the under-fives or same-sex siblings should share bedrooms, but with foster placements in short supply there's sometimes no alternative but to stretch the rules. I knew that if a vacancy became available with a foster carer who could provide the children with a room of their own, it was likely that Bobbi and Archie would be moved on.

'But it's a *rule*,' Megan said with feeling. She yawned and leaned against my leg, looking crestfallen.

I smiled. 'You're right, sweetie, it is.' We'd spent most of yesterday evening at my mother's house and, being New Year's Eve, she hadn't gone to bed until late. I could tell she was flagging so I quickly showed Bobbi the bathroom, pointed out where I'd be sleeping, and then opened the door to the room opposite my own.

'Wow!' Bobbi shouted, running in and diving face down on the sheepskin rug in the middle of the floor. We had spent yesterday afternoon filling the room with Lego and Bratz dolls, Transformers and Brio; anything we thought might appeal to children of Archie and Bobbi's age. There was a large purple beanbag beside the bunk bed and a giant teddy next to the bookshelf in one of the alcoves. Of all the accessories, it was the furry rug that always seemed to appeal most to the children I looked after.

Archie walked slowly around the room, stopping to examine the framed pictures on the wall that I'd put up when he was referred. I wasn't a fan of stereotyping but sports tended to be more or less a safe bet when it came to boys of Archie's age, and several of the pictures around the top bunk were football related. 'It's such a cool room,' he said, straightening one of the slightly lopsided frames. 'Thanks, Rosie.'

I smiled at him and he made an attempt at smiling back, though his eyes once again refused to join in. My stomach contracted with pity. I was beginning to get the sense that his compliments were driven by panic, as if his survival depended on them.

'I thought you could have the top bunk, Archie. Happy with that?'

He nodded. 'We have bunk beds at home.'

I had dotted a few soft toys around the bottom bunk and one of them, a pink rabbit, seemed to take Bobbi's fancy. She dived onto the mattress, grabbed it in her mouth and then rolled back onto the rug with it dangling from her jaws. 'This is the best bedroom in the whole world!' she declared, rolling around. I smiled, wondering what her bedroom at home was like. I looked at Archie, but his expression was unreadable.

After the tour we all sat in the living area to watch *Paddington*. When I say 'sat', Megan, Archie and I sat. Bobbi spun in circles on the rug, threw herself into kamikaze-style forward rolls and snatched every soft toy that Megan chose to sit on her lap. Every time I intervened, she asked if she could have more food.

Broken

Megan lost patience about twenty minutes into the film and began throwing herself around as well. Mungo watched the rumpus from beneath the coffee table, growling softly whenever Bobbi got too near. 'Tell you what,' I said, 'let's get you into your coats and shoes and you can have a bounce on the trampoline while I prepare dinner, okay?' It was only two o'clock, but I had a feeling that late afternoon held the potential for trouble. I wanted to prepare something to throw in the oven so that I'd be free to deal with whatever cropped up.

I watched them through the kitchen window as I fried some mince and peeled potatoes for a cottage pie. Megan and Bobbi dived crazily around the trampoline, giggling and bumping into one another. I felt a jolt of encouragement as I watched them. Archie bounced to one side, slowing protectively whenever they veered close.

After a particularly violent collision Megan fell awkwardly and bumped her ear on one of the posts holding the safety net. She clamped a hand to the side of her head and looked mournfully towards the house. I slipped my shoes on, but by the time I'd reached the door Archie had already given her a cuddle.

About twenty minutes later she climbed, rosy cheeked, through the net and pulled Archie by the hand to the house. 'She wants to show me how to draw a cloptikler,' he said with a wry smile as they came into the house.

'Oh, brilliant!' I mouthed a thank you over the top of Megan's head. He gave me a slow eye roll and shook his head, the sort of reaction I'd expect from someone much older. I tried to remember being nine years old. Shy and home-loving, I knew I wouldn't have coped

23

with such a momentous move the way Archie seemed to have done.

I realised then what Joan had meant when she said that Archie was an unknown quantity. Was it possible that he possessed enough resilience to cope with what the last few days had thrown at him, without the tiniest crack in his composure? As I stood at the sink washing up, my eyes drifted back to the trampoline at the end of the garden. Bobbi was still there but her movements had slowed. She was bouncing lethargically, without the faintest glimmer of enjoyment on her face. All alone, she looked completely bereft.

Abandoning the saucepan I was holding, I was about to go outside and talk to her when Megan shot past me, back into the garden. 'Bobbi, we're back!' she yelled, running towards the trampoline with her arms in the air, jazz hands shimmying all the way. Bobbi's expression brightened. She ran over and parted the net for Megan to pass through, and the pair stood grinning at each other.

'Here we go again,' Archie said, trudging past me. I laughed, but again I was struck by the sense that his words mismatched his age. It was as if he were acting a role, one he didn't have much heart to play.

'Archie, just a second. I thought I might sort your clothes out now. Are you happy for me to go through your suitcase? Or would you prefer to do it yourself?'

He shrugged. 'Not really. You can do it. Not my rucksack though, I can do that.' He went to the door but then stopped and turned. 'Thank you, Rosie.'

A slow shiver ran across the back of my neck as I watched him walk down the path. I took to mashing the boiled potatoes, trying to shake the uncomfortable feeling away. I puzzled over my reaction. I couldn't quite fathom why his apparent maturity should make me feel so uncomfortable.

His sister's struggles were clear to see. Bobbi was in 'flight' mode, so that she literally couldn't keep still. I told myself that, being that bit older, Archie had perhaps managed to devise better coping strategies in dealing with the stress.

At a little after half past four, when I put the cottage pie in the oven, there was still no sign of their play fizzling out. I decided to make the most of the time by sorting through their clothes to see if anything needed to be washed. When children arrive in placement I usually wash most of their clothes straight away, only holding a few items back to retain the comforting smell of their home. I carried their suitcases into the kitchen and set them down in front of the washing machine, but when I opened them up, the fresh scent of washing powder rose to greet me. Joan had washed everything. It was a lovely, welcome surprise.

I watched the children from the upstairs window as I put everything away in their room. They were still playing happily and I began to feel quietly confident that the placement would be manageable, and that everything was going to work out just fine.

Chapter Three

'But I'm still hungry-y-y-y, Rosie,' Bobbi whined an hour later, after making short shrift of two helpings of cottage pie. I could tell she was full because her voracious gorging had slowed to a sort of lethargic nibble, but she didn't seem able to admit to herself that she had had enough. 'I am, I am, you know, Rosie.'

'There's plenty of food on its way to your tummy,' I said cheerfully from across the table. 'You need to give it a chance to go down.'

Reluctant to concede defeat, she was still sitting at the table five minutes later as I rinsed the plates under the tap in the kitchen. Crouched on her haunches on the chair with her knees touching her chest, she kept dropping her head to the table and making loud groaning noises. 'Give it a rest, Bobs, you're doing our heads in!' Archie shouted from the other side of the room. He was sitting on the floor with a mixed box of Lego and Duplo in front of him. Megan was sitting on the other side of the box, Mungo resting his chin on her leg.

Broken

I squirted some washing-up liquid into the sink and turned the hot tap on, vaguely aware though my back was turned of Archie's approach. 'Come on, Bobs,' I heard him say cajolingly. 'Come and play.' The yelp came seconds later. I spun around and saw Archie cradling one of his hands in the other, his face contorted with pain. Behind him, Bobbi was looking thoroughly pleased with herself.

'What happened?' I looked from one to the other. Across the room, Megan wrapped her arms around Mungo's neck, looking startled.

'Nothing. S'okay,' Archie mumbled, though his cheeks were chalky white.

I strode over and drew his forearm towards me. A row of small, angry looking welts had bubbled up across the back of his hand. 'Oh goodness, Archie, she bit you! That must really have hurt.'

'It's nothing,' he snapped, snatching his hand away. 'It's okay, Rosie, don't worry,' he added as he walked back across the room, his polite tone recovered. My gaze fell disap-provingly on Bobbi. She stared up at me, a trace of the gloating smile still on her lips.

'We don't bite in this house, Bobbi,' I said firmly. I pulled out a chair and sat next to her. She sprang frog-like onto the next chair. 'Did you hear me, Bobbi? We use our mouths for eating food, not biting people. Now, would you like to play Lego with the others? Or you could help me with the washing-up.'

'But I'm *so* hungry-y-y-y,' she moaned, banging her head down on the table again.

I winced. 'Bobbi, do you know what? I don't think you are hungry right now. I think you're worried that you might feel hungry later.' She stilled and turned her head to the side so that one ear rested on the table, the other pointed upwards. 'I wonder if that might be because there wasn't always enough food for you at home,' I added softly.

She lifted her head and looked at me. I leaned closer, my head level with hers. 'It's good to know they'll always be enough food for you at Rosie's house, isn't it?'

She frowned, her fair eyebrows knitting together. After a moment she nodded, her mouth offering the faint glimmer of a smile. I stood up and held out my hand. 'Great! Now, how about we go and play with that Lego?'

At that moment, Megan charged across the room. 'Mummy!' she shouted, breathless with enthusiasm. 'We need to put our pictures up in our rooms. Can I have some of that sticky stuff?'

Having used the prospect of playing Lego to tempt Bobbi away from the table, I hesitated for a moment. Thankfully, Megan's excitement seemed to be infectious. 'Can I as well?' Bobbi asked, her eyes brightening as she looked at Megan. Mungo wagged his tail excitedly, though I noticed that he was keeping his distance, staying a few feet away. Archie crouched next to him and stroked his head.

'Of course you can.' I gave them each some Blu Tack and followed them upstairs. 'Stay in your own rooms!' I called out from the bathroom. 'I'll be out in a minute.'

'We will, Mummy!' Megan shouted. I felt a small flip in my chest. It still thrilled me to hear her calling me that.

* * *

28

Broken

Worn out from the excitement of the day, Megan was asleep by 7 p.m. From what Joan had said I suspected that bedtime for Archie and Bobbi might not go quite as smoothly. Most people found it difficult to settle in a strange bed, so I anticipated an unsettled evening. What followed, however, took me by complete surprise.

As Archie was quite a bit older than Bobbi, I gave him the option of staying up to read or watching TV. He seemed pleased with the offer and, after showering, went downstairs to watch *You've Been Framed*. The sound of his laughter drifting up the stairs as I ran a bath for Bobbi made me smile, but it had the opposite effect on his sister. 'Why can't I watch it?' she howled, stamping her feet on the tiled floor. Her cheeks were puce, her eyes red and goggling.

'You know why, Bobbi,' I said, keeping my voice even. While many of the children I have looked after have been largely ignored by their birth parents, they've also rarely been taught what the word 'no' means. Kneeling on the bathmat, I leaned over and swished some bubble bath around in the water. 'I warned you that there'd be no more television today if you bit Archie again.' I hadn't seen it happen, but Archie's yowls had reached me while I washed my hands in the bathroom. He had defended her again, claiming that it hadn't hurt much, but the welts on his arm where she'd bit him were red and angry looking, and his eyes were glassy with tears. I turned to face her. 'Besides, he's much older than you. It's right that he stays up a little bit longer.'

After only a few hours in her company, I already had a strong suspicion that she wasn't going to take any sort of discipline lying down. She stamped her foot again. 'I *am* going down to watch it!' she growled, rocketing out to the stairs.

'Your bath is nearly ready,' I said, staying where I was. I preferred to avoid chasing her around the house if at all possible. 'I have some special toys here somewhere. Now, where did I put them?'

I leaned over and opened one of the low cupboards, sensing that she was back, somewhere behind me. I made a thing of rummaging through the bottles of shampoo and tubes of toothpaste. 'They're there!' Bobbi screeched from the doorway. 'Right there!'

'Where?'

'There!'

'Oh right!' I pulled them out. 'Why didn't you say so?'

She giggled, her eyes settling on the water pistols, ducks and little sail boats in the box I was holding. Relieved, I closed the door behind her.

'No-o-o-o-o!' she bellowed, spinning around. 'I'm going to watch the telly!'

'I think we have some bubbles here somewhere.'

She let out a growl of fury and banged her fists on the door, pummelling with all her might. Lots of children in the care system struggle with an overwhelming, almost pathological need to be in control. I suddenly thought of Taylor, a ten-year-old girl I had cared for about a decade earlier. The witnessing of severe domestic violence against her mother by her abusive father had left Taylor desperately anxious. She was so badly affected that she wouldn't even leave school at the end of the afternoon; even when the building was empty and the cleaners had finished doing their rounds. Though frustrated by her behaviour at the time, I came to realise that Taylor was clasping onto the only things in her life that she had any control over, because everything else was falling apart. As the months passed and her trust in me grew, she allowed me to take over the reins and mother her. She's a grown woman now and sometimes when she writes to me she mentions her 'sit-ins'. They're a standing joke between us.

Some people remain convinced that the relatively new diagnoses of pathological demand avoidance (PDA) and oppositional defiance disorder (ODD) are invented labels demanded by ineffectual parents who are simply incapable of providing consistent boundaries. *You mean they're just not doing as they're told* is a common response to any conversation involving PDA and ODD.

When I first started out as a foster carer it was a view I shared as well. Having cared for chronically inflexible children though, I've become convinced that trauma, both pre- and post-birth, has a profound impact on the brain. In recent years, scientific evidence involving the use of brain scans has confirmed altered brain functioning in children who have been abused or neglected in early infancy.

'Hey, come here, sweetie.' I crawled until I was alongside her then wrapped my arm around her back, holding her close to my side. It was a non-violent resistance (NVR) technique designed to promote a feeling of solidarity rather than confrontation. 'I know you're upset about missing out on TV, but if you come and have a bath nicely we can watch some in the morning, okay?'

Naming a child's feelings sometimes helps to take the sting out of their tantrum, but with Bobbi it only seemed

Rosie Lewis

to fan the flames. With a roar of fury she shook her arms loose. 'I WANT TELLY NOW!' she screeched, ramming home the message by whacking me on the top of my head.

I couldn't help but cry out and she stilled, watching me intently. Her eyes shone and her lips twitched. So much for solidarity, I thought.

'Kind hands, Bobbi,' I warned, but she lashed out again, catching my cheek with one of her nails. Her survival mechanism had kicked in again; the ancient safety net that programmes us to react to perceived threat in a fight, flight or freeze mode. This little girl, it seemed, was going to fight.

I felt a flare of annoyance but I swallowed it down. There was no sense in matching her anger with my own – trying to regulate a child's emotions while in a dis-regulated state was like ironing clothes using a pack of frozen peas – it was never going to work. I cuddled her close, fending off her blows with my arms.

It took a while, but slowly she relaxed, her small body slumping against mine. She allowed me to undress her without further complaint and what followed was the quickest bath I had ever supervised. Her eyelids grew heavy afterwards, when I wrapped her in a warm towel, but when I switched on the hairdryer to dry the damp ends of her shoulder-length hair, she flew into alert, her eyes goggling with distress. I did my best to towel dry it and tucked her into bed, passing her the soft rabbit she had taken to earlier. 'Where's Mummy?' she asked suddenly, her chin wobbling.

'She's at home, sweetie. You'll see her soon.'

She blinked as I covered her with the duvet, then rolled onto her side and closed her eyes. As I stroked some blonde strands behind her ears, I noticed for the first time the picture she had drawn earlier, now stuck on the wall between the bunks. I felt a prickle of unease. It was a childish drawing of several men and women, but what unsettled me were the angry expressions on their faces and the private parts drawn in graphic detail between their legs.

Chapter Four

'Do I have to go to bed now?' asked Archie when I walked into the living room five minutes later. He was sitting on the sofa, Mungo resting contentedly at his feet. A few feet away the credits of *You've Been Framed* were rolling across the television screen.

'What time do you usually go to bed on a school night?' I asked distractedly, still unsettled by the sight of Bobbi's drawings. Mungo nuzzled my hand as I joined Archie on the sofa. I stroked his head and gave myself a mental shake. It was perfectly possible that the drawings were entirely innocuous. Children with older siblings often demon-strated behaviour that was beyond their years.

Jumping to conclusions was one of the pitfalls of foster-ing that I tried to avoid. Like social workers, when foster carers ratchet up lots of experience it's easy to make assumptions. 'Oh, I forgot to ask earlier, Archie. Which school do you go to?'

There was a pause and then he said: 'I don't go to school.'

I frowned at him. 'Oh. You're home schooled then?'

'Mostly,' he muttered, his eyes downcast. I had found a single navy-blue jumper in his case with the letters 'MP' embroidered onto it. A quick Google search had offered a couple of possibilities, but if Archie were to be believed, he wasn't registered with either of them.

'Not to worry. I'll speak to your social worker about it.' A strange expression crossed his face and I wondered whether I had a school refuser on my hands. He ruffled his fringe and rearranged his features, quickly recovering.

'So what time do you usually go to bed on a week night?'

'Between about eight and half past. Mum lets me read in bed though.'

'Oh, you like reading, do you?' It seemed that my strategy for encouraging reluctant readers – allowing them an extra half an hour downstairs after their scheduled bedtime if they read with us – wouldn't be needed for Archie.

He nodded. 'I've just got into Harry Potter. I finished *Philosopher's Stone* a few weeks ago. I can't wait to read *Chamber of Secrets*.'

I stood up and walked to the bookshelf in the corner of the room. 'I have a pack of Harry Potter playing cards here somewhere. Fancy a game now?'

'Really? Yes please!' His voice bubbled with excitement. It struck me as the first genuine reaction I'd seen since he'd arrived.

His fingers trembled when he took the pack from me. He fanned through the cards, exclaiming every time he spotted a different character. 'Who's your favourite? Mine's Professor McGonagall, I think, though I love that ghost as well; the one with the funny voice.'

'Moaning Myrtle!' he cried, flicking through the deck until he found a card featuring Professor McGonagall. He held it up for me to see, his eyes alight. 'Why do you like her best?'

I took the card from him and looked at it. 'Because she's fierce, but in a good way. She's one of those people you'd love to have on your side when you're in a fix. You know the type: firm but fair. How about you?'

He flicked through the cards again. 'I like Harry and Ron,' he said, 'but Mrs Weasley is my favourite.'

'Oh yes, I like her too.' I felt a rush of affection for him. Being one of the most sympathetic and cuddly characters in the Harry Potter series, the archetypal mum, there was no need to ask why she was the one who appealed to him most.

'You remind me a bit of her,' he added shyly, his eyes fixed on the deck of cards in his hand.

I chuckled. 'Well, thank you. At least, I think it's a compliment!' He grinned, fully meeting my eye for the first time since we'd met.

Despite never having played before, he picked up the game of Rummy quickly enough, beating me on his second round. 'Are you sure you've never played this before?'

He grinned as I dealt another hand. 'I don't suppose you got a chance to pack much of your stuff before going to Joan's, did you?' I hadn't seen what was in his rucksack, but there certainly hadn't been any personal items in his suitcase when I'd unpacked it. Bobbi hadn't brought any toys with her either.

'No.' He picked up a card from the deck on the sofa between us, looked at it, then placed it on the discard pile, straightening it until it was exactly in line with the rest. 'The police packed a bag for us and then one of the social workers went to our house and grabbed some more of our clothes. She dropped it at Joan's and said we should ask our social worker if we wanted anything else.'

'And do you know who your social worker is?' It was likely that the children would be allocated a different social worker now that they were looked-after children, rather than children in need.

'I think his name began with a D, but I can't remember. He came to see us at Joan's but I forgot to ask about my stuff.'

I nodded, picking up another card from the deck. 'I can arrange for someone to collect some bits if you tell me what you'd like.'

He bunched his lips together. 'It doesn't matter.'

'How about some books? I mean, we have lots here, but if you were in the middle of reading one …'

He shook his head. 'Mum was going to get *Chamber of Secrets* for me but Jason said reading's for wimps.'

I peered at him over the top of my cards. 'Oh, really? Is Jason your mum's partner?' I usually tried to employ a mild tone whenever a child told me anything about their parents, so as not to deter them from opening up about their home lives. On this occasion, though, surprise got the better of me.

He nodded. 'He says –' he started to say, then seemed to think better of it and gave a little shrug.

When it was clear he wasn't going to say anything else I said: 'Well, we've got a copy somewhere. I'll ask Emily to dig it out for you.'

'Wow! Cool!' he said delightedly, as if I'd offered to take him to Disneyland.

'How about Bobbi? Is there anything she's particularly fond of at home? A cuddly toy or a blanket ... something to help her settle?'

He gave me a blank look. 'She has a duvet in bed, not blankets.'

I nodded. 'Okay. Is she always tricky at bedtime?'

His eyes surveyed his cards and then he looked up, not quite meeting my eyes again. 'Yep. Takes me ages to get her into bed. If she has a sleep in the day it's impossible. She gets up, she rolls around. I have to sleep next to her on the carpet sometimes to get her off.'

Where was his mother while he was doing all of that, I wondered. 'Well, I saw earlier what a knack you have with little ones. You were very good with Megan.'

He smiled, pleased with the compliment. 'I learned skills from dealing with her up there,' he said ruefully, lifting his eyes to the ceiling.

'Ah, yes,' I said, wondering again just how much he might have been left in charge of his sister. Several of the children I've fostered had taken on the responsibility of caring for their younger siblings as well as themselves when they were at home. I'd once looked after an eighteen-month-old toddler who had insisted on changing his own nappy, so adept was he at taking on adult tasks. 'You've got lots of experience then?'

He nodded. 'It's hard though. She never does anything I tell her.'

'Well, now you're here you can leave Bobbi to me. I'll take care of all the grown-up things. Your job is to make yourself comfortable and let me look after you.'

He looked at me. 'Rosie,' he said hesitantly, 'how can I find out if Mum's okay?'

'You're worried about her?'

He lifted his shoulders. 'A bit.'

'Did your social worker explain anything to you about contact?' Contact refers to the regular meetings arranged between birth parents and their children. The meetings are usually held in a local family centre and monitored by contact supervisors who observe the family's interactions and record their findings. In some cases, if there are no security concerns, contact takes place in the foster carer's home. Some birth parents are permitted to spend time with their children unsupervised, although usually only when they have agreed to voluntary care, or during reunification, when their children make the transition from foster carer back to the birth family home.

He nodded. 'He said he couldn't arrange anything until he's had a meeting with Mum though.'

'That's right, that's what usually happens. I expect the holiday period has delayed things a bit, but I'll get in touch with him tomorrow and see if I can find out how she is. Is there anything else you're worried about?'

'Not really. No, wait …' He looked at me hopefully. 'Do you think I might be able to see my dad?'

From the brief conversation I'd had with the placements team social worker, I got the impression that the children's birth father hadn't been on the scene for quite some time. 'I'll certainly ask. Do you see your dad often?'

He shook his head, his expression downcast. 'We used to. He used to come and take us out, but Mum says he doesn't want to see us anymore.'

'How long is it since you've seen him?'

He shrugged. 'I dunno. Ages. I sort of saw him on my birthday.'

'In October?'

He looked at me and nodded. 'He came round with loads of presents, but he had a row with Jason and Mum wouldn't let him in.' He rubbed his forehead brusquely.

'That's tough,' I said.

'I waved out the window but he didn't see me.' A shadow crossed his eyes but then he quickly added: 'Anyway, it doesn't matter. It's nice here, I really like it.'

I felt another twist of sympathy for him. Many of the children I have cared for display hair-trigger anger because it makes them feel less vulnerable than sadness, but Archie didn't seem able to express either. 'Things haven't been easy for you, have they, honey?'

He shook his head stiffly but then gave me a hopeful, not quite meeting my eyes, look. 'Maybe now I'm here though … if I can see my dad?'

I patted his hand. 'I'll see what I can find out.'

Chapter Five

The next day, Friday 2 January, began peacefully enough. I woke at just after 5 a.m. to the gentle sound of glass bottles clinking against doorsteps as the milkman made his deliveries. Hoping for half an hour to myself, I got up immediately and went downstairs. Mungo greeted me, tail wagging, in the hall and followed me as I switched on the computer and went into the kitchen. I made myself a coffee and fussed him while I waited for it to boot up.

With the steaming drink at my side and Mungo at my feet, I sat at my desk to type up the previous day's notes into my foster-carer diary. Foster carers are expected to keep detailed daily notes for each child they care for, recording such things as times and dates when babysitters are used, incidents of difficult behaviour and potential triggers, periods away from home, illnesses, medication, doctor's visits, meetings, any disagreements that may have occurred – either with the child, their birth family during contact or with professionals – damage, theft, or involvements with police, and then email them at the end of each week to the child's social worker for uploading onto social services' computer system.

Record keeping is an important part of a foster carer's role, not only to protect against possible allegations (emailing the diaries provides the foster carer with proof that nothing has been added to the record or altered at a later stage) but also to provide a detailed history for the child in the future, should they choose to read their file when they reach adulthood. When I'd finished, I set the table for breakfast so that it was ready for the children as soon as they came down.

Megan was first to rise, if you discounted Bobbi's six wake-ups during the night. As Joan had mentioned, she talked a lot in her sleep, and every hour or so she called out to me. The first time I went in she complained that she didn't like the dark, so I put a couple of plug-in night lights in the room. I went back to bed and she called me ten minutes later to tell me that the teddies I'd arranged around her bed were too starey. I collected them up and put them in the hall but she still woke an hour or so later.

I went in to her each time and reassured her she was safe, but no sooner had I gone back to sleep than she was calling out again. The noise woke Megan several times as well, who was finding it difficult to sleep anyway because of a stomach ache. I gave her some Calpol and a hot-water bottle to ease her cramps, but she still tossed and turned, groaning whenever Bobbi called out. Tucked away in the top bunk, Archie somehow slept through the entire racket.

'Morning, my angel,' I whispered, lifting Megan into my arms. 'How's your tummy this morning?'

She frowned, her disturbed night all forgotten. She cuddled close as I carried her downstairs, her head resting on my shoulder. I could feel the hard plastic of her hearing aid pressing into my skin and felt a swell of pride at her resourcefulness; over the last week or so she had taken to fitting the aid herself each morning. Sometimes she forgot to switch it on, but negotiating it into her ear was a feat in itself.

I told her how clever she was and she beamed – her reaction evidence that she had managed to switch it on. I gave her some milk and we cuddled up on the sofa, the soft fur of Mungo's head warming my feet. I buried my head in Megan's hair, relishing the opportunity to hug her while she was in a sleepy state of early morning calmness, and so unusually still. It was still only half past six and I was hoping to spend at least half an hour of one-to-one time with her, as I had always tried to do with Emily and Jamie when they were younger. Megan, it seemed, had other ideas.

'No, sweetheart, let them rest,' I said, when she slipped off the sofa and tried to pull me upstairs. 'Let's make the most of some Mummy and Meggie time.' She didn't look entirely convinced on the merits of just having me to play with, but she acquiesced. We read *Felicity Wishes*, one of her favourite books of the moment, and then we read it again.

Just as I was about to embark on a third reading, there was a thump overhead. Mungo's ears pricked up. Megan was off the sofa and at the bottom of the stairs within a few seconds. As I followed her up the sound of arguing reached me, followed by another loud clunk.

Megan stopped short at Archie and Bobbi's bedroom door. At first I thought she was respecting the house rules and was about to congratulate her for being so vigilant, when I caught a glimpse of the room. All of the clothes that I had folded neatly away in the drawers were scattered all over the floor. The wardrobe doors hung open, the clothes inside dangling precariously from their hangers.

Lidless felt-tip pens were strewn here and there, two upended water bottles leaking over them and creating a rainbow effect on the beige carpet. And just visible at the edge of all the mess, I could see a few food wrappers sticking out from under the bed. Megan and I exchanged mutually shocked glances.

I picked my way through the rubbish. Megan followed. She stood next to me, hands on her hips. 'What's happened here?' I asked, trying to keep my tone neutral. Between the ages of eighteen months and seven years, children are convinced that they are responsible for everything that happens to them. This so-called magical thinking, a natural phase of development, leaves children convinced that they are responsible for their own plight when they come into care. Instead of placing any fault with their parents, they assume that they are not worthy of being loved. I was worried that if I made a big deal of it, I could add to the toxic shame the siblings probably already felt. Besides, in my experience, most everyday upsets resolved themselves quickly if ignored.

Bobbi, still in her nightdress and pull-up nappy, was sitting in amongst the mess with a few pens clasped in one of her hands, the rabbit I had given her in the other. She looked blank, as if I hadn't even spoken. I took another step towards her, noticing as I did that her picture had been torn from the wall, a few fragments of jagged paper left behind.

Broken

The drawing, I presumed, lay somewhere beneath her. I wondered who had taken it down, and why. I looked at Archie, who was already dressed and standing by the window. He was staring into the garden, his face angled away.

'We'll clear this up later,' I said firmly. By messing up the room, there was every chance that Bobbi had been unconsciously re-creating her home environment. Home might have been an awful place to be, but it was familiar and probably strangely comforting. Having noticed Archie's fastidiousness, I had already decided that Bobbi was responsible for the mess. 'Now, who's ready for breakfast?' I asked. Archie turned to me in surprise.

Bobbi jumped up. 'Me! I am! I want cornflakes and toast and yoghurt and chocolate.'

'I don't know about chocolate!' I said, laughing. 'Right, we must all try to keep quiet as we go down. Emily and Jamie want a lie-in today. Bobbi, let's get you sorted.' The smell from her soiled nappy was overpowering, even from where I was standing. I wanted to shower her down before we went downstairs.

'No, I want breakfast now.' Bobbi's tone was flat but insistent.

'Yep, soon. Let's go the bathroom and get you cleaned up first.'

She eyed me defiantly. Sensing a sharpening of the atmosphere, I turned to Megan. 'Meggie, would you like to go and choose yourself something to wear?' She nodded enthusiastically and trotted off to her room. I craned my head around the door and called out: 'Don't forget, it's winter!' She loved getting herself dressed but more often than not she'd appear wearing a swimming costume or a pair of hot pants, even on the iciest of days. 'Right,' I held out my hand. 'Come on then, pickle, let's sort you out.'

'Nooooo!' Bobbi yelled, her cheeks turning puce. 'I want food!'

'Tell you what. I'll go to the bathroom and wait for you. If you come within ten seconds I'll give you a sticker. Archie, you go downstairs whenever you're ready. Emily found *The Chamber of Secrets* when she came in last night. She's left it on the table for you.'

Archie tiptoed around the mess to the landing, still looking a bit taken aback. Clearly he was expecting a different reaction to the one I'd given.

Bobbi scooted after him but I caught her around the middle and lifted her up, careful not to touch her full nappy. 'Gotcha,' I said playfully, trying to avoid her kicks while not breathing too deeply; her nappy really did smell bad. She dropped the rabbit and lashed out, catching my cheek in the exact spot that had only just scabbed over. My skin prickled and stung. 'Let's try and stay calm,' I said, my own adrenaline kicking in.

'Nooooo!' she screeched again, pummelling my face and neck with closed fists as I carried her to the bathroom and knelt in front of her. 'Kind hands, Bobbi,' I said, my voice sounding strained as I fended her hands away. She clawed at my arm by way of reply, her nails digging at the bare skin on my wrist until tiny spots of blood appeared.

'Bobbi, you're safe, sweetie. No one's going to hurt you. Let's just calm down and get you cleaned up.'

She was screaming so hysterically that I wasn't even sure she heard me. Even if she had been able to process

what I was saying, part of me knew that 'calm down' probably didn't mean much to a child who had grown up amid
chaos. 'Be kind' was a meaningless instruction to someone
who had, in all likelihood, been mistreated since birth. I
knew that. But with adrenaline surging through my veins,
it was difficult to think of anything else *to* say but 'calm
down'.

I took a few deep breaths and realised that I was staring
at her, probably with a horrified expression on my face. I
forced myself to look away. 'I'm going to cut you!' she
screamed, still trying to run at me. 'I'm going to cut your
cheeks and twist them off your ugly face.'

Another blast of adrenaline shot through my veins. I
wondered what on earth she had experienced to come out
with things like that. I fended her off, my mind flashing to
the pictures in her room. I took a calming breath, grateful
that at least Megan probably couldn't hear any of what was
going on.

'Bobbi, I'm going to hold you close and help you to feel
better.' Being out of control was terrifying for a child. As I
reached out I knew she would fight against me, but I also
knew that she needed to understand that I was the one in
charge. The sooner she realised that I would keep her safe,
the calmer she would feel.

Enfolding her flailing arms with one of my own, I turned
her around and pulled her onto my lap so that her back was
pressed against my middle. Almost immediately I felt a
warm trickle of liquid on my thigh as the contents of her
nappy seeped through her nightdress and over my jeans.
Simultaneously, the overwhelming stench of excrement hit
my nostrils. I held my breath, trying not to gag.

She thrashed around on my lap, arching her back and trying to launch another assault. As gently as I could – I was anxious not to mark her skin – I held onto her wrists and cuddled her close. 'There, it's alright, I will keep you safe.' I tried to force my mind away from the growing brown stain on my jeans. Eventually her screams turned to sobs and her struggles subsided, her body pliable enough for me to gently rock her to and fro.

When she fell silent I stayed where I was. If I moved too early she was likely to remember her anger and start all over again. Besides that, her stiffened features were softening and, with a sting of pity, I realised that she'd probably never been babied before.

In the early days of placement, when children are railing against the sudden changes that have been foisted upon them, it's sometimes difficult to return their aggression with affection. One of the best pieces of advice I've been given is to 'fake it until you make it'. It's near impossible to love a stranger, especially an abusive one, but when you go through the motions of caring for someone, genuine affection usually grows. As the adult, it was up to me to forge a loving attachment with Bobbi.

After a few minutes I eased her gently to a standing position and rose to my feet. Wordlessly, I knelt on the side of the bath and sprayed down my jeans using the hand-held shower head, aware of her hiccoughing sobs behind me. I worked hard to extinguish the look of disgust from my face as I got a nappy bag out of the cupboard and lifted her into the bath. Despite the low soothing noises I was making, she reeled away when I reached for her nappy, her fingers clasping the waistband so tightly that her knuckles were turning white. I felt a slow rolling sensation in my stomach.

I thought back to one of the courses I'd recently attended, when our tutor told us to interpret any difficult behaviour as an expression of fear. I knew that bedwetting and soiling wasn't unusual in victims of sexual abuse – the smell of urine and faeces an unconscious attempt to make themselves less appealing to their abuser – but the fact was, lots of children Bobbi's age still wet the bed. Soiling was more unusual, but perhaps she had been frightened to venture out to an unfamiliar toilet on her own.

'Do you like bubbles, Bobbi?' I asked gently, reaching for Megan's pot of bubbles on the windowsill. I blew a few bubbles into the air above her head. The effect was instantaneous. Her face lit up and then she reached out and took the pot from me. Engrossed in her efforts to blow more bubbles, she was distracted enough for me to remove her nappy and shower her down.

Megan was waiting outside the door when I opened it. I felt a surge of guilt but she looked up at me with an expectant smile and I realised that she probably hadn't heard a thing. Most of the time I felt sad about Megan's hearing difficulties and would gladly have shared my own with her if I possibly could have, but, I have to admit, on that morning it was more of a blessing than a curse.

'Here we are, guys,' I said twenty minutes later, after washing and changing into a clean pair of jeans. I placed a sand timer on the table. 'I have a challenge for you. We're going to see if we can chew every mouthful of our cereal for thirty seconds. The time starts when I turn the timer over, okay?'

Archie, who had been reading, looked up from his book. 'Yay!' Megan exclaimed, grinning at the others. 'I can. I can do it!' I wasn't sure whether Bobbi had even heard me. She started on her Weetabix without even looking at the timer, scooping another huge spoonful into her mouth a few seconds later. My heart sank. I had introduced the 'game' to all of them, but Bobbi was the one most in need of it.

From the wrappings over their bedroom floor, I suspected that both Archie and Bobbi had already eaten something. I hadn't noticed anything missing from my own cupboards so assumed that they must still be working their way through food that had been hoarded at Joan's. I planned to tackle them about it in a day or two – I didn't want them to keep food in their rooms – but I wanted them to feel a bit more secure before I removed that particular safety blanket.

'Bobbi,' I said, 'you can turn the timer over first.' She stopped chewing and looked at me, her cheeks pouched with food. Archie dug into his cereal and held the spoon in front of his mouth, staring at the timer with focussed intensity.

'What?' Bobbi asked thickly, dropping her spoon into the bowl.

'The sand timer. Turn it over and chew your next mouthful until the sand runs out.' Her eyes flickered with interest as she reached out, turned the timer over and plonked it down again. All three of them scooped up their cereal and began chewing.

Bobbi's mouth worked, her eyes flicking competitively between her brother and Megan. 'Done it, Mummy!' Megan shrieked, as the last grains of sand filtered through the timer. Archie grinned then flipped the timer over again. Watching the timer intently, they tucked in again.

I sat with them and joined in, trying and failing to make each mouthful of my porridge last the full thirty seconds.

'That was a really nice breakfast, Rosie. You're the best cook.'

I smiled. 'Thank you, Archie.'

'I want more!' Bobbi shouted, adding 'please' when I gave her a look. Another helping and two glasses of milk later, she was still 'starving'. I told her she'd had enough, repeating my mantra about there always being enough food for her at Rosie's house. A flurry of protests followed but I shook my head, turned the television on and started clearing the table. Megan and Archie went and sat on the rug and watched cartoons, Mungo rolling around on his back between them. Ecstatic with all the attention, his tail thumped noisily on the floor as they tickled his middle.

Bobbi grabbed my wrist and shook it. 'Rosie, I need more, I do, Rosie, I do!'

'You can have some fruit soon, and they'll be lots more food for lunch and dinner. They'll be plenty of food today, tomorrow, the next day and every day that you're here, I promise.'

Her mouth drooped at the edges as if she didn't believe a word of it but she sloped off her chair and stamped across the room. Mungo sprang to his feet before she reached the rug and trotted off to hide under the coffee table.

After clearing away the breakfast things I decided to try and tackle Bobbi's knotted hair. She hadn't allowed me to wash it in the bath the previous night and it was matted at the ends where she'd slept on it slightly damp. Without saying a word, I planted two doll's styling heads on the rug, one in front of each of the girls, along with a hairbrush for each of them and some styling accessories.

Bobbi swooped, scooping everything up for herself. 'There are some for you and some for Megan,' I said, returning half to Megan, who was watching Bobbi peevishly.

'My dolly doesn't want these anyway,' Bobbi said sulkily, sweeping her half back to Megan. 'She has a bad headache.'

'Does she now?' I went to the first-aid cupboard and pulled out some old, out-of-date bandages and plasters. 'Perhaps she needs some of these.'

Bobbi looked thrilled. While Megan covered her doll's head in hair clips and lipstick, Bobbi covered hers from top to bottom in bandages.

Absorbed by the cartoons and the doll, she didn't protest when I got to work on her hair. She kept shuffling forward on her bottom though, only stopping when she was about a foot from the television. I hauled her back each time, wondering whether her eyesight was all that it should be. I made a mental note to book an appointment for her at the opticians.

I used a wide-toothed comb on her hair, trying my best not to pull on the tangled ends. It was as I worked my way back towards the nape of her neck that I noticed something unusual – the back of her head was almost entirely flat. My heart lurched. I knew that since the 'back to sleep' campaign had been launched to reduce the number of sudden infant deaths, more babies had developed flattened spots on their skull as a result of laying in the same position in their cots or car seats, but Bobbi's was an extreme example, her scalp devoid of even the merest hint of a curve. I felt a swell of sympathy for the baby she had been, probably left alone for hours, perhaps even days at a time.

When I'd finished I sat at the table on the opposite side of the room and added a note in my daily diary about Bobbi's flattened scalp to the growing list of worries accumulating beneath her name. The opposite page, the one for her brother, was blank. I wrote 'Archie' at the top and drew a line underneath it. There hadn't been a single incident of difficult or even mildly challenging behaviour from him since he'd arrived.

Even so, I was hoping to speak to Danny Brookes, the children's social worker soon. I had missed a call from him earlier that day. He'd left a message on my mobile to give his name as my point of contact, but when I'd called back, his own answerphone had kicked in. I fired off a quick email to the fostering team listing my concerns and asked them to forward it onto Danny. What I wanted to say about Archie, I couldn't exactly put my finger on. My eyes drifted across the room and settled on the children, all sitting cross-legged on the rug. Beneath his thick crop of hair it was difficult to tell whether Archie's scalp was flat like his sister's. In fact, beneath his smooth facade it was tricky to work out anything about him. I picked up my notebook and pen again and, beneath Archie's name, I filled the space with a large question mark.

Chapter Six

I finally spoke to the children's social worker at 9 a.m. three days later, on Monday 5 January. Most of the children in the borough, including Jamie, had returned to school after the Christmas holidays, but Megan's nursery was closed for an INSET day and wasn't due to reopen until tomorrow. Emily was studying at the library, and I still wasn't sure where to send Archie and Bobbi. I had called Joan to ask if she knew whether the children were home educated, but she had no idea either.

As I listened to Danny introducing himself over the telephone I heard footsteps on the stairs. I turned to see Megan padding down awkwardly in a pair of pink crocs. She had dressed herself again. The thick woolly jumper she had chosen was on inside out, almost covering the pink stripy shorts she was wearing. She jumped down the last two steps and skipped over to me, flinging her arms around one of my legs.

I pulled a funny face as I listened to Danny outlining social services' legal position. Megan giggled and tugged at my hand, insisting loudly that I should come and play. I shook my head and put a finger to my lips, gesticulating for her to go and find the others. She danced around my legs then planted a kiss on my hip and skipped down the hall. Seconds later I heard her chatter cutting through Bobbi's monologue.

From what Danny was saying it seemed that the Bradys' neighbours had tolerated months of anti-social behaviour in the lead-up to the children being removed. On the night the children were removed, they had heard a series of disturbing thuds and lots of shouting, followed by crying that went on for hours. Being the early hours of the morning, it hadn't been possible for the local authority to seek an Emergency Protection Order, so the children had been taken into police protective custody. 'So you're in court today?'

'Yep,' Danny said over a rustle of papers. His voice was deep and warm, his accent bordering on cockney. 'They came in early on the 29th. Strictly speaking the police protection only allows us to keep them for seventy-two hours, so we're out of time on that. I'm meeting Tanya Brady, that's Mum, later today but I've spoken to her over the phone a couple of times. She sounded half-cut the first time, but when we spoke again she told me she's engaged a solicitor. She'll be contesting, but I'm certain we'll get our ICO.'

An ICO or Interim Care Order is a temporary order made by the court when there are reasonable grounds to suspect that a child has suffered or may be at risk of suffering significant harm. An ICO means that the birth parents must share parental responsibility with the local authority until a final decision is made by the courts.

Parents who have had their children removed from their care automatically qualify for legal aid no matter what their financial circumstances, so it's rare for a care order to go unchallenged.

'So how they been then?'

'Erm, well, we're still getting to know each other really. Archie seems to have taken the move in his stride –'

'Oh?' Danny cut in. 'Not sure I like the sound of that.'

'– yes, I know, I know,' I said, lowering my voice. Social workers always reserved more concern for children who seemed not to react when their entire world had tilted on its axis. Some children were highly skilled at concealing their vulnerability beneath a phoney exterior, usually because they feared that their true feelings were too ugly to expose. Such camouflage requires years of practice and monumental levels of self-control. One of my tasks as Archie's foster carer was to help him peel away the protective layers he'd wrapped around himself. I also had to prepare myself to nurture whatever lurked underneath.

'And Bobbi?'

I hesitated for a moment. 'I think it's fair to say that Bobbi and I are still trying to reach an understanding. We've had a few hiccups so far, but we're getting there.' It was a sanitised version, given that the siblings were within earshot. In truth the last few days had passed in a blur of frenzied, violent meltdowns. I was grateful that the children had arrived during the holidays when Emily and Jamie were at home. Whenever Bobbi began to blow, one or the other of them had taken Megan off to play, sparing her the worst of the fall-out.

Broken

The trouble was, Bobbi flew off the handle at the slightest provocation and with very little warning. Most of the time it was impossible to even begin to ascertain the trigger. She refused to comply with the simplest of requests – I had only managed to brush her teeth three times in five days, and even then only for a few seconds while she thrashed around, snarling and snapping. It was like trying to groom a bowl of jelly laced with nitroglycerin.

Archie, on the other hand, spent most of his time either covering up Bobbi's misdeeds or assuming responsibility for them, even when it was clear he'd had not the slightest involvement. He spoke to her in soothing tones and went out of his way to try and calm her down, his parentified behaviour offering an insight into the peace-making role he may have assumed at home. Archie had cleaned up the mess Bobbi made in their room, his sister shouting instructions from the sidelines.

He was always eager to help, though he made an effort at being cool whenever Jamie graced us with his presence. He'd been pleased on Saturday when Jamie and a couple of his mates had allowed him to join in their game of basketball in the garden. Since then it became clear that there was a bit of hero-worship going on. Jamie, having grown up with fostering, took it all in his stride.

Danny belted out a laugh. 'We'll have a proper chat at the Placement Planning Meeting. You home tomorrow? I'm thinking early. I can't seem to get hold of your supervising social worker, a –' There was another rustle of papers. '– Sarah Baker? Is she away at the moment?'

'I'm afraid Sarah left Bright Heights weeks ago. I don't have a supervising social worker at the moment.' Des, my longest-running supervising social worker (SSW) at Bright Heights, had left the agency over three years earlier to gather information on a youth behavioural scheme that had been showing signs of success in Boston. Our friendship had grown over the years and I missed his impromptu visits while he was away, so much so that when he returned to England in 2014, we began spending more time together. We weren't quite in a relationship, but things seemed to be heading that way.

Since Des left the agency I had been assigned to seven different SSWs, each staying in post for such a short time that it had been difficult to build anything other than a polite working relationship with them. 'I'm able to approach the fostering manager if I have any concerns though,' I added in defence of the agency, although if I'm honest I did feel a little cast adrift.

'Yeah, yeah, course you are.'

I sucked in a breath, unsure whether he was serious or not.

'Mate, I'm joking. We'll manage. See you tomorrow.'

I laughed. 'Yes, I'll see you then.' I lowered the receiver but then quickly lifted it to my ear again. 'Danny, sorry, before you go –'

'Jeez, what now? You're gonna be one of those awkward ones, aren't you? I can always tell.'

'Danny, you have no idea,' I said with a grin, already getting the measure of him. A low chuckle came down the line. 'Can I just check, what school do the children go to? Is it Millfield Primary?'

Broken

Danny snorted. 'Yeah. Well, put it this way, that's where they're supposed to go. I'll tell you all about it tomorrow.'

I spent the next half an hour trying to cajole Bobbi into getting dressed. Neither Bobbi nor Archie had a full uniform to wear in the morning and I wanted to get to the school outfitters before lunchtime so that I could label everything and still make it to Megan's swimming lesson, which was due to start at half past one.

I had rolled out every weapon in my armoury to try and persuade Bobbi into her clothes: playfulness, competitiveness – *I bet you can't get your jumper on within the next twenty seconds* – bribery with chocolate. With Megan's enthusiastic help, I'd even involved her in crafting a postbox out of cardboard and red paint, so that we could post pictures of each item of clothing she managed to get on herself. It worked a treat with Megan, who paraded her entire wardrobe in front of me in the time it took to get Bobbi into her socks.

'If you don't get dressed we won't be able to get you a costume and you won't be able to swim with Megan,' I said, kneeling in front of her and holding out her jumper invitingly. I had spoken to Megan's swimming teacher that morning and she'd kindly agreed to squeeze Bobbi into the lesson so that she wouldn't feel left out. I often found people went out of their way to be accommodating for fostered children.

My spirits lifted as Bobbi ducked her head and allowed me to slip her jumper on. I could hardly believe she might finally relent. 'Woo-hoo!' I said, clapping and making a big fuss of her as she slipped her arms into the sleeves. 'Well done, Bobbi!' She beamed.

Megan joined in with the applause. 'Well done, Bobs!' she cheered. 'Yippee!' From beneath the coffee table, Mungo gave a soft bark.

'She'll take it off again in a minute,' Archie predicted morosely from the sofa. He peered over the top of his book and then quickly returned his attention to the page, his eyes eagerly running left to right. Within half a second Bobbi's arms were out of the sleeves, the rest of the jumper hanging like a thick woollen chain from her neck.

I gave Archie a dark look. Ever since his arrival he had been nothing less than accommodating and helpful. This morning, though, he seemed determined to derail my efforts to prepare him for school. He had faked surprise when I told him that Danny had confirmed that he went to Millfield Primary, and since then had dragged his feet at every turn. 'Bobbi,' I said in a low tone. 'Put it back on, please.' She looked at me, her head in a defiant tilt, and then she whipped the jumper right off.

'Back on now or you won't go swimming,' I said warningly. Megan stood close by, her eyes flitting between us. I feigned an interest in the TV magazine on the coffee table, half-aware of Bobbi picking up her leggings as I flicked through the pages.

'Yay!' Megan shouted. 'You can come swimming with me now, Bobs!'

'Ow-a!' Bobbi growled. 'I can't do them.'

'Come here. I'll help.' She crawled over and gave them to me. I lifted her to her feet and told her to hold on to my shoulder. 'That's it, now lift your leg.' She didn't move. 'Come on, honey, lift your leg.'

Half a second later Megan cried out and clamped a hand over her eyes – while I'd been leaning over, Bobbi had slapped her face.

'Right, that's it. No swimming for Bobbi.' I had tried to keep my voice even but it hadn't worked. My patience was drained and it showed. Megan wasn't crying – I think she was more shocked than anything else – but I drew her onto my lap and kissed the top of her head. She leaned into me and rested her head on my chest.

A sickening thud reached my ears a second or two later. I swung around just in time to see Bobbi's head slamming into the floor for a second time, the crack of skull meeting floorboard making my stomach flip. Megan got off my lap and stared at Bobbi in horror. 'It's alright, Meggie,' I said, steering her towards the door. 'You go upstairs and see if you can find a towel and your goggles. I'll take care of Bobbi.'

Megan backed slowly out of the room, her eyes fixed on Bobbi, who was now on her feet and biting her own forearm. It must have been painful, but with the red mist working its numbing magic, she continued to gnaw at her skin. I crouched in front of her, aware that Megan was still staring at us from the doorway. 'Go, Megan, please,' I said, without taking my eyes off Bobbi. I heard her scurry away and my chest tightened with guilt.

'Bobbi, I'm not going to let you hurt yourself,' I said, taking a firm hold of her arm and pulling it free of her jaws. 'I can see that you're feeling cross,' I continued, in a lame attempt at naming her feelings, but she'd already reached a point from which it was going to be difficult to return. She just needed to be held.

'GET OFF ME!' she screamed as I reached out to her, battering me with her fists and then clawing her hands down her own face. I pulled her onto my lap and pinned her arms down with my own to protect us both. She struggled and screamed, her feet slamming repeatedly into the floor. Once again, though, it was Archie's reaction that unnerved me most. He was watching me from the sofa, an expression of suppressed fury on his face.

'What's wrong, Arch?'

'You shouldn't have kept asking her to lift her leg,' he snapped, chucking his book aside. 'You scared her.'

I looked at him. 'How come?' I leaned over Bobbi, who had stiffened on my lap. 'Why were you scared to lift your leg, sweetheart?'

'Jason makes her stand on one leg when she's naughty, that's why,' Archie spat out.

My throat tightened. 'Oh, Bobbi, that's very wrong of him. I'm sorry, sweetheart, I didn't know.' She allowed me to cuddle her to my chest. I gave Archie a regretful look over the top of her head. He glared at me, his cheeks flushed red.

Chapter Seven

Swirling grey clouds hung low in the sky as we drove towards Millfield Primary the next morning. As luck would have it, Megan's nursery opened fifteen minutes earlier than Archie and Bobbi's school, so I had been able to drop her off with confidence that I'd make it to Millfield on time.

It was Tuesday 6 January, Bobbi and Archie's first day back at school after the holidays, and I had woken everyone earlier than usual in anticipation of a major fall-out in getting Bobbi dressed. With careful avoidance of any 'lifting leg' instructions, it wasn't the battle I'd anticipated, as it turned out, and by 8 a.m. everyone had been tucking into their breakfast.

The Jason comment aside, I still knew little about Bobbi's past – my gentle attempt to encourage her to talk about her fears of punishment batted away last night by a loud screechy song – but there was every reason to suppose that she had been neglected from birth. There were all sorts of likely triggers to her panicked behaviour, some I would only ever be able to guess at.

The smell of sour milk, for example, might set off a hysterical reaction in a child who had lain untended in their cot for hours at a time. I knew that some children in foster care flew off the handle whenever they were cold, the sensation reminding them of the terror they felt as babies, when they had been left to go to sleep without clothes or blankets. For others, loud music caused fear, or shouting, or being smiled at in a certain way; a once-used code from Daddy signalling that it was time to join him upstairs. Trauma triggered behaviour was unpredictable by its very nature; I knew it would take some time to decode.

At a red light I glanced at Bobbi in the rear-view mirror as she made an infernal noise. She looked smart in her uniform and older somehow. I had bought two new sets of uniform for each of the children when I finally made it to the shops yesterday, my mother stepping into the breach so I didn't have to drag Bobbi around town in her PJs. 'They've been as good as gold,' Mum announced on my return, a twinkle in her eye. It was often the way with the children I looked after. They seemed to sense the genuine warmth beneath Mum's firm exterior and responded well to her gentle attentiveness. As an unwanted replacement of their birth mother, it often took longer for me to gain a child's trust.

'Maybe you could try being a bit firmer,' Mum had whispered to me on her way out. My mother holds firmly to the view that punishment and retribution are the most effective means of keeping children on the straight and narrow. Though rarely openly critical, I often got the feeling that she believed my own system of using positive praise, consistency and continuity alongside a careful balance of love and discipline was ridiculously soft.

I rolled my eyes at my brother, Chris, who had popped by to pick Mum up and drop her and Megan to the leisure centre for her swimming lesson. When Bobbi had seen Chris on the doorstep she froze. A few seconds later she had wrapped herself around his shins and was planting rapid kisses on his knee.

Stunned, Chris gave her head a quick pat and threw me a '*What's this all about?*' look. I raised my eyes and pulled her gently away. 'Bobbi, this is my brother but you don't know him yet. We keep our cuddles for people we know well. Okay, poppet?' I began to wonder whether she had some sort of attachment disorder. Unscrupulous abusers seemed to have internal radar for vulnerable children like Bobbi. Foster carers are taught to gently dissuade children from being overfamiliar to reduce their risk of sexual exploitation. Bobbi's random friendliness was yet another concern to add to the list in my diary. I was glad that the siblings' social worker was due to visit this morning so I could discuss it with him.

'See, there. That's where I come out, Rosie,' Archie told me as we crossed the colourful springy tarmac of the playground. He pointed to an archway at the far end of the brick building in front of us. 'I'll be there at half past three, but Bobbi comes out five minutes earlier.'

'I know, honey. You've said.' The prospect of returning to school seemed to have cracked his facade. He had been fidgety all morning and extra fastidious, straightening every wonky item in his sight. 'I'll be here, don't worry. You enjoy your day.' He nodded soberly, ruffled the top of his sister's hair and then picked his way through a crowd of children. Not a single one of them turned to greet or even acknowledge him as he passed. My heart squeezed at the sight. Children in care often struggle to make and maintain friendships, their ability to form relationships compromised by their early experiences.

The Early Years play area was separated from the main playground by a multi-coloured fence. Inside the confines I could see a sand pit, climbing frame and, at the far end, a race track with buggies and cars lined up neatly on the starting line. Part of the playground was shaded by enormous sheets of coloured canvas fixed to tall posts, designed to look like sails on a ship. It was a bright, welcoming space, but one that was failing to work its magic on Bobbi. At my side, she was clinging onto my hand so tightly that I could feel her fingernails digging into my palm.

A young woman with crinkly red hair tied into two long plaits appeared at the Early Years gate, ready to welcome the Reception children in. 'Hello, nice to meet you, I'm Rosie,' I said, doing my best to stay upright with Bobbi now clutching at my legs.

The teacher smiled uncertainly. 'I'm Miss Granville,' she said, giving Bobbi a wary, almost fearful look. Any help I was hoping for in coaxing Bobbi away from me wasn't forthcoming, so I went into the classroom with her and gently disentangled myself there.

'That's so thoughtful of you,' the receptionist said when I dropped in my contact information details. 'I think we have these on file already though. The MASH team were in touch yesterday.' A motherly-looking woman with a round face and greying hair, she lowered her tone and leaned closer to the glass partition she was sitting behind. 'Those poor children. It breaks your heart, doesn't it? I don't know how you do it.'

Almost every serious case review triggered by the death or serious injury of a child previously identified as being at risk had highlighted a lack of information sharing as a major failing. Multi-Agency Safeguarding Hubs (MASH) were considered the solution; a co-located arrangement of agencies – social services, police, health and education, with close links to probation, youth offending teams and mental health. It was thought that by bringing the agencies together, information sharing, intelligence gathering and networking would vastly improve. The results were notice-able. Now, if police are called to an incident of domestic violence and children are living in the house, their schools are notified before 9 a.m. the following day. Forewarned of the trauma the child may have experienced, teachers are now in a better position to understand distressed or diffi-cult behaviour.

I thanked the receptionist and made to leave, but before I'd reached the door I heard a tapping sound. I turned to see a tall, bespectacled woman with dark hair at the glass. 'Rosie, sorry,' she called through a grille in the window. 'I overheard you introducing yourself. I'm Clare Barnard, the SENCO. Have you got time for a quick word?'

I glanced at the clock on the wall and nodded. The chil-dren's social worker was due at ten but I had time for a quick chat and the Special Educational Needs Co-ordinator (SENCO) was often a very useful person for a foster carer to get to know. 'Lovely to meet you,' Clare said half a minute later when she joined me in reception. There was a long red sofa behind us and she made a sweeping gesture, inviting me to sit down.

'I've only got a few minutes,' I said apologetically. 'I'm meeting the children's social worker this morning.'

She raised a hand. 'No, that's fine. I won't keep you a minute. I just wanted to bring you up to speed with how things stand from our perspective. We haven't been able to have this discussion with the children's mother because,' she paused, licking her lips, 'well, I expect you can imagine. It's difficult to involve some parents in school life.' I nodded ruefully and she continued. 'The thing is, we've been concerned about Bobbi since she started with us in September. As you probably know, we've not seen much of her, but when she is here she's extremely disruptive. Towards the end of last term we even considered reducing her hours to part-time. That's not something we'd consider lightly. The only reason we didn't is because we were worried about the impact of her spending more time at home.' She looked at me. 'But now she's in foster care –'

'Ah,' I said slowly, the inference dawning on me. 'You're going to reconsider?'

She looked at me over the top of her glasses. 'We haven't made a final decision yet. It could be that she settles down and we won't have to resort to that. We're working hard to encourage her to make good choices, but the level of disruption is quite severe, I'm afraid. She's already bitten her class teacher several times. Miss Granville is newly qualified. It really isn't behaviour we can accommodate in our school.'

'No, I see.'

The SENCO pulled her chin in and blinked in surprise. 'I expected more resistance. The prospect of having a child at home during the day doesn't appeal to some.'

'I'd rather she was here, of course I would, especially as she might regard reduced hours as some sort of rejection. But I appreciate you have a duty of care to the other children. And to Miss Granville,' I added with a grim smile. The young teacher's earlier avoidance suddenly made more sense.

If I'm honest, I had felt a sense of relief when I escaped from Bobbi's class. The opportunity for some time alone to regroup and recharge wasn't something I wanted to relinquish, but if Bobbi wasn't coping well with full-time hours, it wasn't good for her or anyone around her if she wasn't cut any slack. And one way or another, the impact would reach us at home.

Clare smiled gratefully. 'Well, that's one less battle for us to worry about. Obviously we'll do all we can to avoid it. We want her to learn, and with what she's missed already –' She paused, pressing her lips together. 'She has a lot of catching up to do.'

'Being behind isn't likely to help her frustration levels either.'

She looked at me thoughtfully. 'No, it is a worry. Archie's the same. He's a bright boy but he's missed so many days since he joined us in September. Thirty-five in a single term, if memory serves me. We're still liaising with the Children Missing Education Agency because of all their non-attendance.'

'Oh? They're both new to the school then?'

She nodded. 'And we're still trying to piece together what happened before they came here. I'm told they moved into the area two years ago but their mother didn't bother to register Archie with a new school when they relocated. It's only when they came under the radar of social services that his non-attendance came to light.'

'I had no idea. How can that have happened?'

She sighed. 'I'm afraid some children do fall through the net. Archie was registered with a school somewhere down south before the family moved. It seems that Mrs Brady removed him from the admission register down there and gave the receptionist the name of another school when they moved up here, but he was never actually registered.

'As I say, it only came to light when social workers became involved with the family. Our feeling is that they should have been removed from home long before this. I despair of the system sometimes.'

'It's a difficult balance to strike, I guess.' With the benefit of hindsight it's easy to criticise, but I knew lots of social workers who wrestled with their consciences when making judgements that so deeply affected people's lives.

Clare held her hands up. 'Don't get me wrong. I couldn't be a social worker, not in a million years.'

I made it home with ten minutes to spare before Danny Brookes was due to arrive. Given that lateness seemed wired into the DNA of almost every social worker I had ever met, I assumed that I had at least another half an hour before he actually turned up. I made a quick cup of tea, gave Mungo some fresh water and fired up my computer, but just as I sat down in front of it, the doorbell rang.

'Don't look so surprised,' Danny said, when I opened the door. 'Not all of us are muppets.'

I laughed and he shook my hand warmly. Over a foot taller than my five feet, Danny was a large-framed black man with wild Afro hair and the biggest biceps I had ever seen. It was a cold day, about two degrees, but his large hands were warm despite the thin T-shirt and jeans he was wearing. 'You may not be a muppet, but I'm not sure you're human,' I said as he petted Mungo. I showed him through to the living area. 'It's freezing out there and you're dressed for the beach.'

'Big heart, ain't I?' he barked, banging his fist into his chest. 'I don't need nothing else to keep me warm.'

Already at ease in his company, I made him a cup of coffee and gave him a summary of events over the last few days, sparing none of the grisly details. He listened without interrupting, dunking half a packet of biscuits into his coffee as I spoke and letting Mungo lick the crumbs from his fingers. 'So, all in all,' he said, when I'd fallen silent, 'things couldn't be better.'

'We've known worse,' I said with a grin. 'But I really felt myself floundering over the weekend. The tricks I usually employ – you know, lots of praise, sticker charts, removal of privileges – they just don't seem to work with Bobbi. I'm not sure I'm helping her that much. I feel like I'm making things worse, if anything. Then there are the pictures she drew … did you get the email I sent over?'

Danny nodded. 'Yep. It's good you're being vigilant, but I don't think we should worry about it at this stage.'

I looked at him. 'There were quite graphic.'

'Something to keep in our line of sight maybe, but let's not go running away with ourselves yet.' I nodded. Under increasing pressure to place children who are unable to

71

return to their birth families into adoptive placements, some social workers have a tendency to gloss over the more disturbing details of their past through a strong desire not to scupper their chances of finding a forever home. It's a sad fact, but injuries and evidence consistent with sexual abuse makes scary reading for adopters, and sexually abused children are difficult to place. 'And how about Archie?'

I sipped my tea. 'He's doing everything he's asked. He's polite and helpful. Charmingly complimentary, even. But I get the feeling that he's an exceptionally angry young man.' I paused, lowering my cup to the floor. 'I don't know. Maybe I'm reading more into it all than I should.'

Danny handed the packet of biscuits to me. 'They're going down a bit too nice. Get them out of my sight, will you?' He brushed a few stray crumbs from his mouth and let a delighted Mungo mop up the rest. 'Now, listen, there's nothing wrong with that. They've finally got someone on their side. But let's not go over thinking anything at this stage. They've had two major upheavals in the last week. That in itself can cause these sorts of low-level behaviours.'

I knew what he meant. Two moves in one week was undoubtedly a shock to the system, but still I felt my jaw stiffening. What appeared on paper to be low-level behaviours were, in reality, not that easy to live with. He noticed me bristling. 'Listen, I'm sure it's pretty full-on, but you know what I'm getting at, yeah?'

I sighed. 'Yes, I know.'

He nodded. 'Course, there's a lot in their background we just don't know about yet. They've been on our radar for the last eighteen months or so, but it wouldn't surprise me if things weren't a whole lot worse than we thought.' He reached into his rucksack and pulled out an A4 notepad and pen. 'I've just inherited the case from the Children in Need team, so don't know Tanya, their mum, well. She denies it, but we suspect there's a long history of alcohol abuse. She's not with the kids' birth father; they separated when Bobbi was tiny. We're trying to trace …' he flicked through his notes. '… Mr James Brady as we speak.'

I nodded. 'Archie seems very keen to see him.' I told him what Archie had said about his father's visit and his mother's refusal to let him in the house.

'Ah, interesting. According to Mum, he wants nothing to do with them.' Danny tapped his pen on his pad. 'I'll have to do a bit more digging. Mum's been with her latest partner, Jason Keane, for two years. Over the last year and a half there've been a few incidents of domestic abuse. None involving the children in a physical sense but we all know that don't really matter. They were at home at the time, so they're involved.'

I jumped in then, telling Danny about Archie's comment about Jason forcing Bobbi to stand on one leg. He grimaced. 'We've already suggested that separation is the only way for Tanya to get them back, but she's absolutely having none of it.'

I pulled a face. 'Yep,' Danny said with a grim twist of his lips. 'What can you do? The kids both attended the Keep Safe workshop –'

'Yes, I helped out on some of the sessions,' I interrupted again. 'I met Archie there.'

'– oh right, yeah. Mum's been asked to attend the Judy Fights Back course. We want her to wise up to what's happening, but so far she's refusing to engage. She won't go anywhere without Jason. She even wants to bring him to contact with the kids.'

'And is he going to be allowed to?'

'Is he bollocks! No way.' I stifled a smile. Danny was quite different to most of the social workers I knew, but bluntness wasn't a bad trait to have in his line of work, I thought.

'How is Tanya? Archie's worried about her.'

Danny tutted. 'Poor kid. Tell him I've spoken to her and she's okay. What else?' he continued. 'As I said, the kids have shown no physical signs of abuse, but there have been concerns about them getting caught in the crossfire. Bobbi's been kicking off at school so it's clear she's seen something at home. I reckon there's a whole lot more to come out. We've suspected neglect for a while now, and your note about Bobbi's flat scalp would seem to corroborate that. Have you noticed whether Archie's is the same?'

I shook my head. 'It isn't. I made a point of checking when he last washed his hair, and it looks normal –' I stopped, correcting myself, '– I mean, typical, not normal.'

Danny grinned. 'You can relax around me, Rosie. I'm not about to pull you up on stuff like that.' His expression grew serious. 'That would make sense with what we know about neglect. The older kids often fare better than the younger ones, what with addiction intensifying over time.'

I nodded, suddenly reminded of something Greg Keck, a psychologist specialising in the treatment of children who have experienced trauma, had said when addressing a national adoption conference – 'If you have to choose between abuse and neglect, choose abuse; it does less damage.' His audience were shocked, but the psychologist reasoned that when a child was being physically abused, at least they were being noticed, albeit in the worst way imaginable. By making the comparison he was challenging the widely held belief that abuse is worse than neglect and also highlighting the devastating impact of ignoring a child.

Danny filled out some of the necessary paperwork while I made him another coffee and then we went through the Placement Plan and Agreement forms together. 'Contact's been agreed as twice a week with Mum initially, to take place straight after school on a Monday and a Thursday. I've asked for a seamless transfer to the family centre so you don't have too much messing around, but could you pick them up at five thirty when it's finished?'

I nodded, grateful that Danny had given contact some thought. It wasn't always the case. 'How d'you feel about them giving Mum a call, say, a couple of times a week?'

I pulled a face. 'I'm flexible, I suppose, if you think it will help.' Personally I wasn't a fan of telephone contact. Some children found face-to-face contact with their parents unsettling. Shoehorning phone calls into their 'days off' added yet another burden onto their shoulders; another reminder of how complicated their lives were.

'Let's start with once a week then. I'll give you Mum's phone number and you can withhold your number when you call.'

I nodded again. 'Do I need to supervise their conversations?'

'Yep, keep the phone on loudspeaker. Make sure you warn Mum first though, yeah? We'll talk it over at the LAC Review, which, by the way, has been arranged for this Friday.'

I widened my eyes and Danny apologised. 'Yep, sorry. I might be punctual, but I'm not perfect.'

I rolled my eyes. 'Are we inviting Archie to the review?' LAC, or Looked After Children's, Reviews, are meetings attended by everyone involved with the child's welfare – birth parents, foster carers, social workers, teachers and, in some instances, police officers – to ensure that the child's needs are being met and that a reasonable care plan is in place.

Chaired by an IRO, Independent Reviewing Officer, the reviews give everyone an equal opportunity to express their concerns and raise any complaints, as well as a chance to discuss contact arrangements, future plans and the children's day-to-day care. Older children are usually encouraged to join at least part of the review, so that they can share their feelings about the placement and any other concerns they may have. 'Yes, discuss it with him. See if he feels comfortable attending. I'll leave it up to you to decide whether you ask Bobbi or not. Personally I think she might find it a bit much.'

'I agree. I'll ask Archie though.'

'Right. Now we've just got the delegated authority forms to get through.' Delegated authority is the authorisation given by the local authority to the foster carer to make everyday family life decisions on their behalf, without consulting with social workers first. It's a lengthy but useful form covering such things as haircuts, school trips and sleepovers and leaves no one in any doubt as to their responsibilities.

Danny heaved a sigh as he shoved the notepad back into his rucksack and pulled out a bulky manila file, which he referred to as 'more crap'. 'Not a paperwork fan then, Danny?'

'Me? Nah, I'm new to this level of bureaucracy.'

'Oh right? What did you do before?'

'I was in the army. Royal Engineers.'

I smiled. 'Ah, now the timely appearance makes sense.'

He laughed. 'Yep, old habits die hard. I don't do late. This paperwork is a whole different ball game though.'

'Goodness, yes, I bet.' It was hard to tell, but if I had to place him I would have said he was in his late thirties, early forties at the most. 'That's quite a change of direction.'

He scratched his tight curls. 'Yeah well, I'd had enough of travelling around by the time the missus was expecting. I wanted something closer to home, know what I mean?'

It was almost one o'clock by the time we'd finished. After stowing his notepad and files in his rucksack, Danny stretched his arms behind his head, yawned loudly and then slumped back on the sofa. 'I don't wanna move now after all that. You haven't got any lunch knocking about out there, have you?'

Chapter Eight

We ate lunch together and after Danny left I took Mungo for a walk and then spent an hour catching up on the chores that are necessary at the beginning of a new placement; I registered the children with my GP and made appointments for them at the local dentist and opticians. It was standard procedure and something I would be asked about at the LAC Review.

My suspicion that Bobbi needed glasses gained a little more weight when I picked her up from school later that afternoon. 'Look at those sheep, Rosie,' she said as we neared the ironwork gates. A few feet away, two Labradors padded along the pavement on either side of their owner.

'They're not sheep, they're doggies!' Megan said. Bobbi squinted and then the pair of them giggled. By the time we'd reached the car they were at loggerheads though, because Bobbi had accidentally trodden on a snail, and Megan adored snails. 'You're a meanie, Bobbi!' Megan shouted as I strapped her into her seat.

In protest at the insult, Bobbi screamed with such fury that she wore herself out, and a few minutes from home her head began to nod.

'Rosie,' Archie yelled, 'she's falling asleep, quick!'

'Don't worry about it, Arch,' I said soothingly. He really did sound stressed, and then I remembered what he'd said about being responsible for getting Bobbi to bed. He still hadn't adjusted to the idea of handing the reins over to me, bless him. When Bobbi started to scream again, the anguish on his face subsided.

Bobbi tried to kick me as I led her into the house, but I told myself we were making progress. It was a half-hearted attempt and at least I hadn't got the crooked finger from Miss Granville when I'd picked her up, the summons dreaded by foster carers all over the country. When I looked at her home school diary, though, it was clear that she hadn't had an incident-free day – 'BOBBI SCRATCHED A CLASSMATE ACROSS THE FACE TODAY FOR NO APPARENT REASON', the note read, in big attention-grabbing letters. 'WHEN ASKED WHY SHE DID IT, SHE BIT ONE OF THE STAFF.'

Therapeutic parenting experts advise foster carers to assume that the child they're caring for is stuck develop-mentally in babyhood, unable to move on until the unmet needs of their infancy are fulfilled. Telling Bobbi what she shouldn't do hadn't worked out too well so far, so I decided to strip everything back to basics.

'We must use our hands and feet gently,' I said when we got to the living room. 'Shall we try and think of some nice things we can do with our hands?'

'I know!' Megan cried. 'We can clap!' She clapped her

hands together in demonstration, looking from me to Bobbi. She beamed when we copied her and threw her arms around Bobbi. In no mood for a hug, Bobbi shoved her violently in the chest and Megan fell backwards onto her bottom. Mungo half-ventured out from beneath the coffee table with the whites of his eyes showing, growled, then scurried back to safety. Megan looked at me in wide-eyed surprise. As I picked her up for a cuddle I felt a small twist in my heart.

I stoked her back. 'It's best we get to know Bobbi a bit more before we hug her, okay?' I whispered. She gave a small nod of her head. 'Now, Bobbi. We mustn't use our hands for pushing. Can you think of something nice instead?'

'Drawing,' Megan whispered, with a wary glance at Bobbi.

'Good one, Meggie. What else?'

'Painting,' Bobbi offered, beginning to get into the spirit of the game.

'Yes, brilliant, painting's a great one.'

'Can we do it now, Rosie? Please, Rosie, please. I want to paint now.'

'Okay, for a little while, until dinner's ready.'

Megan, who loved anything arty, leapt from my lap and held her hand out to Bobbi. I held my breath, frantically searching my mind for a distraction so that Megan wouldn't feel rejected if Bobbi pushed her away again. Half a second later, to my surprise Bobbi reached out and took her hand. My heart melted as I watched them walk over to the table together.

Through the patio doors I could see Jamie and Archie kicking a ball to one another in the garden. Archie's tense expression had relaxed when he saw me waiting for him in the place we had agreed, but he mumbled something inaudible when I told him that his mum was okay and that contact had been arranged for Thursday. He politely agreed to attend the LAC Review with me on Friday, but had been quiet ever since. When I tried to talk to him he smoothly changed the subject, telling me about the latest fix Harry Potter had got himself into in *The Chamber of Secrets*. Once again I was filled with the sense that something was badly wrong; something Archie seemed desperately keen to cover up. He visibly brightened when Jamie got in from school though and pleaded to play with him.

It was when Jamie finally came in that I first glimpsed the real boy beneath the mask. 'That is one angry kid,' Jamie said as he washed his hands at the kitchen sink. 'He's got a right strop on. I don't know what his problem is. I told him I only had a minute and we've been out there ages.'

I dropped the potato I had just peeled into a saucepan of water and picked up another one. 'I know you have. It's good of you to give him a run-around. Don't worry about it, love, he'll be alright.'

He touched my shoulder and walked away. 'What time's dinner?' he called from the hall. His movements had slowed over the years and our conversations had shrunk at the same rate. At ten years old he used to dart around the place talking for England; now everything about him was measured and unhurried. Even his replies to my texts were abbreviated these days, most of them consisting of a single letter – 'K'.

'It'll be on the table in half an hour.'

At that moment the back door swung open and Archie stamped in, his face like thunder. I lowered my knife and turned around, a half-peeled potato in my hand. 'Disappointed your game's over, love?' I gave him a sympathetic glance. He ignored me. Leaning on one of the worktops for support, he stepped on the back of one trainer with the tip of the other. 'Still, there's always another day,' I added cheerfully, picking up my knife again.

Behind me, he let out a growl of anger. I turned, watching as he ground one shoe into the other in a furious bid to get his trainers off. 'Oh damn it!' he shouted, kicking out at the wall.

'Why don't you just untie the laces instead of going through all that kerfuffle?'

'Why don't you fuck off?' he hollered, yanking one trainer off with his hand. It hit the floor and spun upwards, hitting me on the back of my leg.

'Archie!' He ignored my yelp, stamping away in a furious half-limp, one trainer on, one off. I stared after him, the peeling of the potato hanging in a spiral from my knife, my heart beating fast in my chest.

At the dinner table he picked at his food, pushing it around his plate with a sulky expression. I wondered whether returning to school had upset him, or whether some of his classmates had caught wind of him being in foster care and ribbed him about it. I had expected him to be pleased with the news about his mum, but there was every chance he had mixed emotions about the prospect of seeing her again. After the meal he sloped off to his room, banging the door behind him.

I ventured up there while Bobbi and Megan sat beside

each other on the sofa, watching cartoons. I tapped on the door, opening it when I heard a faint grunt coming from inside. Archie was sitting on the floor below the window, his knees drawn up and one elbow on each, head cradled in his hands. 'I can see you're upset, Archie,' I said softly, taking a few steps into the room. 'Do you want to talk about it?'

He looked up at me and shook his head, a scowl on his face. I waited. 'Did something happen at school today?'

He threw one hand up in the air, fingers clawed. 'Oh, why can't you just leave me alone?'

I held my hands up. 'Okay, but I'm around if you need to talk.'

I closed the door quietly and went downstairs, cursing myself for approaching him too quickly. If I'd left him alone a bit longer, he might have opened up and confided in me.

He was still in his room an hour later. I could hear him throwing something rhythmically at the wall as I read Megan her bedtime story. When I'd finished reading she took her hearing aid out and set it carefully in the box on her bedside cabinet. She glanced up at me from the pillow, a little grin on her face. 'I'm good with my n'aid now, aren't I, Mummy?'

'You're very clever, sweetie. I'm very proud of you.'

She sat up and threw her arms around my neck. 'Love you, Mummy.'

'I love you too, sweetheart. Night night, sleep tight.' I planted a kiss on her forehead, switched her night light on and flicked the main light switch off. She rolled onto her side and gave me a sleepy smile, her eyes already twitching.

I was about to go downstairs when Archie emerged from his room. 'I forgot to say thanks for the dinner, Rosie. It was really nice.'

'Thank you, Archie,' I said lightly. 'But you didn't eat much of it.'

'I said I liked it,' he said, with a ferocious undertone.

'Good. You can have a sandwich or something before you got to bed, if you're hungry?'

He shook his head. 'I'm going to bed now.'

'Okay. Would you like to talk first?'

He looked at me hesitantly, then shook his head.

'Okay, honey. Don't forget to brush your teeth. I'll come and say goodnight soon.'

Downstairs, Bobbi was still in the living room. I could hear her chattering to herself from the hall. It was time for her to get ready for bed but I hesitated before making the announcement, butterflies fluttering in my stomach. I told myself I was being ridiculous – she was only five years old – but I was very tired. The thought of another violent confrontation was setting my nerves on edge.

I took a breath and ventured behind enemy lines into the anticipated combat zone. 'Right, Bobbi. Your turn to get ready for bed now.' In anticipation of a refusal, I had set a sand timer next to the television before taking Megan up to bed, warning Bobbi that she only had fifteen minutes until she had to get ready herself. She was bouncing over the sofa when I reached the living room, adverts playing on the TV behind her. 'Come on, honey, let's go up and get ready.'

Broken

She continued bouncing as if I hadn't spoken so I switched the TV off and went to the door. Her head shot round. 'I was watching that!'

'Your programme has finished, Bobbi. And look at the timer. All the sand has gone. That means it's time for bed.'

She sat still, watching me. 'Tell you what,' I said, summoning my most tantalising tone. 'Race me upstairs.' It was a challenge Jamie could never resist as a young boy, but I had tried several versions on Bobbi over the last week and all of them had failed. I leaned towards the door, one leg out as if on a starting block, and then I shouted, 'Ready, steady, go!'

To my surprise, she leapt off the sofa and charged past me into the hall. I made a thing of trying to catch up, theatrically panting and puffing behind her. 'I don't believe it,' I gasped noisily at the top of the stairs. 'You're so fast!' She grinned, skipping off towards the bathroom. I waited on the landing for a second, puzzling over her willingness to respond to some of my requests, while digging her heels in on others.

The next thing I knew, she was clinging to the towel rail and screaming her head off. I ran to her. 'Bobbi, what's happened?' Worried that she might burn herself, I ran my hand over the rail. It was warm, but not hot. I crouched down in front of her but she tried to bite me, all the while clinging to the bar with the strength of an animal in fear for its life. I couldn't make it out.

Then again, I reminded myself that she might have been subjected to all sorts of triggers as she made her way up the stairs, ones that I knew nothing about.

'I'll be back in a moment,' I said, rushing off to my room. I returned with a weighted blanket and draped it over her shoulders. 'I'm going to sit with you until you calm down,' I said soothingly, kneeling behind her and rubbing her back firmly through the bulky covering. Weighted blankets are quilts filled with pellets that stimulate pressure points in the body and encourage the release of the calming hormone, serotonin.

Bobbi quietened almost immediately, although she continued to cling to the rail for another minute or so. When she finally relaxed her grip I pulled her onto my lap and she slumped back in my arms.

By half past eight, I was exhausted. I still had to clear away the dinner things, type up my daily diary and get the wet clothes out of the machine, but my eyes were stinging and my head felt like a soggy sponge. I couldn't wait to get everything done so that I could climb upstairs and sink into bed.

Chapter Nine

Three days later, on Friday 9 January, I dropped Megan at nursery and Bobbi at school, then drove to the local authority council offices, where the LAC Review was due to be held. Archie sat with a composed expression in the back of the car, though his eyes seemed darker than usual, and his hands tap danced in his lap.

To put him at ease I chattered on about the Harry Potter film we'd watched together the previous night, but if I'm honest, I was feeling a bit nervous myself. The first meeting with birth parents is often a daunting prospect for foster carers. Foster carers are sometimes regarded as usurpers by birth parents, and so a degree of resentment is perhaps inevitable. It's a sentiment I understand. I also appreciate that having your failings as a parent picked over in the presence of a stranger is a humiliating experience. Reactions can vary and, if ever there's a time for keeping a low profile, the first LAC Review is it.

Most parents soften their view when they realise that their children are being well looked after, although there are exceptions. Complaints from birth parents about scuffs on shoes, too much ear wax and the 'wrong nappies' are commonplace when fostering. I once had a birth mother who was oblivious to the irony of complaining about the way I'd fixed her daughter's ponytail, when the cigarette burns she had inflicted on the little girl's skin had barely healed.

Apart from the scant information Danny had given me, I had no idea what Archie's birth mother was like. I tried not to make any assumptions but from the children's behaviour I got the impression that they were used to taking care of themselves. No matter how abusive they may have been, most children frequently ask to see their parents when they first come into care. Apart from a few fretful questions about Mummy around bedtimes, Bobbi had shown little interest in seeing her – a clue, perhaps, to her absence in their lives, even back when they were all living together.

Archie seemed concerned about how Tanya was, but when I broke the news yesterday that she had cancelled their first contact session because she wasn't feeling well, he hadn't seemed surprised, or particularly upset. 'I hope she feels better soon,' he'd said flatly, but nothing more after that.

Running late, I was pleased to find a space in the civic offices' car park. The lift was out of order so we hurried up the stairs, Archie taking the last flight two steps at a time. I could hear Danny's booming laughter as soon as we left the stairwell of the second floor. Archie and I exchanged glances. 'He's so loud,' he said, grinning.

When I gave the door of the meeting room a quick tap the laughter dried up. 'Come in,' came Danny's deep voice.

Inside, the social worker was seated on the far side of a twelve-seater long conference table. He was leaning back in a chair, hands linked behind his head. 'It is you, Rosie,' he said, beckoning us in with a friendly wave. 'Hi, Archie, come in. I'm so pleased you felt able to come, mate. Would you like a drink before we start? Some squash or something?'

'No, thank you,' Archie said politely, moving closer to my side.

'I'm so sorry,' I said, glancing from Danny to the white-haired gentleman sitting beside him. I lifted the long strap of my handbag over my head, took off my coat and piled everything onto one of the empty chairs in front of me. 'I had a few problems getting Bobbi into class this morning. I'll sit here on the end shall I? In the naughty chair?'

Danny boomed another laugh and Archie grinned. 'Yep, and we won't be giving you any stickers at the end of the session either. Ain't that right, Archie?' Archie grinned again and sat down next to me on the chair I'd pulled out for him. 'This is Geoff Parsons, by the way, the IRO.'

I leaned over the table and shook his hand. 'Hello, Geoff.'

Archie did the same. Geoff's white moustache curled upwards with his smile. 'Well done for coming today, young man. It's always pleasing to hear how things are going from young people themselves. How are you getting on at Rosie's?'

'Terrible,' Archie answered sullenly.

I gasped in surprise and turned sharply, realising as I did so that his eyes were twinkling. 'Oh, you!' I tapped his arm. 'You really had me for a second.'

He smirked.

'Ah, we have a bit of a joker on our hands, I see,' Geoff said.

'Seems so,' I said with a laugh.

'Right,' Geoff continued. 'I suggest we make a start.' He turned to Archie, his voice gentle. 'We haven't heard from your mother yet, Archie, and we've had a report from school about how you're getting on but I don't think any of your teachers were able to attend today. We can recap if anyone –' Geoff stopped in mid-sentence as the door behind me flew open and crashed into the back of my chair.

'Oops, sorry,' I blurted out automatically, shuffling forwards and twisting around in my seat. My apology wasn't returned by the tall, slimly built man behind. Slightly breathless from climbing the stairs, he grasped the back of my chair. His head was directly above mine and I could smell his breath; a roux of cigarette smoke and something tangy, like peppermint. As discreetly as I could, I eased forward in my chair. For a second I assumed that he was lost and had blundered into the wrong room, but then I caught the look of recognition on Archie's face.

Danny stood up, all traces of his earlier amusement gone. 'You are –?' he said, ushering the man away from my chair with a sweep of his hand.

I felt the brush of knuckles as the man moved past me into the room. 'Here for the meeting,' he answered bluntly.

'I meant,' Danny said, moving around the table towards him, 'who are you?'

'Jason Keane, his step-dad.' He nodded towards Archie and then, ignoring Danny's obvious objection to his presence, seated himself at the end of the table, a few seats away us. There was no further interaction between him and

Archie. It was as if two strangers had been plucked from the street and deposited in the same room without so much as an introduction.

Somewhere in his forties and smartly dressed in a shirt and suede jacket, Jason wasn't at all what I had expected Tanya's partner to look like. There was nothing directly unappealing about him – one of his eyelids was heavily hooded and he had a cleft chin and thin lips, but his eyes were clear and blue. Somehow, though, his appearance set my teeth on edge. Danny was looking at him keenly but Jason kept his eyes averted, smoothing a hand over his closely cut, greying hair.

'I'm afraid you're not invited, mate,' Danny said, in a tone that was far from friendly. 'You'll have to wait outside.'

At that moment the door behind me opened again, gentler this time. An attractive woman in her early-to mid-thirties stood at the threshold of the room, a sparkly-backed mobile phone in her hand. 'He's with me,' she said, her eyes flicking from Danny to Jason. 'I want him to stay.' There was something Disney about her tone; her voice affected and slightly babyish.

Danny hesitated for a moment then inclined his head grimly. 'Okay. But you should have mentioned before now that you were bringing someone along, Tanya. This is an invitation-only meeting.'

'I'm hardly *someone*,' Jason pointed out with disdain. 'I'm the lad's step-dad and Tanya's partner.'

'I wasn't aware the two of you were married,' Danny snapped.

'I'm sorry I didn't call you, Danny,' Tanya squeaked behind me. 'I wasn't feeling well yesterday and …'

The social worker jerked his head. 'Come on then, get yourself in and let's get on with it.'

As Tanya closed the door I caught the scent of her heavy perfume. Archie turned as she passed and looked up at her. She air-kissed the top of his head. 'Hi, babe,' she trilled, then tottered on to the end of the table. When she reached Jason she shrugged her coat off and draped it over the back of the chair next to his. My skin bristled. She hadn't seen Archie for nearly two weeks – it must have been hurtful for him to see her walking past him to sit next to someone else. Archie stared straight ahead, apparently unmoved, but I felt irritated on his behalf.

Geoff watched the pair with quiet interest as they arranged their phones side by side on the table in front of them and intertwined their hands. He then proceeded to explain the purpose of the meeting and asked everyone to introduce themselves.

When it came to Jason's turn to address the meeting he introduced both himself and Tanya and then tilted his head silently towards her handbag. She let go of his hand and fumbled inside, withdrawing a packet of mints, which she passed to him.

Danny shook his head and opened his mouth to speak, presumably to ask Tanya to introduce herself, but Geoff nodded graciously and the moment passed. He looked at Archie. 'So, the way this works, Archie, is that we'll have a chat with you first, and then we'll ask you to step outside while we talk through some grown-up things. That okay?'

Archie nodded sombrely.

'Good. As you know, you were taken into care on 29 December because we were concerned that your mother and Jason might not be keeping you safe.' Archie glanced at his mother, who was making goo-goo eyes at Jason, then lowered his own gaze to the table. 'Do you feel able to tell us anything about the night you came into care, Archie?'

His cheeks flushed and he shuffled in his seat before shaking his head. My heart went out to him. It was hard enough for a child to speak out in front of a room full of adults, however much confidence they appeared to have. To speak about distressing events in the presence of a neglectful, possibly abusive, parent was a very tall order indeed.

'No, that's fine. I just wanted to offer you the opportunity.' Geoff went on to explain the process of evidence and information gathering, and asked Archie again about life in the Lewis household.

'I like it at Rosie's,' he said, and then launched straight into talking about Jamie's skills with a football and their sessions in the back garden. 'And in the evening me and Rosie play cards. Though last night me, her and Emily watched *Harry Potter and the Philosopher's Stone*,' he said with a smile, which faded quickly when his mother turned to look at him.

Geoff scribbled away on the pad in front of him, minute-taking as Archie spoke. He looked up intermittently, smiling, nodding and making encouraging noises. 'And has Rosie given you the leaflet with the helpline numbers you can call if you're worried about anything, and don't feel you can talk to her?'

Archie nodded. It was one of the first items that foster carers were supposed to give to new arrivals, along with a toothbrush and some clean towels. 'Excellent,' Geoff said, smiling at me. 'It sounds like Rosie and her family have made you very welcome,' he added, with a pointed look in Tanya's direction. 'Now, do you have any questions for any of us before you step outside?' Archie looked thoughtful. I wondered whether he was trying to pluck up the courage to ask about his dad. He glanced towards his mother and Jason, then gave me a beseeching look. I nodded at him to let him know that I'd understood. 'Okay. Well, it was lovely to meet you, Archie. Well done again for coming. We know it's not easy.'

Danny got up then and moved to the door. 'Do you wanna say goodbye to your mum, Arch? Then I'll take you along to the office.'

Archie stood and walked over to his mother. She let go of Jason's hand and half stood up to give him a hug. 'Love you, babe,' she said in a babyish voice, planting a lipstick-coated kiss on his cheek. She made an L shape with her forefinger and thumb and held it to her ear. 'Call me, yeah?'

'See you at contact, okay?' Jason said, although he must have known that it was unlikely he'd be allowed to attend. He reached around Tanya and clapped Archie on the back. 'We'll have you home soon, son,' he said, telling Archie not to worry, but to my ears his words sounded more threatening than reassuring.

Jason fiddled with his phone while we waited for Danny to return, Tanya fawning and stroking his head. When the social worker came back, Geoff asked me to give everyone an idea of our family's day-to-day routine. I started to speak, aware that Jason was looking me up and down. I tried my best not to let his scrutiny get to me and explained how the children were settling in. 'Archie's been fairly quiet,' I said, wondering whether to express my unease around him. I quickly decided against it. How could I find the words to explain it when I wasn't even sure why I felt that way myself? Tanya studied me briefly as I spoke then returned her attention to her partner. 'Bobbi's most definitely been making her presence felt,' I summed up with a smile.

Danny grinned. Jason tore into the packet of mints. 'Can you expand on that a bit, Rosie?' Geoff asked.

'Erm, well, she's a little uncooperative at times,' I said, chuckling inwardly at the understatement. I avoided any mention of ADHD, using the alternative code word 'active' instead. 'She's also funny and bright,' I continued, not only because it was true, but also because her mother was sitting just a few seats away from me. It was important for Tanya to know that her daughter was staying with someone who appreciated how very special she was, in spite of her difficulties. I scanned my mind for some other positives. 'And she's got great stamina,' I added, remembering her most recent monumental meltdown.

I told them about my meeting with the SENCO and her concerns about Bobbi's behaviour in class. 'I'm hoping that her new glasses might help her in that respect though. It can't have been easy trying to cope when she was that long-sighted.' A visit to the optician a few days earlier had confirmed my suspicion that Bobbi needed glasses, something I had reported to Danny in an email as soon as we got home.

Considering her aversion to getting ready in the mornings, my heart sank when the optician broke the news – I imagined that I'd have to dream up all sorts of cunning ruses to get her to wear them. As it happened, she fell in love with a bright purple pair on sight and couldn't wait until they were ready to collect. Archie, who had been hoping for a pair like Harry Potter, was devastated when diagnosed with twenty-twenty vision.

'You didn't get her an ugly pair, I hope?' was all Jason had to contribute on the subject. 'Those minging NHS ones that make kids look a bit special needs.'

We all stared at him wordlessly. He crunched on a mint and stared back, Tanya ignoring everyone else and stroking his hair. It was becoming clear that Archie's good manners weren't modelled on behaviour he'd witnessed from this pair.

After a heavy pause I ran through some of the things we'd been doing in the last nine days or so, including going to the park, playing board games together and doing craft. 'So that's your method, is it?' Jason said between crunches. 'Bribing them so they'll turn against us. Hear that, Tan?'

Tanya, who had nodded along with his every word, turned and hooked her arm over the back of her chair. 'Yeah, kids get used to things, don't they? It's not really fair.'

I stared back at her, struggling to formulate a reply. Luckily, Danny stepped in. 'We're not talking a trip to Florida here, Tanya. The kids have been to the park a few times.'

'Yeah, then you've got ice creams and all that,' Jason complained. 'We can't be shelling out for all that when they come home.'

'What's that gonna cost?' Danny said. His eyes flicked to Jason. 'Less than a packet of fags, I'd wager.'

Jason gave a slow blink. Tanya's eyes flicked nervously between the social worker and her partner. She bit down on her lip and shifted in her chair, all the while making a sort of squeaky placatory noise in her throat.

'Anything else to add, Rosie?' Danny asked, his voice softening when he spoke to me.

'No, nothing.' I was still smarting over the fact that Tanya seemed to begrudge her children a trip to the park, after all they'd been through in the last couple of weeks. I felt my throat tightening. I swallowed and added: 'Except that Archie is keen to see his father.'

Tanya stiffened. Jason gave me an icy stare. Geoff looked at Danny, who lifted a hand to indicate he had something to say about that. Geoff ticked something off on the wad of papers in front of him and then smiled at me. 'Thank you, Rosie. That gives us some idea of how the children are settling in. It sounds like they've coped quite well, under the circumstances. Now, Danny, would you give us an idea of where the local authority stands in terms of moving forward?'

'Yep, sure.' Danny summarised the incident that had led to the removal of the children, Jason shaking his head and making loud scoffing noises as he crunched on another mint. The social worker went on to list the dates and times of every police welfare visit in response to incidents of domestic violence, as well as reports of concern filed by Millfield Primary. 'So, our plan is to carry out some checks, parenting assessments and what have you, on both Tanya and her ex-husband, James Brady,' his eyes flicked to mine, 'who we've recently managed to locate, by the way. He's working an extra shift this afternoon, which is why he's not here today, but he's keen to see the kids as soon as he can. It seems he's made valiant efforts in the last two years since Jason and Tanya moved away, but he's only managed to see the kids a handful of times since. The last time was five months ago, in August 2014.'

Geoff looked at Tanya. 'Are you reluctant to allow access, Tanya?'

I noticed as I looked at her that Jason was shaking his head. 'We don't want them confused,' Tanya told Danny, her eyes on Jason.

Geoff frowned. 'I don't understand.'

'She *said*,' Jason took over, 'we're not happy about that tosser seeing the kids.'

Danny gave them a cold look. 'Oh, and why's that?'

Tanya opened and closed her mouth like a goldfish. 'Look,' Danny said, 'if there's a safeguarding issue around the children seeing their father then you need to let me know about it, pronto. If not, he has a lawful right to see them.' Jason and Tanya exchanged glances.

'I'm telling you,' Jason said, pointing his finger at Danny. 'The man's a wanker. He shouldn't be allowed anywhere near kids.'

Danny stared at him. 'We need to carry out some checks on you, actually, Mr Keane. Can you tell me now if you have a record?'

Jason's expression filled with scorn. 'What?'

'I'm asking if you have a criminal record. Are you known to the police?'

Jason rubbed his nose briskly. 'No, course not.'

'Are you sure?' Danny persisted. 'Absolutely no run-ins with the law?'

Jason frowned. 'No, none that I can think of.'

Danny kept his eyes fixed on him. 'Funny that, cos I was speaking with Harriet from the Children in Need team, and she says you've got at least nine convictions under your belt, ranging from driving while intoxicated to common assault and possession of cannabis. She got that wrong then?'

Jason's eyes narrowed to barely more than slits. He began to nod. 'Oh, I get it. So that's your game, is it? Raking up every bit of shit you can find and slinging it at us, is that right?'

'That's about the size of it, yep,' Danny answered calmly. 'But only shit in the shape of facts.' I lowered my gaze, beginning to wonder if the smell I'd noticed when Jason had walked into the room was cannabis. I knew that local authorities no longer underestimated the use of cannabis by birth parents; evidence of the correlation between its regular use and psychotic illness now difficult to reason away. 'And since we're setting all our cards on the table, have you been drinking, Mr Keane?'

'Hark at you, giving it large,' Jason said with a harsh laugh. 'You pen-pushing prat.'

Danny remained silent, the look of contempt on his face more powerful than any reply he could have made. After a moment he addressed Tanya in a business-like tone. 'You do realise, Tanya, that as things stand it's going to be difficult to return the children to you, positive parenting assessments or not.'

Jason's downturned mouth hardened into a slit so tight that it rivalled his eyes.

'What's that supposed to mean?'

Rosie Lewis

The temperature in the room seemed to drop but, unlike myself, Danny appeared supremely unfazed. 'Exactly what it sounds like.'

Jason jabbed a forefinger at Danny. 'You can piss right off,' he spat, and then to Tanya: 'I've had it.'

Tanya watched him leave and then turned to Danny. 'What do you mean, "as things stand"?' she asked tearfully. 'You mean with me and Jase?'

Danny nodded. 'Unless and until you demonstrate a willingness to safeguard the children and put their needs first, they're likely to remain in foster care.'

'But that's not fair!' she wailed. 'Jason's my life.' I could feel her eyes on me, perhaps hoping to garner support from a fellow woman. 'You've got to follow your heart, haven't you?' she asked in a wobbly voice.

I turned to look at her. Mascara was spilling from the inside corners of her eyes and running in dark rivulets down either side of her nose. I got the impression she was genuinely upset and I felt a wave of sympathy for her, but only a tiny one. 'That depends, I suppose,' I answered vaguely, hoping to steer the conversation away from myself. I didn't go along with the idea that a partner's needs should be prioritised over and above the needs of children but I knew not everyone shared my view and I was, after all, divorced. *And* I was going to be caring for Tanya's children for the foreseeable future. I didn't want a confrontation.

'Do you think that's fair though?' she persisted. 'The last few weeks have been really stressful for me and now they're trying to split me and Jase up. We're entitled to a bit of happiness, aren't we?' Her voice, high with indignation, was squeakier than ever.

100

Broken

'Not if it comes at the expense of your children,' I said flatly, giving her my honest opinion.

Tanya put a hand to her throat. 'The kids are fine,' she said weakly, dabbing her nose on the back of her hand.

'To be honest, Tanya, I don't think they are.' Somewhere in the back of my mind I was aware I might be overstepping the mark, but not enough to stop myself continuing. 'They're very troubled. It seems to me that they've seen too much.' It felt good to speak out. Sometimes it was simply too hard not to.

Tanya continued to stare at me, but a new emotion crossed her face. There was a subtle adjustment in the line of her jaw, a few faint creases beneath her eyes that told me that she wasn't entirely convinced by her own argument. I turned away, expecting to see a line of disapproving glances from the men opposite. I was relieved to see that Geoff's expression was mild. Danny was staring at me, but, if anything, it was with a touch of admiration.

At that moment Jason opened the door and gave an aggressive jerk of his head. 'Tanya, out!'

Chapter Ten

The weekend that followed was difficult, with Bobbi erupting over the slightest upset. Archie was as polite as ever, but anger simmered beneath his good manners. It was a curious combination; one that left him ingratiatingly livid or furiously polite. Funnily enough, I think Mungo also sensed that something was wrong. Ever since Bobbi's arrival he had avoided her, but there were times when he veered away from Archie as well. It was as if he could smell the tension and knew that, sooner or later, it was going to demand an outlet.

The hoarding issue seemed to have escalated as well. On the morning of Sunday 11 January I noticed a packet of sixteen KitKats missing from the kitchen cupboard. I found five of the bars stashed under the children's bunk bed, along with a large jumble of chocolate-smeared foil and red wrappings.

It was as I gathered the soggy contraband into a ball that I noticed something solid in amongst it. I spread the wrappings over my open palm and rummaged around. There, in the middle of the haul, was one of the silver bracelets I usually kept in my bedside cabinet drawer.

Unsettled more by the thought of the children in my bedroom than the 'theft' itself, I asked Emily to take Megan upstairs after lunch and invited Archie and Bobbi to join me at the table. 'I found this under your bed,' I began gently, producing the bracelet from my pocket. Archie flushed and looked away. Bobbi began 'singing' in a high-pitched wail.

'Be quiet a minute, Bobbi,' I said, but silence for Bobbi was an abstract notion and she carried on regardless. 'Bobbi, big breath in.' I modelled the action with a theatrical hand on my chest. She sucked in a lungful of air. Her eyes bulged, looking bigger than ever through the thick lenses of her glasses. 'Good. Now see if you can hold the breath and count to ten while you listen to me.' I wasn't confident that she was listening at all, but at least I was able to make myself heard. 'Right, so I'm not going to go on about this. One of you took my bracelet and it belongs to me, so you shouldn't have. But most importantly of all, you mustn't go into any bedroom but your own, do you understand?'

Bobbi exhaled then gasped noisily, slumping down in her seat until her chin touched the table. Archie gave a small nod, his face still averted. 'Bobbi, did you hear me? You must never go into anyone else's bedroom, okay?'

She sat up and looked at me, suddenly sharp-eyed. 'Why not?'

'Because I'm a grown-up and my room is private.' I shook my head. 'But it's not just me. We all have our own private space.'

She frowned. 'But we go into Mummy and Jason's bedroom. We have to sleep on the floor in there sometimes, cos Jason's friends come round and there's not enough room.'

I frowned. Archie's head shot round. 'It's fine if Mummy lets you into her room,' I said, my eyes trained on Archie. He was watching his sister carefully, his shoulders tense. 'But while you're here, you must stay out of any bedroom that's not your own, okay?' Bobbi glanced at her brother and then nodded.

'Good,' I said with a firm nod of my own. 'Also, we must keep food out of the bedrooms. If you're hungry, let me know. There will always be food for you here. Do you remember me telling you that?' They both nodded, Archie's eyes still fixed on Bobbi's face.

His reaction to his sister's comment about Jason's friends stayed with me and by Sunday afternoon, the creeping discomfort I felt around him escalated with a vengeance. I used the prospect of school to nurse myself through the last few hours of the day, but by eight o'clock on Monday morning, even getting there on time seemed to be a feat beyond my capabilities.

Emily, home on study leave in lieu of her nursing exams, kindly offered to walk Megan to nursery so that she, at least, wouldn't be late. Temperatures had plummeted in the last few days and the living-room windows were clouded with mist. I rubbed the glass with the sleeve of my cardigan and watched them leave. Bundled up in hat, scarf and gloves, Megan smiled up at her sister as they walked along, hand in hand. My heart lifted at the sight. It was such a joy to see Emily embracing her role as older sister and little

Broken

Meggie revelling in her doting attention. I felt a moment's pride in them.

When they disappeared around the corner I exhaled a long breath and knelt on the rug, where Bobbi was sprawled out on her front. 'Come on now, love, please,' I said, holding her pinafore dress out in front of her. Wearing only a vest and a pair of navy-blue school tights, she looked up and gave a tiny shake of her head. 'Right, I'm going to have to pick you up and dress you myself.'

Bobbi was on her feet in seconds. On tiptoes, she scurried away and dived behind the sofa. With the opening notes of the *Pink Panther* theme tune drifting along the hall as Jamie practised on the saxophone for his A-level Music mock exam, her antics should have been amusing. I usually loved listening to Jamie play, but after a weekend of constant battles, it was like being serenaded by Black Sabbath when you'd booked Céline Dion.

Jamie was due at the dentist in half an hour. I had offered to give him a lift, but at this rate there wasn't going to be much chance of that. 'Bobbi,' I said, summoning my most enticing tone. 'I wonder what you might do at school today. Painting, maybe?'

She crept out from behind the sofa, her fingers hovering threateningly over the waistband of her tights. 'Oh no you don't, young lady,' I warned. The fact that she was wearing tights at all was no small triumph in itself. It was only after I had worn them on my hands and performed a puppet show that she had capitulated and allowed me to pull them on. I wasn't sure whether it was the spectacle itself that had won the day, or the fact that my hands had loosened the wool and warmed them up. It had worked a treat, and Megan had thought it hysterical.

I sighed, dropping the pinafore dress dejectedly onto my lap. Archie, who was laying prostrate on the sofa with his shirt sleeves rolled up his arms and his school jumper screwed up in a ball under his feet, yawned loudly. Though never keen to go to school, he had always got ready when asked. Today, though, he seemed particularly reluctant. I wondered whether it had anything to do with the fact that contact had been arranged for straight after school. I looked at him. 'Archie, come on. Show your sister how it's done, will you?'

He blew out his cheeks and sat slowly up, but made no further move to get ready. 'What on earth is *wrong* with you two today? If you don't go to school you won't be able to meet Mum afterwards for contact.'

I watched Archie's face for a response. He twisted his lips into a pout. Bobbi blew a raspberry. 'Right, that's it. Up you come.' I strode across the room, picked Bobbi up and held her at arm's length in case she lashed out. Surprisingly, she held onto my shoulders and remained serene as I sat on the floor and eased her arms into her blue checked blouse. At that moment Jamie ducked his head into the room. 'I'll load their stuff in the car, shall I, Mum?'

'Yes please, love.' He turned to leave. 'Oh, Jamie, just a sec, before I forget. I got an email from school about the prefect applications. Apparently the deadline's last thing today.'

Capitalising on my straying attention, Bobbi pulled away from my grip and scooted to the sofa. Jamie took a few steps back into the room. 'Well, whoopee-do! I'd best get onto that straight away. Wouldn't wanna miss my chance of being prefect, would I, Mum?'

I grinned up at him, half-aware that Bobbi was now trying to expel Mungo from his refuge under the coffee table. 'Hey, drop the sarcasm. I thought we agreed that you'd apply? It'll look good on your university applications if you're a prefect.'

'Well, that saves me a job then,' he said casually. 'Cos I've decided not to go to uni.'

I stared at him. 'What?'

'I'm not going,' came his reply from the hall. 'I'm gonna devote myself to the band full-time.'

I got to my feet and pulled Bobbi away from Mungo, who was making small, panicked growls. 'Oh you are, are you? And when was this decided?' There was no answer. I wasn't even sure whether he'd heard me. At my side, Bobbi was trying to sink her teeth into my leg. Along the hallway the *Pink Panther* theme struck up again. Momentarily stunned by Jamie's revelation and the storm of noise around me, it was only when her teeth made contact with my shin that I shook her off.

'I'm a Barbie girl in a Bobbi world,' she screeched, veering towards Mungo again. A volley of ear-ringing barks shot out from beneath the table and for the first time since the siblings had arrived, the reality of what I had taken on began to dawn on me. It was a disorientating feeling and my stomach swooped. I felt so tense that the sound of a key turning in the latch sent my pulse racing. I spun around as Emily walked into the room. 'Still here then, Mum?'

I rolled my eyes. 'I think it's fair to say we're making minimal progress at the moment.'

She slipped her arm around my shoulder. 'Oh dear. You okay?'

I forced a laugh. I was being ridiculous. 'Yes, fine thanks, love. Did Meggie go in okay?'

Emily smiled. 'Yep, she skipped in, telling anyone who'd listen that I was her big sister.'

I laughed, my pulse returning to normal. 'Ahh, that's sweet. Thanks, Ems.'

'No problem. I'm going up to study now. See you lot later.' At least four inches taller than me, she leaned over, kissed the top of my head and left.

I glanced at the clock. 'Right, come on, guys, it's five to nine now.' I clapped my hands together and knelt back on the floor. 'Tell you what, Bobbi. You can have five minutes television if you get ready nicely, and then we have to go, agreed?' She nodded and plonked herself down on my lap. I fumbled with the remote, squinting and trying to find the right button.

Archie sighed. 'I'll do it, Rosie.' I threw it over and, after catching it one-handed, he flicked a button on the remote and put CBeebies on. Mesmerised by the screen, Bobbi moved her arms and legs robotically, and within five minutes she was finally dressed. 'Right, Bobbi, you have another two minutes of television and then we're going, okay?'

'No, I'm watching this.'

'We'll record the rest and you can watch it later. Two minutes, then we're leaving.'

She gave me a sidelong glance then scooted off my lap. With her eyes fixed on mine, she began unzipping her dress. 'Oh no you don't, young lady. You keep it on!' I could hear the impatience in my tone. I knew it wasn't going to help, but I was too irritated to even think about the impact it was likely to have. Bobbi stared at me with supreme indifference and whipped her cardigan off. 'Bobbi, no! This is getting beyond a joke now. You must KEEP YOUR CLOTHES ON!'

Kaboom! The touch paper ignited. Throwing her head back, she let out a furious rip-roaring scream. On the sofa, Archie dropped his head back on a cushion and let out a deep groan. Along the hall, the *Pink Panther* theme tune was reaching its crescendo. In hideous synchrony, Bobbi threw herself onto the floor and smashed her forehead into the bare boards. When I went to her and pulled her to her feet, she whipped her glasses off, threw them across the room and then clawed at her own face, digging her nails in and screaming at the top of her voice.

'Bobbi, Bobbi, no, you mustn't hurt yourself. Come on now.' She struggled when I picked her up but I held fast and staggered into the hall. 'Archie, grab her cardy, please,' I called out over her screams. 'And her glasses.'

At that moment Emily came charging down the stairs. 'For zarking sake, can't you lot keep the noise down? I'm trying to study!' Emily was the loveliest, most gentle person you could ever meet for three and a half weeks of the month. Catch her on the wrong day, though, and she was an absolute menace.

As she turned and stamped back up the stairs, Archie sloped back to the living room. 'Get back here!' I snapped. 'We're leaving right this minute! And where do you think you're going, Jamie?' I said, noticing that Jamie had ducked out the front door, no doubt hoping that

I wouldn't notice. I opened it a second after it had clicked to a close.

'Dentist!' he said, already halfway up the path.

'Oh, come back, will you? Help me get them into the car and then I'll give you a lift.'

'It's alright,' he said at the gate. 'I don't mind walking.'

I stood on the step. 'Jamie, please.'

He stopped, dropped his head back and closed his eyes. 'Thanks, love.' I slipped my feet into my shoes, draped Bobbi's coat around her squirming body and stumbled out the door. Archie sloped sulkily behind, Bobbi's glasses in one hand, her cardy in the other. Jamie walked back and closed the door behind us. 'Bunny, I want Bunny!' Bobbi wailed as I shut the car door.

I pulled the driver's door open and leaned in, talking to her over the top of the headrest. 'You'll see Bunny later, honey.'

She burst into tears. 'No! I want Bunny now!'

'I'll get it,' Jamie offered. 'Then I'm going to walk.'

I watched as he groped for his keys. 'We need to have a chat, Jamie.'

'There's nothing to talk about, Mum. I've made up my mind.'

'But you're not using your head, love. How many musicians end up making anywhere near a decent living? You need to get your studies in first. Then you can do whatever you like.'

He shook his head and pushed his key into the lock, letting himself into the house. He reappeared with a stony expression half a minute later, the soft toy dangling from his hand. It was a rabbit, but not Bobbi's one. I stood aside and he leaned silently into the car, passing the toy to Bobbi. She took one look at it and let out a squeal. 'That's not real Bunny! I want *my* Bunny!'

Jamie groaned. 'That one will do for now, Bobbi,' I called out vaguely, my gaze still fixed on Jamie. 'At least think about it, Jamie,' I said, trying to block out the wailing behind me.

'Mum!' he moaned. 'You're just not listening!'

'And you're not listening to *me*.' I paused, softening my tone. 'I never imagined that you wouldn't go to university.'

'Well, sorry I didn't turn out as advertised,' he muttered under his breath.

I stared at him. 'I can't believe you're just throwing the chance away, that's all, without giving it proper thought. Crikey, what I wouldn't have given for the opportunity to go.' When I was at school, going to university had seemed like an impossible dream, something that only the well-off might consider.

'It's not throwing it away if I never wanted it in the first place, is it?'

I struggled to think of an answer to that. My mouth just flopped uselessly open. Eventually I found my voice. 'Let's just –'

'I'm going,' he cut in, breaking into a half jog down the path.

'Jamie, come back!' I called out, Bobbi screaming hysterically behind me. It was as I watched Jamie disappear from view over next door's hedge that I noticed her; a smartly dressed woman with long blonde hair and colourful bangles on each wrist. Holding her key fob aloft, she locked her car

Rosie Lewis

and walked towards me. The colour drained from my cheeks.

'Rosie Lewis?' she called out, a slightly puzzled expression on her face.

'Erm, yes, that's me.'

'Gabby Waldon,' she announced, glancing from me to the hysterical child in the back of my car. 'Social worker with the local authority. I'm here to carry out your unannounced inspection. Now isn't a bad time, I hope?'

Chapter Eleven

'It has to be up there with the worst ones yet,' I told Des as he followed me into the living area that evening, Mungo sniffing at his feet. It was just after seven thirty and with the girls tucked up in bed, the house was quiet but for the low buzz of the washing machine on a spin cycle in the kitchen. Emily was out for a meal with her grandmother and I wasn't expecting her back until late. Archie was in the shower and Jamie at band practice with his friends. Throughout the day my mind had returned to our row, my throat tightening with regret. Jamie was usually such a cheerful character. I hated falling out with him. We'd had a brief chat when he got back from school that afternoon, but things were still a bit cool between us.

Des was the perfect distraction. Loud and gregarious, he sat next to me on the sofa and chuckled as I relayed the entire mortifying fiasco. 'Par for the course in the Lewis household, I would have thought,' he joked, his loud voice booming despite his efforts not to disturb the children. Mungo sat at my feet, his feathery whiskers tickling my legs.

I groaned. 'It was awful. Then she came in and saw the fall-out from the weekend. Toys everywhere, smalls that had spent the entire weekend draped over the radiators stiff with rigor mortis. Honestly, it was bad.'

Des boomed a laugh and threw a hand to my shoulder. 'Ach, it cannae have been that bad,' he said in his soft Scottish lilt. It was a lyrical tone, one that never failed to cheer me. 'I expect she's seen worse. I once turned up to do an unannounced on a couple having the mother of all smash-ups. There were household objects flying across windows and everything. They didnae last long as foster carers after that.'

'Oh, heavens! I don't feel so bad now.'

'I'm sure t'was fine. She didnae express any concerns, did she?'

'She was very kind actually. She said she got the sense that ours is,' I paused, hooking the air, 'a "proper family home with plenty of evidence of children's play". Now there's a creative way of describing it.'

'Spot on, I'd say,' he said, leaning forward and opening the bottle of wine on the coffee table. Left over from Christmas, I had retrieved it from the cupboard when Des had texted to let me know he was popping in. He poured me a glass and lifted his own. 'Here's to your proper family home, warts an' all,' he said, holding his glass up in front of me.

'Cheers,' I said with a smile. We clinked. I took a sip, shuddered and passed it back to him. I liked the idea of sharing a bottle of wine but had never found one I liked the taste of and rarely managed more than half a glass. Des, a true Scot, took a much larger swill of his own, gulped down the rest of mine and banged the glasses back on the table.

'So how is everything? Any better?' Des had been train-ing in Edinburgh since the children had arrived almost two weeks earlier. We had spoken on the phone during that time, but only briefly. Absorbed with the needs of my own family, his manically busy lifestyle suited me.

I tucked my legs up next to my hips. 'They're gorgeous children. Absolutely lovely.'

Des shifted around until his back was pressed against the arm of the sofa, so that we were facing each other. 'But –?'

'But – I don't know. Bobbi's behaviour is familiar, although a little more extreme than I've experienced before. She's aggressive, impulsive, difficult to manage generally, the little cherub. But I think she's calming down. She's not talking ten to the dozen anymore. I think she'll settle with time. She has a hard time coping with school, but she's showing some attachment to me; clinging in the mornings and reaching out when she's upset.' Miss Granville had written another note in SHOUTY capitals in the home school diary again, Bobbi having antagonised her classmates all morning. Totally overwhelmed, she had apparently spent most of the afternoon under one of the desks, refusing to come out even when the headmistress was called in.

'And Archie?'

'You'll meet him in a minute. He's a bit of an enigma. I don't quite know what to make of him. One minute he's civil and well mannered, effusive with compliments, the next brooding and sulky. He was very withdrawn after contact this afternoon.' When I'd picked the children up from the family centre earlier, the contact supervisor told me that there had been a lot of whispering in corners between Tanya and Archie during their ninety-minute contact session. The supervisor had intervened several times, but Tanya had taken little notice. 'He barely ate a thing when he got home. Well, nothing at the dinner table at least.' I gave him a rueful look.

'They're still hoarding?'

I nodded grimly. 'Rubbish mainly. Crisps, chocolate bars, cheese. I even found a fondue fork under a box of Junior Scrabble earlier.'

Des chuckled, though his expression quickly grew serious. 'The body craves sweet, salty, fatty food when in an alarmed state. Perhaps they're just taking what they need. You might havetae forget healthy eating for a wee while, or ride both horses for now.'

'I hadn't thought of that.'

'Sometimes, sweetheart, you have to swim with the tide.'

I felt a spark of heat in my face and quickly looked away. The fact that we were becoming more than just friends still took me by surprise. He reached out and touched my sleeve. Mungo eyed him from my feet.

'It's not only food though, Des. One of them took a bracelet from my room. I found it under their bed.' Some foster carers were able to tolerate all sorts of abuse – kicking, spitting, biting and punching – but I knew quite a few who struggled to continue with a placement after a child had stolen from them.

'Don't take it personally,' Des said mildly, slipping into supervising social worker mode. 'They're communicating with you. Telling you their deepest fear; that they'll be left to die. Kids steal either to fill the unfillable hole inside them, or to hold onto something physical, because everything else around them is disintegrating. The fact that they chose something of yours says something – it tells me that they see you as their anchor at the minute, the person who's going to keep them afloat.'

'Oh, Des,' I said, feeling quite emotional, 'I hadn't thought of it like that.'

'You said that Bobbi's scalp is flat at the back. We both know what that means. Who was it who said that children adopted today are the Baby Peters who dinnae die? Hoarding is the kids' way of securing their survival.'

'But they don't need my bracelet to survive,' I protested weakly, already entirely convinced by Des's argument.

He dipped his head. 'Aye, that I'll grant you. But it's likely they're both functioning at least two, possibly three years younger than their actual age, in terms of emotional development, like most looked-after children. What age is Bobbi? Five? So adjusted, she's two or three years old at most. And Archie, maybe six or seven?' I nodded. 'So if we're thinking toddler in terms of Bobbi, suddenly taking a bracelet isnae stealing, but natural inquisitiveness.'

I gave him a sceptical look. 'So I should have just ignored it?'

'I'm not saying that. I just mean do what you'd do with a toddler. Explain that they mustnae take things that don't belong to them and then forget it. The last thing you want to do is shame them.' I knew Des was talking sense. Shame was often the fuel that ignited difficult behaviour in fostered children. Responding with anger, though a natural response, was a sure fire way of fanning the flames and getting every-one caught up in a downward spiral. 'Anyways, at least –'

He stopped as Mungo jumped to his feet and gave a low yap. The sound of a key in the front door followed. 'Jamie,' I said, standing up and brushing myself down. Mungo belted into the hall.

'Hey!' Des said as Jamie walked in, Mungo weaving excitedly around his legs. 'It's the main man. How you been, fella?' He jumped up and pumped Jamie's hand heartily.

'Hiya, Des,' Jamie said with a grin, flicking a glance in my direction.

'Hungry? I can warm some lasagne up for you.'

He nodded and thanked me quietly, his reserve eliciting a look of puzzlement from Des. He glanced between us fleetingly then clapped a hand on Jamie's back. 'Course he's hungry. He's a growing lad, look at the size of him!' A natural with kids of all ages, Jamie and Emily had always liked Des and he doted on Megan. When he sat back on the sofa, Jamie took the opposite end and launched into an update on some booking or other he had arranged for the band. I could hear their easy conversation as I heated Jamie's dinner in the microwave, the odd raucous laugh.

Des had been lead guitarist in a rock band in his youth and often regaled Jamie with tales of touring and after-gig parties. Their shared passion for music meant they were never short of something to say to each other. I pulled some wet clothes from the machine and hung them on an airer then went back into the living room, listening in bemused silence as they argued the merits of Gibson Les Paul guitars against Fender Stratocasters, Jamie tucking into his dinner on a tray on his lap.

'You shouldn't encourage him,' I said later, when Jamie was in the shower.

'Huh?'

I dipped my head towards the door. 'You know. All that talk about the band. I'd rather he concentrated on his exams at the moment.'

Des scratched his wavy hair. 'I thought he was doing okay at school.'

'At the moment he is. But he won't if he spends all his time trying to revive The Bad Natives.'

He fixed me with an appraising, half-amused look. 'There are worse ways to make a living, you know. The Natives never went hungry. And we were never short of groupies either.'

I raised my eyebrows. 'Hmmph!'

'Oh, come on, sweetheart,' he said, laughing. 'You can't let go of your sense of humour or you'll never stay the course.'

I pulled a face. He was right, again, but I wasn't quite ready to admit it yet. He reached for my hand and laced his fingers through mine. I gave him a reluctant smile.

At that moment Mungo's ears flapped back. When the door opened, expecting to see Jamie, I snatched my hand away. Jamie and Emily's amused glances whenever I mentioned Des weren't lost on me. However much they liked him, I was quite certain that the merest whiff of any canoodling between us would have been a bit disturbing for them. Instead of Jamie though, Archie stood in the doorway, his expression grim. 'What is it, Archie?' I said, springing to my feet. I was surprised to find that my pulse was racing, though I wasn't sure why.

Archie glared at Des, his jaw tightened as if his teeth were grinding together. His arms hung poker straight at his sides, his thin hands clenched into tight fists. I cleared my throat. 'Archie, this is Des.' I paused. 'A friend of mine.'

'Hi, mate,' Des said softly, a cheery though slightly puzzled smile on his face. Archie blinked and stared. There was a look of fear in his eyes, as if Des's presence was somehow a threat.

I cleared my throat. 'Archie's a whizz at Rummy, Des. Do you fancy joining us for a game?'

'Fantastic,' Des said with a smile. Archie continued to stare at him wordlessly, his eyes finally straying to the bottle of wine and glasses on the coffee table. Something about the angle of his shoulders made the hairs on the back of my forearms stand on end. Mungo began to bark.

'What's wrong, Arch,' I said gently. 'Has something upset you?'

He turned his eyes on me, his lips twisted in disgust. 'You slag,' he said slowly. His words were cool and measured but his cheeks were crimson. 'You horrible, dirty slag.' Taken aback, all I could do was stare at him. Wisely, Des stayed where he was, his face angled away.

'Archie,' I said, at a loss as to where all this had sprung from. I glanced at Des. He raised one eyebrow and then looked away again. 'What's this about, honey?'

Archie's chest began to heave. Without warning he kicked out at Mungo, catching his soft underbelly. Mungo yelped in pain and hid behind my leg. 'Archie!' I shouted, crouching down and wrapping my arms around the trembling pup. Archie glared at me then turned on his heel and disappeared.

* * *

Broken

'You sure you donnae want me to stay?' Des said quietly in the hall a minute or so later. 'Just as back-up if you need it.'

'I'll be fine, really,' I whispered. 'Outbursts are my bread and butter. It's the phoniness I find hard to cope with.'

'If you're sure.' He touched the pad of his thumb to my cheek. 'Text me if you need a wee hand and I'll come straight back.'

I rested my forehead against his, patted his hand. 'Thanks, Des.'

When he left I leaned back against the front door and glanced up at the banisters, my legs trembling. There was no sound coming from upstairs but, despite the confidence I had expressed to Des, for a second I regretted asking him to leave. I took a breath, trying to compose myself. I knew that any sign of stress on my part would only escalate Archie's own.

Sometimes being a foster carer is a bit like being a detective. Archie was suffering, but the reasons for his distress were, for now, closed off from me. I had sensed that something was wrong when I first met him, and now it was becoming clearer that Archie's inner world was broken. I pushed myself away from the door and rolled my shoulders back. No matter how distressing a place it might be, I had a feeling that if I wanted to understand him, I was going to have to join him there.

Chapter Twelve

I found him sitting on his pillow, his legs dangling over the ladder of his bunk. After a soft tap on the open door, I walked into the room and stood a few feet from his bunk. 'Archie?' I ventured carefully, turning his name into a question.

Archie kept his head hung low, though he kicked out with his bare foot, warning me to stay away. 'Do you want to talk about what's upsetting you, Archie?' I said, working hard against my racing pulse to keep my voice low.

'No!' he snarled. 'Leave me alone!'

I waited, listening to the even tone of Bobbi's breathing. It seemed strange that she was able to sleep through such loud disturbances when she woke so often through the night. I wondered whether selective deafness was another protective mechanism at work, one that had allowed her to sleep through some of the chaos of home. 'I can hear how upset you are. I want to help you if I can.'

He leapt from the bunk and landed a foot from me. I stood my ground, returning his furious glare with a neutral one. 'You're nothing but a dirty slag,' he breathed, a nasty twisting sneer on his face. 'I don't even want to look at you.'

I gave him a long, steady look. His words were not those of a nine-year-old from a loving or even barely functional home. 'I'm guessing that you've heard and seen some difficult things in the past, Archie, but those sort of names don't belong here, in this house.'

He leaned forward until his face was only a few inches from mine. 'I could cut you up in your sleep, you know,' he blasted, louder now. 'I could take a knife and slit your throat.'

My chest fluttered. It was so hard to reconcile the furious boy in front of me with the one who had chatted so easily in the kitchen as he'd helped me wash the dishes just a couple of hours ago. I was so knocked off balance that I just stood there, staring at him in disbelief. Over his shoulder I could see that Bobbi was beginning to stir. From the bathroom came the tell-tale groan in the pipes as the water was turned off. I felt my pulse racing again. Jamie would be out of the shower soon. I didn't want him to get involved.

'We'll talk in the morning,' I said calmly, though my heart was beating fast. I turned and walked across the room.

'You ugly, stinking slag!' Archie shouted. I could sense him following, his shadow looming up behind me. 'I don't want to stay with you. Tell Danny I wanna go somewhere else. You make me sick.'

'What's going on?' came Jamie's voice from the hall.

My chest tightened. 'Nothing, Jamie, everything's okay.' I swivelled around to face Archie again, ushering him back with my hand. 'Go to bed now, Archie. I'll talk to you in the morning when you've calmed down.'

'Doesn't sound like nothing,' Jamie persisted, his voice closer now. I turned and saw him standing in the doorway, his hair dripping wet, dark patches appearing on his T-shirt where he hadn't dried himself properly. He dragged the towel he was holding over his forehead, draped it round his neck and glared at Archie.

Archie's cheeks flushed a deep red. 'Tell him to get out!' he screamed. 'Get out of my room!'

'Take it easy, you loon,' Jamie said disgustedly.

I turned to Jamie, taking pains to look unshaken. 'Go downstairs, Jamie, will you?'

'Yeah, and you get out too, bitch!' Archie bellowed. Jamie's eyes widened. He started forward, the tendons in his neck straining with fury.

I held my hand out, pressing it against his damp chest. 'Jamie, please. I'm fine. Go downstairs. I'll join you in a minute or two.' It was a struggle to keep my expression unruffled.

Jamie gave a sigh of exasperation and made a move to leave, his gaze lingering for just a second on the furious boy behind him. 'What a fruit loop,' I heard him mutter as he went downstairs. I felt a prick of guilt, knowing how hard it must have been for him to hear someone shouting abuse at me like that. The fact that aggression was something Archie had perhaps had to witness himself many times in the past wasn't lost on me.

I closed the door and took a few steps back into the room. I stopped about two feet away from Archie and looked at him. He met my gaze. 'Archie, we don't know each other very well yet,' I said, 'but hopefully you'll come to trust me and realise that I'm here to help you.' He lowered his eyes and stared at the floor. 'I understand that you're feeling very angry about lots of things, and I want to help you figure it all out, but for that to happen you need to understand that my house is a place of safety, for you and for Bobbi, but for all of us as well, and that includes Mungo. That means there are rules that must never be broken. Calling me names like the ones you just used is not allowed, ever. And what happened downstairs with Mungo must never happen again either.'

He flushed still deeper and looked quickly away. 'That's all I want to say for tonight. We're all tired. I think we should try and get some sleep.' I reached out and gave him what I hoped to be a reassuring pat on the arm.

His eyes darkened, turning from deep hazel to brown. 'You smell,' he said in a contemptuous tone. 'You smell just like her.'

I pulled my hand away slowly. 'Like who?' I asked, aware of my pulse beginning to race again. 'Who do you mean, Archie?'

I hadn't realised quite how much of a toll Archie's outburst had taken until I got ready for bed that night. Entirely sapped, I abandoned an attempt at reading the paperback on my bedside table and dropped off to sleep almost as soon as I switched off the lamp. I woke in the small hours though, Archie's words foremost in my mind. When he'd said that I smelled just like 'her', he had sounded so venomous and hateful, using a level of spite unusual in someone so young.

Refusing to engage any further, he had pivoted on his heel and lunged at the ladder of his bunk, throwing himself up onto his mattress and pulling the duvet over his head. I presumed that the smell he had found so repellent was alcohol. But what had he seen when he looked at me, I wondered. Had it been his mother, or was it possible that the 'her' he referred to related to someone else?

My heart lurched when I thought about how confused his feelings for his mother seemed to be. It put me in mind of something I'd read by the American writer Judith Viorst about a small boy who had been doused in alcohol and set on fire. Frightened and in pain, the boy cried for his mother from his hospital bed, even though it had been her who had set him alight. What stuck in my mind at the time of reading was that the boy wholeheartedly wanted his mother regardless of anything she had done and of the danger she represented. Or as Viorst put it, 'Whether she hurts or hugs'.

By morning Archie's mask was firmly back in place, so much so that it might have been easy to convince myself that last night's fall-out was a figment of my imagination. 'Good, thank you,' he'd said, when I asked him how his night had been. Having washed and dressed without prompting, he sat at the breakfast table and lavished fuss on Mungo, who had taken a fair bit of coaxing out of his basket earlier that morning. Archie tensed when Jamie walked past him to the kitchen though, his eyes lowering sheepishly to the table.

'See you,' Jamie said a moment later, emerging from the kitchen with a banana in his hand. He was going into school early to practise for an inter-county football match that was taking place later that afternoon.

'Bye, love, good luck,' I said when he patted my shoulder.

'Bye, Jamie,' Archie said quietly. He brushed a few invisible crumbs from the table and straightened the placemats, keeping his eyes lowered.

'Laters,' Jamie said casually, with only the slightest hesitation. Archie looked up then, seemingly surprised at being forgiven so easily.

Bobbi came down a few minutes later, bleary-eyed but belting out a monstrous tune at the top of her voice. Still in her pyjamas, she threw her arms around me then leapt onto the chair next to Archie. 'Rosie, can me and Meggie do some painting after school today? Can we, Rosie, can we?'

With a sudden jolt I realised that, for the first time since she'd arrived almost two weeks earlier, she hadn't demanded food the moment she set eyes on me. It was an encouraging sign; she was beginning to trust that I would take care of her needs without reminders. 'That sounds like a plan,' I said, kissing the top of her head and straightening her glasses on my way to the kitchen.

She cheered and started singing again. I watched her as I poured milk into a large jug and carried bowls and spoons to the table, marvelling at Archie's ability to switch off from her antics. Studiously examining the back of a cereal box, he barely glanced her way, even when she bumped into him and screamed in his ear.

'In fine fettle again this morning, Bobbi?' Emily said with a grin as she and Megan came in.

'Isn't she just?' I said, giving Emily's shoulder a squeeze as she took a seat at the table. 'And you, madam,' I said, squatting down in front of Megan and giving her tummy a tickle. 'I thought I asked you to get your uniform on?' Sporting a purple leotard and pink tutu, she grinned and performed a wobbly pirouette. 'I suppose we can get ready after breakfast. In fact, girls, as you're both full of beans, maybe you could help me serve the cereal this morning.'

'Huh?' Bobbi said, her eyes popping open in surprise.

'It's so good when we make it to school on time. I think if you help me we might be able to get there on time again today. What do you think?'

Bobbi frowned, her mouth falling open.

'Oooh, I will, Mummy!' Megan said, her hand up in the air as if in the classroom. 'I'll help!'

'Great! Perhaps you could give everyone a bowl and spoon then, Meggie, and Bobbi, you can pour the milk.'

'Huh?' Bobbi said again, but she had already climbed off the chair and was looking at me expectantly. When everyone had chosen their cereal she moved between us, holding the jug of milk in a stately manner, her head tilted at a regal angle.

'Thank you very much, girls,' I said, adopting a tone of serious gratitude as they returned to their seats. They gave each other a comradely grin and tucked into the breakfast, oblivious to the look of amusement passing between Emily and me.

Miracle upon miracles, we made it to Millfield Primary with five minutes to spare before the bell, Bobbi and Archie both correctly attired, teeth brushed, hair in place. 'Have a lovely day, Archie,' I called out as he picked a path through the small groups of children standing between him and the school building. Despite the frozen air, Bobbi shrugged her coat off and swung it over her head, spinning around like a drowsy insect on a hot summer's day.

As on other days, there was no interaction between Archie and the children he passed. He stole a surreptitious glance around the playground as he neared the entrance to his Year Five classroom, perhaps to see if there was anyone he might engage with. After a moment he dropped his rucksack on the ground, leaned back against the wall and closed his eyes.

My heart lurched as Bobbi pressed her head against my stomach in one of her semi-aggressive hugs. I leaned over and patted her back absentmindedly, my eyes still settled on her brother. I made a mental note to speak to his teacher to see if she could suggest a likely pairing with someone else in his class, someone kind-hearted who might be willing to take him under their wing. I thought back to some of the kindnesses he had shown Megan since he'd arrived – he was a thoughtful soul and would make a nice friend for someone, I was sure of it. All he needed was a helpful nudge in the right direction.

I was so absorbed in my plans that I started when one of the mums, a woman with shiny black hair and a long face, tapped me lightly on the arm. We both laughed. 'Sorry, I didn't mean to make you jump. I've been meaning to come and say hello. I'm Lisa, Rory's mum.'

'Oh, hi, Lisa.' I realised that I sounded slightly vague, but neither of the children had mentioned Rory, or any other classmates for that matter. 'Is Rory in Archie's class?'

I began to wonder whether I might be able to make use of this mum's friendliness to get some sort of playdate arranged.

'Oh no, Rory's in the year above. No, it's just that I've spoken to his mum, Tanya, a few times and –' she stopped, eyeing me speculatively. At the sound of her mother's name, Bobbi stilled and looked at us over the top of her glasses. Her eyes narrowed. I looked at Lisa and waited, beginning to suspect that she was on a mission to unearth some gossip. It often happened when children came into care and remained at the same school. Most people respected the birth family's right to privacy, but some simply couldn't resist the urge to uncover the juicy details. A few more seconds passed and Lisa's gaze began to waver. She glanced down at Bobbi and opened her mouth to speak, but then the bell rang.

Lisa raised her hand. A young boy, presumably Rory, gave her a quick wave in reply and headed off towards the opposite end of the building. I turned back to Lisa. 'It's just that we were wondering –' she said in response to my raised eyebrows. She hesitated, her eyes flicking across the emptying playground to where a handful of mothers were standing by the main gate, watching us. She licked her lips and leaned in conspiratorially, her voice lowered to a loud whisper. 'We were wondering whether everything was alright?'

I gave her a bright smile and looked down at Bobbi to remind her that a pair of little ears were flapping. 'Yes, fine, thank you.'

She frowned. 'But Rory says he's heard that you're a foster carer?'

'Yes, that's right.' I shoved my hands in the pockets of my coat and turned slowly towards the Early Years gate. Lisa fell into step next to me.

'So you're looking after the kids full-time then?'

Aware of the sharpening gazes from the mothers at the gate, I quickened my step and herded Bobbi towards her classroom. 'Yes, the children are staying with me for now,' I said in a friendly tone, but one that I hoped invited no further enquiry. I gave her a quick smile and then leaned over to talk to Bobbi. 'Right, sweetie, almost time to go in.' Bobbi found it so stressful to leave me in the mornings that I still spent the first ten minutes or so in class with her in the mornings. It was a gentler start to her day and one the teachers didn't object to. In point of fact, Miss Granville usually shot me a panicked look when I made a move to leave. I straightened. 'It was nice to meet you, Lisa. Enjoy your day.'

'Yeah, you too. Do you mind me asking why they've been taken off their mum though?' she persisted. I noticed the other mums still watching me with interest.

I pulled my keys out of my pocket. 'I'm afraid I'm not allowed to go into the ins and outs of it all,' I said, beginning to feel irritated with her thoughtlessness. The removal of children from their parents was a shocking act, one that was bound to spark interest. It was natural for people to wonder what had happened, but unfair to think it was a subject that should be publicly debated, and especially in front of a child.

'But she must have done something to them,' Lisa whispered close as we joined the back of the line waiting for the Early Years gate to open. 'The social don't take kids off you for nothing, do they?'

'I can't discuss it,' I said bluntly before leaning down to make a fuss of Bobbi. Lisa gave me a slightly resentful look and then walked away to join her friends.

Chapter Thirteen

The next two weeks passed relatively peacefully, if you glossed over Bobbi's meltdowns and overlooked her unpredictable assaults. There were no further confrontations with Archie and, though he seemed even quieter than usual, he was mostly back to his polite, contained self.

The suspicion of the children's former foster carer Joan that Bobbi might be an ADHD sufferer gained some ground when I took the children for their LAC medical – the statutory check-up with a paediatrician that all looked-after children are obliged to have when they come into care. Having spoken to Bobbi's teacher over the telephone, the paediatrician was of the opinion that traits of hyperactive disorder were present, although he told me that a diagnosis was rarely confirmed before the age of seven.

Interestingly, he also explained that many of the symptoms could be alleviated by following a sensory diet. He told me to work half an hour of intense physical exercise into Bobbi's day, both morning and evening. He also recommended giving her deep-pressure back massages as well as heavy chores to carry out throughout the day, plus tough objects to chew and thick drinks to suck through a thin straw. At the end of the consultation he also suggested that I should buy a spinning egg chair from IKEA. 'Works better than Ritalin,' he told me with a wink.

Our weekly attempts at telephone contact with their mother had mostly failed, her answerphone message immediately cutting in. It seemed to me that Tanya Brady was slowly withdrawing from her children. I had little doubt that she would continue to contest their removal through the courts, however. With the availability of legal aid, most parents objected, even those who preferred life without the restrictions that children bring.

I will always remember the look of horror on one birth mother's face when she received the news that her three young children were being returned to her care. Her jaw dropped, her eyes goggling in panic. She was so gobsmacked that she fled to the nearest pub for a bender. When she turned up to afternoon contact with the children, she could barely stand upright.

Often, the absence of contact with birth parents helps children to settle quicker. I certainly sensed a softening in Bobbi's outbursts and she rarely asked to see her mum, even at bedtime. I suspected that she had begun grieving for her mother the day she came into the world, never having experienced what it was really like to be loved.

My new ploy of engaging her in helping us to get ready in the mornings was working a treat as well. She and Megan seemed to revel in the challenge of making it to nursery and school with time to spare and loved the new routine of half an hour's frantic bouncing on the trampoline before washing and dressing for school. Most of the time they hurried me along with an encouraging: 'Come on, Rosie, come *on*!'

By the end of their first month with us we had it down pat, arriving at Millfield Primary, on Friday 30 January, more than five minutes before the bell was due to ring. The morning was bright but very cold and I stamped my feet to try and warm them up as we stood in the playground. Bobbi copied me, her heart-shaped face crumpling into a grin when I picked up speed. She struggled to keep pace, giggling as she lost balance.

It was as I reached out to stop her from toppling over that I noticed a couple of mothers looking at us askance. I straightened, Bobbi pulling on my hand and hopping from foot to foot as she tried to get me to copy her. As soon as they caught on that I'd seen them they turned away, but as I joined in Bobbi's game I was aware of their eyes on us again. I wasn't sure whether it was the same mothers I had seen last week at the gates, but there was something unfriendly about the jut of their chins, something far more potent than mild curiosity.

When I returned to the school that afternoon no one seemed to pay me any interest, negative or otherwise, but there was a general frostiness amongst the group of mothers waiting outside the Early Years playground. Even an unfettered rendition of 'Let it Go' from Megan as she skipped at my side did little to thaw the tight smiles coming my way.

'Where's Bobs?' Megan asked a few minutes later, as the last stragglers emerged from the Reception classroom.

'I've no idea,' I said, frowning. Bobbi was usually at the front of the queue at the end of the day, though I wasn't sure whether that was through her own eagerness to leave or by Miss Granville's design. I reached out for Megan's hand and was about to go to the Early Years' gate to enquire, when I heard someone calling my name. The voice was vaguely familiar and I wondered whether it might be Lisa again, eager to have another try at bagging some gossip. I turned to see Clare Barnard hurrying across the emptying playground. 'Sorry, Rosie,' she puffed, wrapping her cardigan tightly around herself and folding her arms against the cold. 'Could I have a quick word?'

I glanced over at the Early Years' gate where Bobbi's teacher was standing. Miss Granville gave a tiny shrug and lifted empty hands in an apologetic *What can you do?* gesture. 'Bobbi hasn't come out yet,' I said, my eyes still resting on Miss Granville.

'No, that's what I've come to talk to you about. She's running around the PE hall at the moment with the headmistress.'

I turned sharply to look at Clare. 'Running around the hall?' I repeated, frowning. For a second I wondered whether they'd decided to chase her around as a way of releasing some of her pent-up emotions. 'What, you mean, running around and having fun?'

'We-ell,' Clare said slowly, pushing her glasses further up her nose. I noticed a twinkle of amusement creeping into her eyes. 'Bobbi may well be having fun, but I think it's safe to say that Mrs Cullum-Coggan isn't enjoying herself very much.'

I stared at Clare, still not comprehending. 'Bobbi's spent the majority of the day in the toilets, I'm afraid,' she said in explanation, turning towards the school building. I fell into step beside her, Megan's hand in mine. 'As you know, we're not allowed to physically manhandle her out. She emerged a few times of her own free will, but as soon as someone said something she didn't like she scrambled back in again.'

I grimaced, waiting as Clare punched a code into the keypad beside the door to the main reception. She pulled the door open and gestured me in, but I hesitated. 'What about Archie?'

'We've sent him to Chess Club. He was happy to go and we thought we could use all hands on deck for now.'

I gave her a grim smile and walked past her into reception. The plump, round-faced receptionist stood up from behind her glass partition as soon as she saw us. 'Would your daughter like to play with me for a few minutes?' she asked, smiling at Megan warmly.

I leaned down to speak to Megan, who was already vigorously shaking her head. 'Do you want to play here for a minute, Meggie?'

She leaned closer to me, regarding the woman shyly. 'No, thank you,' she said, with polite firmness. She clutched my hand tight and looked up at me, her bright hazel eyes clouded with concern. 'I want to stay with you.'

'Oh, that's a shame. I have an iPad here,' the woman said, lifting a thin screen enticingly into sight. 'I thought you might be able to help Mamma Panda find her babies on *Panda Pop*.'

Megan bit her lip and looked at me uncertainly. 'I won't be long, Meggie,' I said brightly. 'I'll get Bobbi and then come straight back for you, I promise.' She nodded, unable to resist a request for help and the lure of technology.

The tiny glance she threw over her shoulder as she walked away made my heart constrict. I gave her a reassuring wave through the glass and she smiled and waved back, allowing herself to be lifted onto the swivel chair that the receptionist had just vacated. Clare opened an adjacent door and I followed her into a long corridor, the walls decorated with brightly coloured paintings and Star of the Week charts, photos of smiling children beaming as they held the coveted Champion's Cup.

We passed several open doors leading to different classrooms before a high-pitched screech reached my ears. The noise, classic Bobbi in tone, grew louder with each step. I began to gain a sense of the gravity of our ensuing conversation when Clare bypassed a set of double doors that led to the hall and continued along the corridor, stopping outside a closed door marked 'SENCO'.

Clare showed me into her office, a small room with fluorescent lighting and cork boards arranged on the walls. 'Please, have a seat,' she said with a half-smile, gesturing towards the hard-backed chair positioned alongside her desk. She took the swivel chair opposite, clasped her hands on top of her desk and looked at me. 'So, as I said, it's been a difficult day.'

I nodded, waiting for her to continue. She lifted her eyebrows. 'In fact, it's been a difficult day at the end of a very difficult week.'

I frowned. 'Oh, really?' As far as I knew, the children's last week at school had been relatively trauma-free. There certainly hadn't been any notes written in glaring red capitals in the home school diary, or any crooked fingers at the gate.

She nodded. 'Has Bobbi said anything to you?'

'No,' I said, slightly surprised to find myself bristling with defensiveness on Bobbi's behalf. Though I always felt protective towards new children when they came to stay with us, it took a while for genuine affection to grow. Strangers to me a month ago, until that moment I hadn't registered any particular attachment towards the siblings, other than a sincere commitment towards helping them heal. 'And neither has anyone else,' I added in a slightly barbed tone.

'Well, I think perhaps Miss Granville has been trying to get on with things as best she can, but there have been several incidents of unacceptable aggression from Bobbi since we last spoke, both towards the other children and Miss Granville herself.'

'Ah,' I said slowly, the hostile glances from some of the mothers in the playground suddenly making sense.

'She targets three or four children in particular, and some of the parents are now baying for retribution,' Clare said unapologetically. 'Whenever we report an injury to parents we have a policy of not mentioning the child responsible, but more often than not the child tells all when they get home. I'm afraid our Bobbi's making quite a name for herself.'

Any resentment I felt towards her melted away at the inclusive-sounding reference to 'our Bobbi'. 'That's awful. I'm sorry to hear that. Can you separate her from the children she's clashing with? Perhaps sit her with someone else?' It seemed a simple solution, one I was sure they'd probably already considered, but it seemed worth a mention.

'Our child-led learning approach for Reception children means that they work in a free-flow environment,' Clare said, picking up a pen and opening the notepad on her desk. 'Some of their learning will be adult initiated but, apart from carpet time, they're free to move around the classroom as they wish.' She paused, her pen hovering over the empty page as if waiting for me to come up with some other helpful gems.

I looked at her in silence, already out of ideas. 'Of course, as they're now in care we're organising a Personal Education Plan (PEP) for both Archie and Bobbi. You'll be invited to a meeting soon, but in light of what's happened today, on top of the week we've had, we can't wait until then to discuss what to do about Bobbi.'

'No. I see.' I glanced out of the small window into the now-empty playground. I knew that, in an effort to close the attainment gap between disadvantaged children and those in the general population, schools were provided with additional funding from the government – nearly two thousand pounds for each adopted or looked-after child, and those entitled to free school meals – to benefit pupils and aid their learning.

Thanks to a well-established system of social pedagogy – building a team around the child in need and nurturing well-rounded personal development – I knew that looked-after children in Germany, Denmark and Norway were far more likely to achieve educationally than their British counterparts, as well as moving into either employment or further education in far greater numbers.

I also knew that, unless challenged noisily, many schools in England tended to absorb the pupil premium into their mainstream budget. Archie and Bobbi were entitled to receive extra support to help them in the classroom, and I was determined to make sure that's exactly what they would get. 'What about using the pupil premium to get some one-to-one help for Bobbi? She's clearly in fight-or-flight mode. She might feel less fearful if she's with someone she feels she can trust.'

Clare's eyes flickered. 'Erm, well, yes –' she faltered, perhaps surprised that I knew anything about the premium. 'We have two teaching assistants who float between the Reception classes. They're there for the children whenever they need it.'

'But every Reception class has a TA,' I argued, keeping my tone reasonable. 'They would be there whether Bobbi was in the class or not. I'm talking about using Bobbi's pupil premium to get some extra help in, specifically for her.'

Clare folded her arms and rested them on the desk. 'Well, as I said, the TAs are there to help any of the children when they need it.'

'Well, it doesn't sound like they're helping Bobbi very much,' I said, tilting my head towards the door and the school hall beyond.

'I don't think there's much anyone can do to help her if she won't come out from under a desk.'

'But perhaps she wouldn't have fled in the first place if someone had been sitting with her,' I argued. School was often a haven for children whose home lives were traumatic; a port in a storm and the one place they felt safe. Not so for Bobbi, or so it seemed.

Clare pressed her lips together. 'Look, I appreciate you're looking out for her, really I do, but we have to balance the needs of twenty-nine other children against those of Bobbi. At the moment she's draining all of the class teacher's attention away from them.'

I felt myself becoming annoyed. I glanced out of the window again to rein my irritation in. It wasn't Clare's fault that Bobbi's needs were greater than the other children, or that there were limited resources to go round. It was simply that the system was geared to helping the majority of children, those capable of learning quickly or those with needs so significant that they needed full-time one-to-one help. Children like Bobbi had a tendency to fall through the net. I decided it might be best to shift the onus onto the school, or at least frame it so that they accepted some of the responsibility. 'How do you think we might help her then?'

Clare paused, picked her pen up again. 'I think we're going to have to consider reducing her hours to part-time, as I mentioned before. At least for now. We can review again if she settles.'

'And if she doesn't?'

'Well, then she'll have to go to the behaviour unit.'

I stared at her. 'At five years old?' After all that she'd been through, the last thing Bobbi needed was more rejection. I could understand their wish to reduce her hours, but to throw her out of the school would be like telling her *we can't cope with you, we don't like the way you are*.

Clare levelled her gaze. 'Sometimes we have no choice. We have to protect the welfare of *all* our children. We've had to exclude a child from nursery before now.'

I grimaced. The idea of expelling a child from nursery seemed ludicrous to me. I was beginning to suspect that

Millfield Primary might be a little trigger-happy in their approach to discipline.

'None of the local specialist behaviour units have space for Bobbi at the moment anyway. It would be a case of trying to keep on top of her education at home while the local authority figures out the best way forward.' Clare held up a hand. 'Don't worry, we're not quite there yet, but unless we have a better week next week we're going to have to reset her schedule, for her sake as well as the other children.'

I gave her a tight nod and looked away, wondering whether the headmistress had managed to catch Bobbi yet, or if she was still in mad pursuit in the hall. As if reading my thoughts, Clare eased her chair away from her desk and said: 'Miss Granville spent her morning break blocking the backs of all the desks. When Bobbi noticed she ran out of the classroom and shut herself in the toilets. We locked the outer door to the toilets at lunchtime and that's when she ran off. We've been taking it in turns to try and catch her ever since.'

'Oh no, poor Bobbi.' The one haven she had found outside the classroom had been cut off from her. No wonder she had panicked and fled.

Clare's eyes widened in surprise. 'Poor Bobbi?'

'It's terror that's made her run, Clare, not naughtiness. If you deny her a safe space in the classroom, she'll find one somewhere else, even if it is the loo.'

She gave me a thoughtful look. 'Right, I think perhaps we should see if Mrs Cullum-Coggan needs some help.'

* * *

The school hall was empty when we got there, but there was a high-pitched wail coming from further along the corridor. We followed the sound and found a smartly dressed woman of about fifty standing in the doorway of one of the class-rooms, her cheeks flushed a deep shade of pink.

'Mrs Cullum-Coggan, this is Rosie Lewis,' Clare said when we reached the open door.

'Hello,' I offered tentatively. She was a stern-looking woman, her features sharply defined.

'Over to you, Rosie,' she stated flatly. In the classroom, Bobbi was squatting on top of a cabinet near the far wall, her arms wrapped around her knees. My heart caught at the sight. 'I'm out of ideas. We've tried everything to calm her. She appears to be having some sort of manic episode.'

'Maybe you should have called me.'

'If we rewarded every pupil for behaving badly by send-ing them home we'd have an empty school,' Mrs Cullum-Coggan said, drawing the back of her hand along her forehead. I could see her point, but this wasn't bad behav-iour. Bobbi looked distraught.

I gave a small nod and walked into the classroom. 'Bobbi, love, it's time to come home.' She looked up sharply. The glazed look in her eyes took a moment to clear, but then when recognition struck she sat back on her bottom, burst into tears and held her arms out to me. I sat beside her on the cabinet, took her glasses off and pulled her onto my lap. She sobbed in my arms for several minutes as I rocked her and stroked her hair. 'What is it, sweetie?' I asked when she'd quietened.

She turned her tear-streaked face towards me. 'Everyone says Archie's weird,' she said, hiccoughing a sob.

Broken

I frowned. 'Who says that?'

'Freya says it. She's got a brother in Year 6, and Connor and Jessica.'

'Why would they say that?'

'Don't know,' she squealed, tears rolling down her cheeks again. She kicked out at the cabinet. 'But he's not. They're lying. It's not fair!'

I cuddled her close, thinking, no, little one, none of this is fair. Mrs Cullum-Coggan and Clare exchanged surprised glances at the door. They looked slightly choked themselves.

Chapter Fourteen

As soon as I got back from dropping the children off on Monday 2 February, I switched my computer on and searched for some adoption forums on the Internet. I had attended all sorts of courses in the last decade covering a diverse range of issues, but had always found the advice from adopters and foster carers on the forums of far more practical help.

I rested my head on the desk as I waited for the page to load, my eyes stinging. Mungo yawned, stretched his front legs out and then made a pillow of my feet. I tickled his ear, enjoying the unspoken camaraderie between us. Bobbi had remained on full throttle all through the weekend and was still calling out to me at 4 a.m. this morning. As on other nights she settled quickly after I'd stroked her hair, but barely an hour passed before she was crying out again. It was only nine thirty but I felt thoroughly drained.

As the screen flickered above my head my mind rewound over the last few days, juddering to a stop here and there as if trying to bring something to my attention. My old computer tower whirred noisily at my side as my thoughts returned to our visit to my mother's house yesterday afternoon.

Archie had greeted Mum politely and offered her a string of effusive compliments about her house and the quality of her orange squash, but there was a lethargy about him. As soon as they'd exhausted the pleasantries he slunk off to one of her armchairs and sat holding a book up in front of his face. There had been no more outbursts from him since the evening he'd met Des, but in a funny way I regretted the calm. His fury had offered me a rare glimpse into his inner world, one that I felt sure was close to shattering.

Every attempt I'd made since then to get him talking had been deflected away with light-hearted chatter about Harry Potter or other distractions, but I wasn't fooled. My sense of foreboding was growing with each day that passed.

Bobbi had thrown herself into my mum's arms as soon as she saw her. 'Well, what a greeting,' Mum chuckled breathlessly, patting her gently on the back. 'More than I get from some, I might add,' she said with a pointed look towards her grandson.

Jamie, stretched out on the armchair opposite Archie with a jar of her peanuts open on his lap, threw her a grin. 'Oh yeah, sorry, Nan,' he said thickly. 'Hiya.'

Soon after I began fostering, my mother applied to become one of my back-up carers. After being interviewed by one of the agency social workers, she attended a weekend Skills to Foster course, submitted to various background checks and childproofed her home. Having covered for me countless times in the last decade, she had plenty of experience of the different behaviours that could arise in children from difficult backgrounds. As Bobbi wrapped her short arms around Mum's middle she gave me a knowing look over the top of her spectacles.

'That's *my* nanny,' Megan grumbled possessively, her bottom lip pouting as she stood nearby.

'Oh, come here, little yellow belly,' Mum laughed, holding out her other arm. Megan ran forward and Mum drew her into a hug. 'How's my special granddaughter today?'

'Okay,' Megan smirked, enjoying the fuss. 'This is my friend, Nanny,' she said, patting Bobbi's chest. 'Her name's Bobbi, like a boy.'

Bobbi scowled and began throwing herself around. Mum instinctively shrank away, protecting Megan from Bobbi's stray blows. 'Crikey, be careful, lovey, you'll do yourself a mischief if you carry on like that. We've already met, haven't we, Bobbi?' she added quickly, artfully distracting her from escalating into a full-blown meltdown. 'Do you remember? I came and sat with you while Rosie popped to the shops.'

Bobbi stopped screeching and looked at her. 'We played with the farm,' she said, patting Mum softly on the cheek. It was an affectionate gesture, a reminder of the special bond that often develops between the older generation and the young.

'We had fun, didn't we?' Mum said to Bobbi, giving her shoulder a squeeze. She turned to Megan. 'Bobbi can be a boy or a girl's name.' She stood up with a soft groan and glanced at me over the top of her glasses. 'Mind you, I suppose any name can be, these days. I heard someone called their daughter Tofu the other day. I've never heard anything so ridiculous in all my born days.' The girls, still either side of her, made a competitive grab for her legs. 'Careful, you'll have me over in a minute. Now, get out from under my feet so I can get the kettle on. Dinner won't be ready for a while so we've got time for a cup of tea.'

Megan skipped off and got the colouring pens out. 'Come and do drawing, Bobs,' she said cheerfully, laying on her front on the rug near the hearth.

Bobbi released Mum and began dancing manically around the room. It was a bright, open space, with tall bookshelves fitted snugly into the alcove on one side of the fireplace and an old-fashioned dresser in the other, but there were lots of trinkets around. It wasn't the ideal place for one of Bobbi's raves. 'Bobbi, let's find a game to play,' I said invitingly, holding out my hand to try and catch her mid-lap. She stopped near the dresser and picked up one of Mum's ornaments. Megan dropped her pen and sat up. 'Ooh, no!' she piped up, eyes boggling in astonishment. 'You *mustn't* touch Nanny's things!'

The warning drew my mum back from the kitchen. 'That's right,' she said, brandishing a teaspoon in the air with mock sternness. 'You leave my ornaments alone, young lady, or I'll chop your fingers off.'

I cringed. The Skills to Foster training course Mum had attended all those years ago hadn't done anything to soften her tongue. I held my breath, expecting Bobbi to react badly. To my surprise, she restored the china horse she was holding to its place on the shelf with exceptional caution, her eyes fixed wide on my mum's face.

'That's the ticket,' Mum said with a firm nod and a quick, not unsatisfied, glance in my direction. She waggled the teaspoon at Megan. 'And you make sure you keep those pens away from my new rug, madam,' she said, tapping her slippered feet on a thickly piled cream-coloured rug at the foot of the sofa. 'I don't want to come in and find it all colours of the rainbow, d'you hear?'

Megan grinned. 'Okay, Nanny.'

'Well done, Bobbi, good listening!' I said, taking her hand and leading her towards the rug.

'Well done, Bobs!' Megan repeated, patting her on the top of the head.

'She's not a puppy, Megs,' Jamie said with a momentary glance away from the screen of his iPhone.

'She sounds like one sometimes though, don't you, Bobbi?' Megan returned, leaning close to Bobbi's face and smiling broadly. Bobbi yapped and bobbed on her heels. We all laughed.

'Tell you what,' I said, passing Bobbi some paper. 'Let's play Follow the Leader. You take a pen and follow mine as closely as you can, okay?' It was a game I usually played with children who were fearful of intimacy, since it offered a non-threatening way of making a connection. Bobbi was already a dispenser of frequent cuddles, but I thought the game might help to get her used to following instructions.

'Huh?' Bobbi pressed her glasses further onto her nose with a flattened hand and stared at me with her mouth open.

'I'll show her, Mummy!' Megan chose a felt-tip and began drawing some wiggly lines across the page. I followed her pen closely behind with my own. Bobbi, itching to join in, bobbed up and down on her knees as she watched us.

Broken

We each took turns in following one another across the page, the girls giggling whenever my pen bumped into theirs.

With my mum taking care of dinner I was able to spend the next couple of hours with the girls, focussing on all the games I'd been meaning to play since Archie and Bobbi arrived. Archie declined my offer of joining in, but when I stuck eight sheets of A4 paper together with Sellotape and drew the shape of a large person in the space, he lowered his book and showed some interest. 'Who's that?' Bobbi asked, watching me with intrigue.

'It's a people,' Megan said. She had seen me play this game with several other children and had always been an enthusiastic participant.

'That's right,' I said, inviting the girls to draw circles all over the body. 'Now what we have to do is think of all the different parts each of us has inside, the bits that make us who we are.'

'Huh?' Bobbi said, frowning.

'Well, inside all of us are lots of different thoughts and feelings. At the moment you're confused, so I'll write that in one of these lovely circles you've drawn. Can you think of any other parts you have inside you?'

'Bobbi has screechy parts,' Megan offered earnestly.

'Erm, we-ell, she does make a funny noise sometimes, don't you, Bobbi? Can you think of how you might be feeling when you make that noise?'

Bobbi bit her lip. 'Erm,' she said, looking around the room. By offering Bobbi a visual representation, I was hoping to help her to recognise and then begin to regulate her emotions. I was about to offer up some ideas when she lookcd back at me. 'Sad,' she said levelly, taking me completely by surprise. Clearly she was more in touch with her own feelings than I'd realised.

'You feel sad sometimes. Right, so we'll put that down in one of our circles.'

'My tummy was always sad at home,' Bobbi said, her tongue poking through her lips as she drew some features on the face. 'It hurts when it's sad,' she added matter-of-factly. 'It growls and grumbles and keeps me awake. But it's happy now I'm at your house.'

'Ah, interesting,' I said mildly, aware that Archie was now glaring at his sister. I joined in with the colouring, making a mental note to record her comment in my diary when I got home. Children often begin to open up and talk about their difficult experiences once they feel safe. Foster carers are encouraged to record all disclosures as accurately as possible but are warned against asking probing questions which might prejudice any future inquiry. 'Charlie used to love playing this game,' I said eventually, when it was clear that Bobbi wasn't going to enlarge on what she'd said.

The girls, absorbed in decorating the head with a mass of bright orange curls, didn't say anything. Archie slid from the armchair onto the floor. 'Who's Charlie?'

When children are taken into care they're often convinced that they're the only ones who have ever been removed from their families. The news that other children have gone through similar experiences comes as a revelation to them and they seem to draw comfort from knowing they're not unique in that way. It's one of the reasons that our fostering agency encourages regular social events for carers and their families.

'Is it someone you looked after?' Megan said, her pen now chasing Bobbi's over the circles they'd drawn. I nodded and was about to open my mouth to speak when she jumped to her feet and put the lid on her pen. Bobbi dropped her own pen and began rolling across the floor. 'Can I tell him, Mummy?' Megan asked.

I grinned. 'Of course you can, sweetie.'

'Arty, Mummy helps children. And I help too.'

'That's right. Charlie was a little lad who came to stay with us before you were born though, Meggie, and he used to love drawing pictures with us.'

'Why did he stay with you?' Archie asked, his eyes shining with interest.

'His mum wasn't able to keep him safe,' I said, aware that he was watching me intently.

'Why not?'

'Well,' I said slowly. I wasn't about to share the confidential details of a real child's past, so I hastily invented a plausible scenario to share. 'Charlie's mum was addicted to some bad medicine. Not the sort of medicine you get from a doctor, the kind that makes you well. This medicine makes you ill and so she couldn't take care of Charlie, and he became ill too.'

Archie's eyes were burning with intensity now. 'How ill? What happened to him?'

'He was cold and hungry and lonely. No one played with him or took care of him when he was unwell.'

'Mum,' Jamie said, a note of urgency in his voice. For a second I thought perhaps he felt that I was sharing too much. I turned to look at him, but he was gaping across the room, his eyes bulging with horror.

I followed his gaze, a band tightening around my breast-bone. The smell hit me before I managed to process the sight; the acrid, overwhelming and unmistakable stench of faeces. And there, squatting right over the middle of Mum's new fluffy rug, was Bobbi, her face red as she strained. Drawn by the chorus of gasps in the room, my mum appeared at the doorway a few seconds later. 'Well, that's the limit, it really is,' she had said, shaking her head in disbelief.

On screen, one of the adoption forums had loaded. I logged on under the username Mrs Doubtfire and scrolled down the different subjects being discussed. The option 'DAILY STRUGGLES (a space to vent your fears and frustrations and search for answers)' seemed most relevant.

I browsed the list of most recent threads but there was nothing related to education or difficulties at school. I was a regular reader of the forums but rarely posted, usually finding the answer to whatever issue I was having after a short trawl through the older threads.

Today, though, I decided that some specific advice might be more helpful. I clicked on 'Start a new thread' and went for it, explaining that I had an AD (adopted daughter) and a FC (foster child) of a similar age, then detailing Bobbi's behaviour and her difficulties at school – the constant interrupting of the teacher, the crawling under desks, her refusal to follow basic instructions, as well as the SENCO's proposal of reducing her hours and their general reluctance to provide additional support. For the benefit of the easily revolted I left out yesterday's fluffy rug episode. Known as 'code brown' in fostering circles, faecal smearing is potentially a sign of previous sexual or physical abuse, but might just as easily be dismissed as a one-off 'accident'. Bobbi was still only young and, Mum's initial horror notwithstanding, it wasn't something I felt worthy of too much alarm.

After making myself a coffee I refreshed the page and was touched to find that several members had already taken the time to answer my post:

6 replies

Submitted by SLUMMYMUMMY – You have my sympathies, Mrs Doubtfire! We've been trying to get Cherub's school to agree to additional support for the last 3 yrs. Now they're threatening him with expulsion. Have you read *The Explosive Child* by Ross W. Greene, PhD? That book changed our lives – if only I could get Cherub's teachers to read it.

Submitted by TIREDMUM – Ditto Mrs Doubtfire and Slummy Mummy. No luck on accessing the pupil premium here either. AD now at the stage of school refusal. I've had to give up my job and home tutor her. Every day I'm screamed at, smacked, punched and abused. I wake each morning with a ball of panic in my chest. Sometimes I fear we won't make it. I've heard good things about *The Explosive Child* and also *Inside I'm Hurting* by Louise Bomber. Now all I need to do is find the time to read them. Sending you warm wishes and wishing you luck x

Submitted by MYSTERYFC – I am a teacher, foster carer and adopter. You have the right to insist that your FC is provided with a full-time education, Mrs Doubtfire. Schools are not allowed to reduce hours willy-nilly. Get some legal advice!

Submitted by WHISKERSONKITTENS – Tired Mum, I feel for you, I've been there too. We almost didn't make it but these forums gave me strength through the darkest times and somehow I managed to keep going. Keep posting. You WILL find the support you need on here. My AD is now 23, she is my best friend and I love her more than I can say. There is always a way forward. Please know that your AD's attacks are not personal. She's hurting and you are her safe base. Hold her while she rages at the world, watch her while she sleeps.

Submitted by SCOOBYDOO – Discipline, discipline, discipline! Mrs Doubtfire, if FC doesn't behave at school send her to her room when she gets home and make her stay there! Tired Mum, my motto has always been 'If you hit, you sit!' I can't believe that you allow a child to hit you! Send her to her room until she learns to control herself. Whiskers on Kittens, get a life! While AD sleeps, watch the soaps, not her!

Submitted by ISITWINEOCLOCKYET? – Scooby Doo, just one question – how the f*ck did you ever manage to get through the approval process?

I sat motionless for a moment, moved by the depth of love and devotion these parents had for their children. It was so inspiring. Drawn towards the post about *The Explosive Child* for obvious reasons, I downloaded the eBook and spent the next two hours glued to my Kindle. It was as if the book had been written specifically for Bobbi.

In it the author, Ross Greene, explains that there are a minority of children, often those who have suffered trauma and loss or in-utero injuries from alcohol or drug exposure, who are simply unable to respond to adult imposed sanctions. Their difficulties render popular parenting techniques such as reward and punishment, sticker charts and the removal of privileges futile and redundant.

Greene, a child psychologist, suggests that there are three options available to carers dealing with difficult behaviour. The first is to plough ahead with adult-imposed sanctions that are unlikely to ever work, the second is to ignore all but the most troubling behaviour and the third is to compile a list of triggers for the child, those incidents most likely to result in confrontation – perhaps cleaning their teeth, keeping their room tidy, or dealing with transitions such as leaving a park or turning the television off – and then prioritise those behaviours that are most important to deal with first.

'Striking when the iron is cold', the author advises the carer to wait until the child is calm and then say something like, *I understand that you find it difficult to turn the TV off when your programme is over – what can we do to make it easier for you?*

The carer and child then work together, solving the problem collaboratively, rather than combatively. Besides making the child feel involved and consulted, they also feel under pressure to make any solution they suggest work, because their own idea is at stake. I had to admit, the logic was difficult to argue against.

Some of the suggestions sounded familiar and I remembered Des telling me about new techniques used in US schools, designed to interrupt the 'school to prison pipeline', a phrase coined to describe the seemingly inevitable trajectory for problem kids in the classroom.

The other book that had been recommended, *Inside I'm Hurting*, wasn't available on Kindle but, astonishingly, when I refreshed the thread, someone with the username LIONKING had kindly summarised the book, bullet pointing the tips they had found most helpful for their own children.

I printed everything off and put it into a folder then telephoned Millfield Primary. Megan was due to spend the whole day at nursery on Friday and so I made an appointment with the SENCO for 2 p.m. at the end of the week. I also sent an email to the head of the virtual school, the organisation responsible for overseeing the education of looked-after children, asking if there was anything I could do to persuade Millfield to spend the pupil premium they were receiving for Bobbi on additional support for her.

It was only when I began to feel lightheaded that I realised I hadn't eaten anything since early morning. I checked the time, amazed to find that it was a quarter to twelve, almost time to pick Megan up. I grabbed a banana and ate it while I refreshed the forum page one last time. There were some new responses to my post.

2 replies

Submitted by GOOSEYLOOSEY – Have you tried
using memory cards for the constant interruptions,
Mrs D? AS needs to feel I keep him constantly in
mind. When he interrupts I give him a memory card
– a visual reminder to show him that I know he needs
me and he'll have my attention very soon. Handy
when I'm on the phone or in the loo!

Submitted by LEMONSHERBERT – Have you
considered that your FC might have a processing
difficulty? Early trauma slows processing speeds. We
find giving short, specific, simple choices to our AS
works wonders. We'd never leave the house in the
morning without them.

I scribbled a quick note of all the suggestions, typed a quick
message to thank everyone for their replies and then pulled
on my coat. Feeling empowered and optimistic, I grabbed
my keys and raced out the door. I couldn't wait to pick up
the children and try out my new techniques.

'Bottom on sofa or floor?' I told Bobbi later that afternoon,
after a dangerously executed cartwheel over the footstool.
'Which one?'
    She looked between the two and then threw herself into
a handstand on the sofa. It was an approximation of success
and I gave an inward cheer, my silent celebration faltering
when she collapsed sideways and crashed into Megan. 'Ow!
You poophead!' Megan complained, clamping a hand over

her head and giving me a teary look. Still adjusting to nursery, her usual effervescence was absent in the late afternoons, her skin chalky and pale. I pulled her into a hug and kissed the top of her head. 'Try to be a bit more careful, Bobbi,' I said. 'How about you both help me to get the dinner ready?'

'I want to bounce with Arty,' Megan said wearily. Of the two siblings, Megan seemed to prefer Archie when she was tired. However badly they were behaving, he always seemed to have a reserve of patience for the girls.

'You look fit for bed and not much else, sweetie,' I said gently, glancing across the room to where Archie sat, his books open in front of him on the table. 'And anyway, Archie's still doing his homework.'

'S'alright, I'll go,' he said amiably, closing his book and getting up. 'I've almost finished anyway.'

Tonic to her ears, Megan immediately perked up. She ran into the hall, grabbed her coat and shoes and then took Archie's hand, steering him towards the back door. Mungo followed them out. Still a bit wary of Archie, he kept a safe distance as he trotted along the path after them.

'Wait, Bobbi.' I reached for her hand as she leapt off the sofa to follow them. 'Before you go outside you need to put your coat on.'

She yanked her hand away and spun around, heading for the door. Remembering one of the suggestions on the forum about breaking instructions down into short, specific nuggets, I knelt down in front of her. 'Bobbi,' I said, taking her hands in mine and gently steering her to face me. She craned her neck away, keeping her eyes fixed on the garden. 'Hey, Bobbi, look at me.' Reluctantly she turned around to face me. I let go of her hands. 'Good girl. Now, hat on,' I said, miming the action by pulling closed fists down either side of my head. 'Coat on. Wellies on. Then outside.'

She frowned, looked around, then trotted off and grabbed her hat. To my amazement, she pulled it down over her ears then grabbed her coat and shoved it at me. I held it up and she wiggled her way into it, catching my smile and returning it with a big beaming one of her own. I couldn't believe it.

'What a good girl! Give me a high five.' She clapped flattened hands against mine and then threw her arms around me. My heart melted. 'Aw, that's lovely,' I said, giving her back a brisk rub. 'Now, glasses.' I held out a flattened hand. She hooked her glasses off, dropped them into my palm and then ran to the patio door, slipping her feet into her wellies before running out.

Progress in the early days of a placement often feels slow. I find it helpful to cherish every success, however tiny it may be. The mystery of Bobbi's ability to respond to some of my requests, presumably those I had kept short and sweet, while ignoring others, had been solved. In the world of fostering, it was undoubtedly a moment worthy of celebrating.

I couldn't understand, then, as I watched her run across the frosted grass to join the others, why I felt as though we were all standing on quicksand, further away from solid ground than that first day back in early January.

Chapter Fifteen

I arrived at Millfield Primary just before 2 p.m. on Friday 6 February. It was a bright day, a few stringy white clouds stretched across an otherwise clear blue sky. There was a sharp bite in the air though, the frost-covered sails shading the Early Years playground billowing noisily in the wind.

'Rosie, you're freezing,' Clare Barnard said, grasping my icy fingers in her own warm hands. Her eyes strayed to the books and papers tucked under my arm.

'You've come armed, I see,' she said, but her smile was as welcoming as her handshake and she chatted pleasantly as she escorted me along the corridor towards her office. 'Mrs Cullum-Coggan has asked to join our meeting,' she said, stopping and tapping on the open door of a different, much larger office.

My heart sank. It seemed that the outcome of the meeting might already have been decided, the SENCO enlisting reinforcements to shore up her position.

Mrs Cullum-Coggan stood up as we came in, walking around her long desk and shaking my hand. 'Please, sit down,' she said, gesturing to one of the empty chairs in front of her desk. I took the nearest one and Clare sat on the chair next to me. Mrs Cullum-Coggan eyed the thick wad of papers on my lap and raised an eyebrow.

'I've been doing a bit of research.'

'So I see,' she said with a half-smile. Her severe features softened significantly. She sat down behind her desk and leaned her elbows on top, her fingers pressed together in an arch. 'Well, there is a lot we need to discuss, but perhaps if you start, Rosie, and we can take it from there.'

I looked down at my notes and quickly gathered my thoughts. 'The first thing we need to do,' I said, 'is to get Bobbi seen by an educational psychologist.' I went on to explain my reasoning using inclusive language to encourage them to view the issue as a joint one and careful phrasing to trigger all their safeguarding alarms.

Mrs Cullum-Coggan sucked in sharply. 'There's a long waiting list for ed psychs',' she said, shaking her head as if already dismissing the idea.

'So can we shuffle Bobbi up the list?'

Clare opened her mouth but the headmistress spoke first. 'We can't do that. Some of our children have been waiting almost a year.'

'A year?' I looked between Mrs Cullum-Coggan and Clare. 'Why so long? Aren't there enough to go round?'

The headmistress lifted her shoulders. 'Demand is high.'

I paused, wondering whether her reluctance had more to do with tight budgets than high demand. 'Well, can I pay for Bobbi to see one privately then?'

She frowned. 'Could do, I suppose, but assessments done privately aren't worth the paper they're written on.'

I gave a small laugh of disbelief and shook my head. 'Really?'

Clare turned in her chair towards me, her stance more conciliatory than that of her boss. 'Parents who go privately tend to get the diagnoses they've paid for. Local authorities rarely place much store in privately sought consultations.'

Temporarily knocked off course, I looked down at my list and decided to move on to the list of classroom tactics I had printed out, summarised by my new virtual pal LIONKING. 'I'm not trying to teach grandma to suck eggs,' I said, giving Clare an apologetic glance, 'so please tell me if you've already tried this stuff.'

'We've seen more of Bobbi in the last month than we did the whole of last term, so we haven't had all that much time to get to know her,' Clare said encouragingly. 'You live with her. You're the one who knows her most out of all of us; that was demonstrated to us very clearly last week. So please, go ahead.'

'Thank you,' I nodded, grateful that at least they were willing to listen to what I had to say. At least, Clare seemed open to it. Mrs Cullum-Coggan sat listening quietly, her expression impassive. 'So firstly I'd like to send her into school with a learning friend, a small item from home that she has an attachment to.' I was thinking of Bunny, of course. According to LIONKING's notes from *Inside I'm Hurting*, the use of a transitional object as a link with home could help to ease a child's anxiety in the classroom, and Bobbi's attachment to Bunny had undoubtedly grown since her first night with us.

'We have a strict no toys policy,' the headmistress cut in, before Clare could respond. 'Things get very messy otherwise. Lots of arguments over what belongs to whom and tears over lost items. I'm sure you understand.'

'I appreciate that,' I said, trying to sound reasonable but firm. 'But Bobbi has a specific need for reassurance, bearing in mind all she's been through. Bringing some small token from home might make all our lives easier.'

Out of the corner of my eye I could see that Mrs Cullum-Coggan was shaking her head, but my eyes were on Clare. The SENCO glanced at the headmistress and then looked at me. She licked her lips. 'If the object were small and discreet, and not a toy as such, perhaps that might be something we could consider?'

I avoided Mrs Cullum-Coggan's disapproving stare. 'Yes, I'm sure I can come up with something.'

Clare smiled. 'Excellent.' Her eyes fell to my lap and I moved on to the next item on my list.

'You said that Bobbi keeps crawling off under the desks or hiding in the toilets.'

Clare gave a grim nod. 'Yes, that's right. We unblocked the desks after what you said last week about her need to flee, and she spent most of this morning under one of them, I'm afraid. We tried to coax her out again but –' she pressed her lips together and let her words hang in the air.

I felt a band of sympathy tighten around my chest. Poor Bobbi. 'Would you consider having a small tent in the classroom? Or one of those cloth wigwams? They don't take up much room and –'

'We hardly have space for a tent in our classrooms!' Mrs Cullum-Coggan cut in, scoffing, as if it was the most ridiculous suggestion she had ever heard. 'And even if we did, we can't have children diving into a tent willy-nilly, the second someone does something to upset them.'

'Bobbi could hold a card up to ask permission to take a break when she's feeling overwhelmed,' I pressed on, ignoring the note of heavy sarcasm in Mrs Cullum-Coggan's tone. 'All it would take is a small nod of agreement from Miss Granville and then she could take herself off. At the moment she's scarpering regardless. This system would increase the teacher's control, not weaken it.'

'That may be so,' the headmistress said. 'But we simply don't have the space to indulge every child's whim.'

Beside me, Clare's fingers were strumming her lap. 'If I might interrupt, Mrs Cullum-Coggan?' Her boss inclined her head minutely. 'We do have a book corner in the Reception classrooms. Perhaps if we were to come up with a way of closing the area off somehow, we could provide a bit of a sanctuary without stealing away any more space from the classroom. Children do like to tuck themselves away so I'm sure it's something that would benefit everyone.'

I smiled at Clare gratefully. 'That's a wonderful idea. I'll see what I can come up with.' I was already picturing some willow screens around the outside of the bookshelves, with some sort of canopy hanging from the ceiling.

Mrs Cullum-Coggan gave a stiff nod. 'Very well. Anything else?'

'Well, yes, quite a lot actually.' I ploughed on through my notes and those of the LIONKING, telling them that Bobbi was most likely to flee whenever there was a deviation from the usual routine. I suggested that she might benefit from being given a structured activity during 'off timetable' periods; perhaps colouring-in or tracing, a predicable exercise that would help to soothe her.

'We can certainly try it,' Clare said helpfully, nodding as I continued to reel off all the interventions recommended by the online adoption and fostering community. There was an unmistakable change in her demeanour from the last time I'd spoken to her. I suspected that the change had something to do with that day in the classroom when Bobbi had sobbed in my arms. Perhaps the sight had transformed her view of Bobbi, and she now saw her as a very frightened little girl rather than a troublesome one. Far from being irritated or insulted by my interference, as I had feared she might, Clare seemed energised by my ideas. I got the impression that Mrs Cullum-Coggan, on the other hand, regarded me as a bit of a nuisance. She kept glancing at the clock on the wall above Clare's head with each new suggestion I made, her stern features overwritten with weary impatience.

'Is that everything?' she asked, when I'd fallen silent. I nodded. 'Well, you certainly have some interesting ideas. I'm not sure how useful they'll be, ultimately, particularly in light of recent events.' I gave her a blank look. She unfolded her arms and lifted her hand, palm upwards, towards Clare. 'Perhaps you can bring Mrs Lewis up to speed, Miss Barnard?'

'Yes, of course.' Clare rolled her lips in on themselves and then looked at me. 'Rosie, I'm afraid there's been an incident this morning that's quite concerning.'

'O-kay,' I said slowly. The hackles on the back of my neck began to prickle.

'It happened at break time,' Clare continued. 'On the far side of the playground near the sand pit. Bobbi pinned another girl to the ground, and some of the language she used was' – she stopped, licking her lips – 'well, let's just say it was highly inappropriate.'

I stared at her, waiting for her to elaborate. 'What did she say?' I asked, after a few seconds of silence.

'We can't be sure exactly. This only came to our attention because a teaching assistant heard some sort of scuffle going on. The other girl involved is too upset to talk about it, but the TA says she heard Bobbi say something like' – Clare flushed as she flicked a glance across the desk at her boss – '"You're going to fucking get it", and then she called her a "dirty girl".'

My heart plunged into my stomach. I groaned and looked away, the reason for Mrs Cullum-Coggan's presence beginning to make more sense. It was a serious incident, one that would be reported to the local authority. With my sights adjusting to this new information, my thoughts started to spin, spooling back to Bobbi's early days with us. I suddenly pictured her graphic drawings and the terror in her eyes when I first put her in the bath.

A lump rose in my throat. I glanced around the room to compose myself, concentrating on the framed certificates on the wall between two mahogany glass-fronted cabinets. When I turned back to Mrs Cullum-Coggan her features had softened. 'It's clear that you care about Bobbi,' she said gently. And then she gave a deep sigh. 'And believe me, we have every sympathy for her ourselves. I dread to think what she might have been through, but we have to safeguard the well-being of *all* of our pupils. What we're dealing with here is peer-on-peer abuse. We can't allow this sort of behaviour to continue.'

'No, I understand,' I said quietly. I had already felt a pressing need to help Bobbi with her struggles at school. Now I felt thoroughly sick.

'We're going to reduce her to part-time hours with immediate effect, and consult with the local authority on whether Millfield is the right place for her.' I nodded in agreement. However much I wanted to avoid Bobbi feeling rejected, I understood that the other children had to be kept out of harm's way.

I didn't leave the meeting until almost ten to three and made it to Megan's nursery just in time to pick her up. I was back at Millfield Primary at just gone twenty past, Megan chomping hungrily on an apple beside me. I kept my eyes trained on the outside door leading to Bobbi's classroom; after hearing about the incident in the playground, I couldn't wait to hug her.

As soon as I caught sight of her expression though, I shelved the idea. With her forehead crumpled and lips pouted in a deep scowl, she stamped across the playground, dragging her coat on the ground behind her. Stopping a few feet away, she chucked her book bag at me. I caught it reflexively, one of the rough corners catching me in the corner of my eye. 'Owph, careful, Bobs,' I said, blinking rapidly. I rubbed my eye briskly, eager not to make a song and dance over it. 'Would you like an apple while we wait for Archie?'

'I want chocolate!' she snapped, turning in circles to avoid Megan, who was holding her arms out and following her.

'She won't let me huggle her,' Megan complained, spinning one way and then the other with her arms outstretched.

I drew a forefinger under my watering eye and leaned down. 'Just give her some time, Meggie. It looks to me like Bobbi doesn't want a cuddle right now.'

Affronted, Megan scowled and took an angry bite of her apple. Bobbi caught my sleeve and waggled it. 'I *said*, I want chocolate!'

'I don't have any on me, Bobs,' I said, catching sight of Archie as he crossed the playground towards us. I pulled an apple out of my coat pocket and held it out to her. 'Have this for now and maybe we'll have chocolate pudding after dinner. What do you think?'

She smacked the apple out of my hand and sent it spinning up into the air. To my amazement, after a few staggers this way and that, Archie caught it in his outstretched hand. He gave a shout of glee and jogged over to us, a beaming smile on his face. 'That was unbelievable, Archie,' I said, laughing. I rubbed his shoulder and gave it a squeeze.

'You wait till I tell Jamie!' he said with a smile. 'He'll think it's so cool!'

Megan waved her arms in the air, meeting Archie's outstretched hands in a high five. Singularly unimpressed, Bobbi screeched all the way along the road and was still whining when I helped her into the car. 'Chocolate, chocolate, chocolate!' she screamed angrily, arching her back and making it difficult for me to secure her seatbelt around her.

'Bobbi, I don't have any chocolate,' I said, keeping my voice even. 'But if you sit nicely you can have one of those chocolate puddings you like after tea, okay? And you can help me make some chocolate custard to go with it if you like.'

'I. WANT. IT. NOW!' she screamed. She pulled her glasses off and threw them at me, her cheeks turning puce. I folded them without a word, slipped them into my coat pocket and then strapped the seatbelt around her again. As soon as I did, she pressed on the catch and released it, her contorted features loosening with satisfaction.

'You won't have it at all if we can't get home,' I warned, still blinking to soothe my smarting eye.

The pantomime continued for the next fifteen minutes. Every time I drove a few yards she popped the button on her seat belt so that I had to pull over onto the side of the road. After several stops I sat in my seat and pulled my fingers through my hair. I was unsure what to do. I was half-tempted to pull over and go the rest of the way on foot. Tired, Bobbi would be unimpressed with that, so it might deter her in the future. On the other hand, it was freezing outside and Archie and Megan were exhausted as well. Megan yawned as I pulled over for the umpteenth time, her head wobbling as she tried to stay awake. I felt a stab of guilt. Fostering was hard on your own children sometimes.

'Sorry, Meggie, sorry, Archie,' I said as I leaned into the car. 'We'll soon be home.' Megan nodded and rested her head against the cold glass of the window.

'It's not your fault, Rosie,' Archie said kindly before taking another bite of his apple.

It was as I climbed back into my seat that I noticed something floating across the windscreen. I squinted, my heart sinking at the sight of smoke rising from the engine. 'Right, that's it,' I announced, almost grateful that the decision had been made for me. 'We're walking the rest of the

171

way.' We were only two roads from home, three hundred yards at the most. I grabbed my bag and climbed out of the car to a chorus of groans.

Bobbi's jaw dropped when I opened the rear door. 'Walking?' she said in a disbelieving tone. 'Why walking?'

'Because it's not safe to ride in a car with no seatbelt on,' I said in a mild, matter-of-fact tone. I shivered and zipped up my coat. The wind was bitingly cold and it was already getting dark.

'Bobbi!' Archie and Megan groaned in unison. 'It's your fault we've got to walk.'

I held out a hand to help Bobbi out of her car seat but she shrank away. 'I won't take my seat belt off no more, Rosie,' she said. 'I promise.'

'No, I gave you lots of chances,' I said briskly, shaking my head. 'Now we walk.'

'To be honest, Rosie, any child who's been exposed to five minutes of MTV might do something like that,' Danny said, when I telephoned him later that afternoon. 'Kids are bombarded with sexual images from the minute they wake up. Music videos, billboards. Christ, only this morning I saw a woman's naked bottom stretched across the side of a bus. What you've told me isn't indicative of anything really, in itself. Schools have a duty to be vigilant, but we get reports like this coming in almost every day. Unless Bobbi tells you something explicit, I wouldn't worry too much about it. Read *My Underpants Rule* to her so that she understands boundaries, but don't go quizzing her.'

'No, I wouldn't do that,' I said, uneasy with Danny's dismissal of the incident.

Broken

'By the way, before you go,' Danny continued, 'the kids' dad, James Brady, has been in for a meeting and his police check has come through all clear, so contact's been arranged for this Saturday. There aren't any safety issues so would it be okay to pass on your address and phone number? He'd like to pick them up around nine.'

'Oh, surely not Saturday, Danny? We're usually busy at weekends.'

'I know, sorry, but he can't do weekdays. He's a doorman, he can't see the kids after school and make it back in time for work.'

'I don't mind if you pass on my details but –'

Before I had a chance to continue, Danny thanked me and ended the call. I stood in the hall with the receiver in my hand, the dialling tone buzzing through the air. Weekend contact was a frequent bone of contention between social workers and foster carers – it wasn't unusual for contact sessions to be double-booked and cancelled at the last minute, contact supervisors were notoriously unreliable, and birth parents often didn't even bother to turn up – but I told myself I shouldn't really complain, not yet.

Archie was keen to see his father and there was a chance that contact between them would work well. At least, I thought to myself, Bobbi and Archie would be thrilled when I told them.

Chapter Sixteen

It was two very excited children that I left under Emily's watchful eye early on Saturday 7 February, while I walked to fetch my car. It was another freezing day and the pavements were glistening with frost, the tips of my socks already soggy inside my boots and clinging uncomfortably to my toes. Stiff with cold, my fingers fumbled clumsily with the catch to release the bonnet of my car.

It was as I leaned over the engine that I first heard them; male and female voices tumbling over one another so that, even as they drew closer, it was difficult to distinguish anything that was being said. There was an urgency to their tones that made my stomach tighten, though, and the muscles in my legs began to tense.

I straightened at the sound of footsteps and risked a glance over my shoulder. A woman wearing tight leggings, high-heeled ankle boots and a cream fur coat rounded the corner at speed, closely followed by a coatless, heavy-set man, who was trying to grab her arm. Swearing loudly, she span away and flailed out her arms, nearly losing her handbag in the process. I only glanced at them for a second or two, but the snapshot in my mind was one of a prostitute and either a dissatisfied client or her pimp.

Either way, I didn't want to bring attention to myself. I ducked my head quickly back under the bonnet and made a vague attempt at loosening the oil cap. I grasped the cap and twisted hard, aware that their footsteps were slowing and their voices fading away. Slowly I straightened and saw that they were looking directly at me. 'Oh, hello,' I said lightly, as if I'd only just noticed them.

'Will you be wanting a hand there, darlin'?' the man said, peering over my shoulder at the engine. His thick southern Irish accent was so informal and friendly that the picture I had drawn of him in my head vanished instantly.

I smiled. 'It's okay, thank you. I'm just trying to get the oil cap off.'

'Will I give it a try? They can be a bit stiff.'

'Oh no, I wouldn't want you to get mucky.' I held out my oily hands and looked down at the black residue clinging to my unzipped coat and jumper.

'I'll not be bothered about that,' he said, waving me out of the way. He leaned over the bonnet and released the cap easily, his companion looking bored on the pavement behind him. Her inky black hair was glossy with wax and pulled back, Beyoncé style, from her face, her sharply defined brows prominent above her dramatically outlined eyes.

'That's wonderful, thank you,' I said with a grateful smile. He nodded, handed the cap to me and turned to walk away, but when I leaned down to pick up the carton of oil from the pavement that I'd brought from home he stopped abruptly.

'Now what would you be doing with that?' he asked, taking a few steps towards me. The dark-haired woman stayed where she was and sighed loudly.

I looked from the carton to him. 'I'm going to put it in the engine,' I said slowly, unable to comprehend why he was so interested.

'Jaysus Christ! You can't be serious!' He grabbed the container roughly. I stared at him with my mouth open.

'You can't do that!' he raged. 'The engine'll seize up.'

'Oh, really?' I took the container back from him and stared at the label. 'It says engine oil here.'

'It's bloody two stroke, look,' he said, jabbing a finger at the label. 'For lawn mowers and the like. Jaysus!' He was shaking his head and speaking with a tone of such exasperation that he sounded almost offended, as if he'd caught me in the act of trying to poison one of his children. 'Someone sell this to you for your car, did they?'

'No, I found it in the shed.'

'She found it in the shed,' he parroted to his companion, as if she might find the admission hilarious. She stared at him stony-faced and then blew on her fingers, making a show of the fact that she was feeling cold.

He turned slowly away from her and fixed me with narrowed eyes. 'Your oil light came on, you say?'

'Erm, no.'

'What makes you think you even *need* oil then?'

I hesitated, beginning to feel a bit defensive. 'The engine was smoking yesterday. I just assumed that I needed a bit of a top-up.'

'A bit of a top-up?' he repeated disbelievingly. It was a revelation that heralded another telling-off. 'A bit of a top-up, she says! You can't just guess a thing like that! Especially when you've got young kiddies.' I frowned. He raised his eyebrows, indicating the car seats in the back.

'Oh, yes, well normally I take it in for a half-service but I've been busy and –' I stopped, watching as he turned and leaned over the bonnet again. 'Got a cloth, have you?' he said, pulling on the dipstick and lifting it into the air. I shook my head. 'Trace, got a tissue there?' She glared at him.

'Don't worry, I can check it later,' I said, feeling bad for holding him up.

'S'alright,' he said, running the probe through his armpit. His companion's mouth contorted in disgust. After re-dipping the probe, he lifted it up to examine it and then tutted loudly. 'Unbelievable!' he exclaimed, shaking his head again. 'Bone dry. Look.' He shoved the incriminating evidence in front of my face. 'Not a drop on it. Another half a mile and you'd have blown your engine.'

'Sorry,' I said automatically. 'Thank goodness you were passing.'

He nodded and grunted, as if he'd accepted my apology, but only grudgingly. Considering he'd been a complete stranger to me minutes earlier, the whole situation felt a bit surreal. 'Tell you what, I've got a Fiat meself and a couple of litres of oil in my boot.' He pulled out his phone and started tapping on the screen. 'I'll check to see if your'n is compatible with mine –' he glanced up from his handset and looked at me. 'There are different oils for different engines, you see. You can't go mixing them.'

'Ah.'

He held my gaze for a second and looked at me thought-fully, as if wondering whether I was all there, then glanced back at his screen. 'Yep, it'll be alright with yours. I'm parked in the next road but one,' he said, already walking away. The dark-haired woman rolled her eyes again, pulled her handbag higher onto her shoulder and flounced off after him.

'Let me give you something for that,' I insisted a few minutes later, as he emptied the last few drops of his own oil into my car. 'I'll dash home and get my bag. I only live around the block.'

'Away with you,' he said, slipping his arm around his companion and propelling her across the pavement. She scowled and shrugged him off.

I watched the unusual pair as they walked away, marvelling as I often did at the generosity of strangers.

I was in my bedroom and changing out of my oil-smeared top when the doorbell rang. I frowned. It was just before half past eight and James Brady wasn't due for another half an hour or so. I opened the door, my hair still tucked into the collar of a clean jumper. 'Oh, it's you!' I exclaimed, recognising the man who had stopped to help me with my car.

'Oh, for the love of God!' James Brady exclaimed, his eyes wide. 'Would you bloody believe it?' He turned to the dark-haired woman, who was standing at his side. 'It's the oil fiend,' he said. He grinned, but one of his eyelids flickered. He hadn't seen his children for months, and I sensed that he was eager for the wait to be over.

Broken

I laughed. His companion smiled for the first time then, though not with any warmth. Despite the heavy make-up she was wearing her skin was pale and I thought perhaps she was still resentful that she'd had to wait around in the freezing cold while her partner dabbled with my car.

'It's nice to meet you properly, Mr Brady,' I said, shaking his hand. 'I'm so grateful for earlier, really. Please, come in. You look so cold.'

'This is Tracy, by the way, the other half,' he said, joining me in the hall. 'And call me Jimmy.'

'Down the end,' I called after him, though he was already half-jogging down the hall. Tracy remained just inside the front door, checking her appearance in the mirror. She turned her face from side to side and rolled her lips in on themselves. 'Nice to meet you too, Tracy,' I said when she turned around. She gave me a disinterested smile and smoothed her hair.

'Sorry we're so early; we live fifty miles away, you see,' Jimmy said, running his eyes around our open-plan living area. 'We sat outside for a while in the car then went for a walk. Good job we did as it turned out.'

'Well, yes,' I said with an embarrassed grin. 'The children are still getting dressed. They'll be down in –'

'Daddy!' Bobbi screeched, her footsteps hammering on the stairs.

'Ahh, come here, you little darlin',' Jimmy called out. Bobbi ran into the living area and Jimmy's eyes filled with tears. He strode forward. 'Oh, would you look at those glasses! You look so cute, darling!' Grabbing her sides, he swung her high above his head. She giggled and shrieked, pleading for more when he finally lowered her to her feet.

'That's enough for now, my girl,' he said, crouching down so that his face was level with hers. 'God, I've missed you so much.' They rubbed noses and then he shifted his weight and pulled her onto his lap. Somewhere in his late thirties, Jimmy had an open, slightly careworn face and closely cropped hair. He was so burly and strong looking that it was easy to imagine him sorting out drunken revellers on a Friday night. He beamed at Bobbi with the enthusiasm of little boy though, warmth oozing from every pore.

Tracy, in contrast, stood at a distance with her arms folded around the fur coat she had just removed, her lips pressed tightly together. She watched silently as Jimmy lavished affection on his daughter, the smile on her lips still devoid of any real warmth. She was an attractive woman and from her svelte figure and unlined skin, I guessed that she couldn't have been more than twenty-eight, at most.

'Hi, Dad,' came a quiet voice behind me. Archie had been thrilled when I told him that Danny had managed to contact his father, but it had been six months since they'd last seen each other and shyness seemed to have overtaken him. He stood at my side, his head close to my shoulder.

Jimmy looked up. His eyes were shining with emotion. 'Come here then, fella. Let me have a look at you.' Easing Bobbi off his lap, he beckoned his son over.

Having been ousted, Bobbi ran over to Tracy and hugged her. 'Hi, Bobbi,' Tracy said in a tight voice, patting the child mechanically on the back. Bobbi started jumping up and down on the tips of Tracy's high-heeled boots and grasping at the wrap-over top she was wearing. 'Careful,' Tracy said, adjusting herself and looking annoyed.

Broken

Archie glanced at Tracy as he made his way over to his father. 'Hello, Tracy,' he said politely.

'Hi, Archie,' she said, offering him a brittle smile.

I coughed. 'Can I get either of you a hot drink to warm you up?'

Jimmy, who had enfolded Archie in a bear hug, opened his mouth to speak, but Tracy quickly cut in. 'We really need to get going,' she said.

With their exams fast approaching, Emily and Jamie spent the day in their respective rooms, emerging periodically when they grew peckish. It was lovely to spend some one-to-one time with Megan, and the hours flew by quickly. She began flagging mid-afternoon, so around three o'clock I suggested a ride on her scooter to the corner shop, so that she could choose a magazine. We were just pulling on our coats when the doorbell rang.

I was surprised to find Jimmy standing on the doorstep, one arm draped over each of his children's shoulders. Bobbi looked close to tears and Archie was pale. 'Oh, hello!' I said, standing aside to let them in. I peered outside but there was no sign of Tracy. 'You're lucky you caught us actually. We weren't expecting you back so soon.'

'No,' Jimmy said, as the three of them came into the hall. 'I meant to call but I forgot to programme your number into my phone.'

I hesitated. 'Tracy not with you?'

'Nah, she's in the car.' He spoke quietly, with no trace of his earlier enthusiasm. 'She developed an aura about half an hour back. It means a migraine's on the way. We have to get home before it properly hits. She gets them bad, you see.'

I nodded sympathetically. I wasn't a regular migraine sufferer though I had experienced a few headaches over the years that were severe enough to affect my vision and upset my stomach, so I could imagine how disabling they might be. Entertaining Bobbi in full-on party mode while feeling that way wasn't exactly what the doctor might order.

'Would she like to come in and take some tablets before you head off?'

'She's taken some already, thanks,' Jimmy said, pulling Archie and Bobbi into a tight hug and kissing their heads. He released them and turned to me, Bobbi climbing onto his shoes and clinging to his legs. 'Thanks for all you're doing for the kids. They tell me they really like it here.'

I smiled, realising that this was where Archie's good manners came from. 'No need to thank me. I'm pleased to help.'

'Right, I'll be off then. I'll see you next week. We'll go see a film then get pizza, okay?' Archie nodded glumly. Bobbi burst into tears and rubbed her face on his trousers. Jimmy picked her up and she snuggled into his neck.

'Oh right, so contact is every Saturday then?'

Jimmy craned his neck around Bobbi's head and nodded. 'That's what I've been told. That okay? I work during the week, you see, and what with living so far away …'

'No, I understand,' I said with a smile. The children clearly adored him. I was only too happy to fit around his working hours. It was when parents who didn't work insisted on weekend contact that I tended to feel less accommodating. 'Come on then, sweetie,' I said, holding my arms out to Bobbi. She came to me willingly and cried on my shoulder. 'They'll be fine,' I told Jimmy as he ruffled Archie's hair. He nodded, looking choked.

Archie was distant and uncommunicative during dinner. With one elbow on the table, he cradled his head in his upturned palm, his other clutching his fork, which hovered above his untouched plate.

'Not hungry, love?' I asked softly, more as an acknowledgement of his feelings than any sort of prompt. His cheeks were pale with a greenish twinge. I wasn't about to encourage him to eat if he didn't fancy it. He moved his head and made a little noise, dropping his fork so that it clanged against the edge of the plate.

He wasn't quite gloomy enough to show disinterest when I got the chocolate fountain out though, asking for some of the fruit kebabs I'd prepared earlier with almost as much urgency as the girls. They drained the chocolate tiers with enthusiasm but as I cleared the table, Bobbi burst into tears again. Emily's face crumpled with sympathy and Megan stretched across the table to offer a hug. 'No, you stay with Emily, Meggie,' I told her, and then to Bobbi I said, 'Come here, love.'

I led her into the hall, sat on the second stair and pulled her onto my lap. 'What's up, sweetie?'

'I want Daddy,' she croaked, her small chest heaving. Tears rolled down her chocolate-streaked cheeks and fell onto her lap. I took her glasses off and rocked back and forth. After a minute or so she shrugged me off. 'I just *wish* I could be a good girl,' she burst out passionately. 'Why am I always so bad?'

'Oh, honey, you're not bad,' I said spiritedly. 'You mustn't think that. You're a wonderful, lovely little girl.'

'Why does Mummy not want me then? And nor Daddy neither?' She thought that being taken away from them was a punishment – her magical thinking at work – something that really broke my heart.

'They *do* want you, Bobbi. They want you and they want Archie as well. It's just that Danny's not sure yet whether they can keep you safe. That's why you're staying with Rosie.'

She gave a small nod and cuddled into me docilely. She played animal hospital with Megan before her bath, but became tearful again as I got her ready for bed. 'My tears are not going away, Rosie,' she said, clasping Bunny to her cheek. I leaned into the bunk and stroked a few blonde strands away from her forehead.

'Think of nice things,' I said, giving her a smile. 'Like fluffy clouds and rainbows and ducks. They'll chase those tears away.'

Archie went to his room about ten minutes after Bobbi dropped off to sleep. I tapped on his door just after 8 o'clock. 'Do you want to talk, Arch?' I said, leaning my head into the room.

'No,' came a grunted reply. He was sitting in his usual position with a book in his hands, a stack of pillows piled up between his back and the wall, his legs dangling over the ladder of the bunk.

I waited at the door for a moment. 'Okay, that's fine. It's just that I noticed you came back a bit earlier than planned. If I'd been looking forward to seeing someone and didn't get as much time with them as I'd hoped, I'd feel a little sad too.'

He looked at me but didn't say anything. 'Well, that's it really. I'm here if you want to talk.' He gave a curt nod and returned to his latest book – *Harry Potter and the Prisoner of Azkaban*. My hand was on the door handle when he next spoke.

'It's not fair!' he blasted. 'Tracy moans about us being bad all the time, but *she's* the one who's mean!'

I walked into the room. 'Is that why you came back early? Because of Tracy?'

He slammed his book to a close and tossed it aside. '"They're so rude, Jim",' he mimicked, rocking his head from side to side and pecking at the air with fingers and thumb. '"I can't get a word in edgeways, Jim; they're giving me a headache, blah, blah, bloody blah."' He looked at me. 'She didn't have a headache, Rosie. It was just a lame excuse to get rid of us.'

I bit my lip. There were certainly no flies on him. It was easy to imagine Tracy pouting and complaining and drawing Jimmy's attention away from his children and onto her. I felt a bubble of irritation at the thought. While I appreciated that Bobbi and Archie were perhaps not the easiest of children to step-parent, it seemed hard to believe that Tracy couldn't stand aside for a few hours, so that the children could enjoy the rare moment with their father. 'We don't know that for certain, honey.'

'Yes we do!' he shouted, angry tears glistening in his eyes. 'She can't stand us! She's the reason we're not living with Dad. I hate her.'

I walked over and patted his leg. Part of me wanted to utter platitudes to console him but I resisted the temptation. As much as I wanted to try and make him feel better, it was no use misleading him with a lie. If Tracy's earlier demeanour was anything to go by, what Archie had said wasn't so very far from the truth.

Chapter Seventeen

Archie was withdrawn when I dropped him off at Millfield Primary on the morning of Monday 9 February. He trudged across the playground in slow motion, his shoulders so heavily stooped that it appeared as if his rucksack was laden with rocks instead of books.

Accompanied by her new little learning friends – a small colourful pouch containing three worry dolls that I had ordered on the Internet – Bobbi was less reluctant than her brother to go in, though perhaps that had more to do with the fact that she knew she'd be out again before lunchtime. The reduced hours certainly seemed to help her, and Megan was thrilled with the idea of having Bobbi to herself each afternoon. It was a relief that they were getting on well, particularly as the half-term holiday was just a week away. Bobbi and Mungo seemed to have reached an understanding as well. Sensing her increasing calm, he was beginning to follow her around, only fleeing to the coffee table when he sensed that a meltdown was imminent.

As soon as the gate to the Early Years playground opened Bobbi gave me a fleeting hug and pounded off, eager to check out the safe space I had built in the classroom yesterday.

Armed with willow screens from our local garden centre, a canopy and a spinning egg chair from IKEA, I had left my mum in charge at home and met Clare Barnard, the SENCO, in the Reception classroom. We got to work straight away, clearing the floor around the book corner so that we could fix some hooks to the wall and ceiling. 'It's so good of you to give up some of your weekend, Clare,' I said as I climbed a small stepladder.

She looked up at me. 'I'd only be at home, marking,' she said, passing me a cordless drill. 'Besides, I felt bad after our meeting the other day. Mrs Cullum-Coggan's a bit of an old-fashioned disciplinarian, I'm afraid.'

I drilled a small hole in the ceiling, narrowing my eyes against a fine sprinkling of plaster. I climbed down a step and passed the drill back to Clare. 'No need. I appreciate the position she's in. And Bobbi can be a handful.' In truth, Mrs Cullum-Coggan's belief in discipline probably wasn't very far from my own. I remembered a social worker telling me recently that some local authorities were coming to realise that many of the children leaving the care system were, sadly, unemployable. Accustomed to being handled with kid gloves, they expected to receive the same treatment when they entered the workplace. As soon as they realised that they had to adhere to the same rules as their workmates, some left in disgust. Others smashed up the office. One of my duties as foster carer was to ensure that the children I cared for learned that actions have consequences. It was a simple but crucial lesson and, without it, they stood little chance of functioning in civilised society.

Clare handed me a large hook. Climbing up to the top rung, I pressed a raw plug into the hole I'd made and began screwing the hook into the ceiling. 'She certainly demands a lot of our attention,' Clare said when I climbed down. 'The reduced hours have helped though. She's been a lot calmer. And there hasn't been a repeat of the playground incident.'

I pulled a face. 'Thank goodness.'

She looked at me. 'Actually, Rosie, it's Archie I'm most worried about now. It sounds strange, I know, especially as I can't put my finger on why, but … do you know what I mean?'

I pressed my lips together. 'I know exactly what you mean.'

'He's polite and charming, helpful to the teaching staff, but the other kids avoid him. It's as if they sense something in him. It's worrying.'

I cleared the floor of debris with a heavy heart. Archie had been with us for just over five weeks, and it still seemed that I was no nearer to discovering what was troubling him than I had been back on New Year's Day.

We set to work securing the willow screens to the hooks I'd screwed into the walls using cable ties, then squared off the book corner, leaving a small gap as access for the children. I hung the canopy I'd bought from the hook in the ceiling, draped the white voile over the outside of the screens and put the egg chair inside, in front of the shelves. We stood back to admire our work.

'It looks amazing!' Clare cried, her cheeks flushed with effort. 'I'm almost tempted to spend the afternoon in there myself.'

I laughed. 'Let's hope Bobbi feels the same. Mrs Cullum-Coggan could do without her wandering at large again.' As we left the classroom we talked about arranging a meeting to specifically discuss Archie. What we would say though, I don't think either of us was entirely sure.

My mobile rang just as I reached my car. I slipped the handset into my hands-free holder and flicked it to loud-speaker mode. Bright Heights had managed to book a place for me on one of the oversubscribed local authority thera-peutic parenting courses at a conference centre in a neigh-bouring town. It was due to begin in half an hour and I didn't want to be late. 'Hello?' I said, indicating to pull onto the main road.

'Rosie, it's Danny. How did contact go?' I could hear the rush of passing traffic coming down the line and guessed that Danny was also on the move.

I ran through a quick précis of events, making sure to tell him about Jimmy's Samaritanly act. 'I'm afraid I've been a bit neglectful of my poor old car,' I said, owning up to the fact that it had almost run out of oil. Some birth parents file complaints against their children's foster carers for the most trivial faux pas, and I had handed Jimmy a golden opportu-nity, should he decide to try and cause trouble for me.

I was relieved to hear that Danny wasn't interested in making an issue of it. 'You sound as bad as my missus,' he said mildly.

I went on to tell him about the warmth of Jimmy's inter-actions with the children. 'The same can't be said about his

Broken

partner though,' I said, pulling up at a red light. I stared at my phone and waited for a response, as if Danny were sitting right there in front of me on the dashboard.

'No? You don't think they get on?' Danny sounded disappointed.

'I don't know. Maybe she was having an off day,' I offered, backtracking a little. Assessments would be carried out on both Jimmy and Tracy before a decision was made about the children's future. While it was important for foster carers to report children's feelings about their birth parents and wider family, I didn't want to colour Danny's view when all I had to go on was a few comments made by Archie at the end of an emotional day.

'I'm holding out hope that things might work out with Dad,' Danny said, his deep voice booming out in my small car. 'The assessment on Tanya isn't looking too good. I'll be very surprised if she comes out as viable at the end of it, what with the missed contacts and her refusal to entertain the idea of a future without Jason. With his past, there's no way we can let the kids go back there. She also insisted she's substance free, but her hair-strand test says different. We now have proof of a lie and, well, you know what that means.'

I did. When social services had incontrovertible proof that they had been lied to, it didn't look good when the case came to court. It seemed increasingly likely that Archie and Bobbi would never return home.

'Oh dear, poor kids,' I sighed, my heart going out to them. It was difficult enough for children to accept that they were unable to go home through parental addiction or mental health issues, but to discover that you were destined to spend the rest of your childhood in care because your mother chose a man over you – well, that *was* a difficult pill to swallow.

'We've got an interim court hearing next week,' Danny told me. 'In light of Tanya's unreliability – oh yeah, before I forget, she's cancelled today's contact as well –'

'Why this time?'

'Oh, I dunno, something about having to visit Jason's mother in hospital or something. Anyway, in light of her messing around with the contacts and her reluctance to engage, I'm going to try and get the sessions reduced to once a month. All future contact is suspended for now anyway because of her failures to attend. I'll pop over later if that's okay, about five-ish. I need to sit the kids down and explain to them that they won't be seeing their mum for a while.'

Chapter Eighteen

I knew I'd located the correct training room inside the conference centre when I read the quote on a whiteboard positioned just inside the door:

A thing which has not been understood inevitably
 reappears;
like an unlaid ghost. Freud.

I sat next to a young woman with a long dark fringe hanging over one side of her face, the other side of her head shaved close to her scalp. She smiled, introducing herself as a student social worker on temporary placement within an adoption team.

Our tutor, a thin, bookish man named Stuart, spent the first twenty minutes of the session trying to get the overhead projector and his laptop to communicate. When the white screen at the front of the room finally flickered into life, he stood in the centre of our semi-circled chairs, his forehead shiny with perspiration.

Local authority courses often began with an introduction that resembled a party political broadcast, and this one, it seemed, was no different. 'As you'll have read on your booking forms, lunch isn't provided,' Stuart told us, 'so I hope you've brought your own. If not, there's a cafe in the lobby but it's pricey. We do still provide tea and coffee, but no doubt they'll squeeze every last drop of that out of us soon as well, so make the most of it while you can.'

I exchanged a wry smile with the woman next to me and pulled a notepad from my bag. After introducing ourselves, Stuart asked us to share some of the difficulties we experienced in our day-to-day lives with the children we cared for. After a few minutes most of us had shouted out, 'Yes, I've had that! I've had that too!' Whenever adopters and foster carers are gathered in the same room they always end up playing Behaviour Bingo or Tantrum Top Trumps.

'Excellent,' Stuart said, trying to draw us back to the agenda. 'I think you probably all noticed the quote on the board on the way in. Can anyone tell me what it means to them?'

'That it's difficult to move forward if the past is unresolved?' the young woman next to me offered.

'Absolutely,' Stuart nodded. 'Yes. We have a lot of adopters in the room, as well as foster carers. When a longed-for child arrives in your home it's a time of joy for the whole family, but do you think the child feels like celebrating?' We shook our heads. 'No, of course not, many of them don't. Most children remain stuck, emotionally and developmentally, at the point of their greatest trauma.

'Most people think that adoption means happy ever after because they view it through a pre-1960s lens, a time when young women gave up their babies through fear, shame and lack of support. Nowadays relinquished babies are so rare that it's almost unheard of. Modern-day adoption involves children who've experienced the most severe trauma and neglect.

'That may be something that happened to them when they were three or four, or damage wrought on them before they were born. An infant's brain weighs about 400 grams at birth. By the end of the first year it weighs about 1000 grams.' Stuart surveyed the room. 'Our every interaction with the babies we care for is recorded in their tiny cells, our every word firing new connections between the neurons; connections that will stay with them their whole lives. Now, that's all well and good if they're with a loving, or at the very least, sympathetic caregiver.'

He paused and began pacing back and forth. 'But what happens if they're thrust into the arms of someone who isn't? Coming into foster care or moving into a forever home isn't a magical process that suddenly wipes the slate clean. As Dr van der Kolk, a director of the Trauma Center in Boston says, "the body keeps score". What he means by that is that the abuse, neglect and trauma that a pre-verbal child experiences stays with them. When a small child reaches safety they may not have the language to express what they've been through, but the sensory memories – the terror in their hearts, the fear in their gut – it stays with them, stored at a cellular level deep inside themselves.'

He fell silent for a moment and I thought about Bobbi lying abandoned in her cot, and possibly Archie too. I thought about their struggles at school and all the special moments of infancy that were lost to them. I almost wanted to cry.

'If a child spends their early years in a secure and stable environment with a loving caregiver sensitive to their needs, they develop strong foundations on which future relationships and learning can be built. When a child who has experienced trauma in their early years comes into foster care, their foundations remain wobbly.

'Children who have been neglected or abused have a powerful cocktail of toxic bio-chemicals coursing through their veins,' Stuart continued, 'the most prominent two being cortisol and adrenaline. Both leave their mark on the brain. The media coverage of soldiers returning from war zones has increased public knowledge of post-traumatic stress disorder, but very little attention is paid to the legacy of child abuse. Depression, flashbacks, nightmares, irritability, sleep problems, shame, guilt; these are all difficulties our children face daily. Then there are the physical symptoms; the stomach aches, the headaches, the dizziness and sweating. And then we wonder why our children are struggling to study in school.'

Stuart went on to describe the wire-monkey experiment carried out by an American research psychologist, Harry Harlow, in the mid-twentieth century. Investigating the impact of maternal deprivation, Harlow removed some infant rhesus monkeys from their mothers and introduced each of them to two surrogate mothers, one made of cloth and the other wire. Even though the wire monkey was the one offering food, the monkeys overwhelmingly preferred the cloth surrogates, leaving it only when needing to feed. 'The infant monkeys all experienced developmental trauma,' he told us, 'the ones removed from their mothers highly fearful and often aggressive.

'Interestingly, Harlow's own mother was a distant figure, so perhaps he invented the experiment to try and understand his own past. Crucially though, what his experiment tells us is that humans are social beings who crave – no, not only crave, they *need* a sense of belonging; a connection to a significant other. It also tells us that one of the most traumatic experiences we as humans will ever face is the loss of a loved one. Recovery can only come by reconnecting to another person, but that's difficult to do when the person you love is also the one that hurts you.

'Children are able to grow physically when they are denied love and security, as I'm sure many of the children we care for have done. But their survival comes at a cost. They might refuse to interact and withdraw into themselves, they might try to control everything and everyone around them, or they might develop a phoney persona, closing their true selves off from the world to keep themselves safe.'

I thought about Archie and my chest tightened with sympathy again. As Stuart continued to talk about the false sense of self projected by some trauma victims, I became utterly convinced that Archie was hiding something, something so traumatising that the only way he could possibly function was to pretend it didn't exist.

'The good news,' Stuart continued, 'is that brain matter has a plasticity to it. What we have to do is encourage new neural pathways to form in the pre-frontal cortex, the part of the brain necessary for empathy, logic and reasoning, so

that the reptilian brain stem – the part of the brain responsible for our fight/flight/freeze reflex – only kicks in when
absolutely necessary to our survival.

'And whatever strategy a child's mind has put in place to
protect them, the remedy is always the same.' Stuart
wheeled the whiteboard closer to the group and turned to
the next blank page. 'Parenting with PLACE,' he said,
writing the letters in capitals in a column down the page,
'is one of the most effective ways to reach the troubled
child. Buried deep down in every child's brain is a yearning
to be loved. Our task is to help them to build enough trust
and confidence in us so that they're able to take the risk,
reach out and grasp it.'

Stuart asked us to guess what each letter of PLACE
stood for and after a few minutes of discussion he had
completed the list:

PLAYFULNESS
LOVE
ACCEPTANCE
CURIOSITY
EMPATHY

During the last part of the morning we discussed practical
ways of expressing love to the children we care for as well
as using playfulness to help them to appreciate that,
however difficult their particular circumstances, there is a
positive, lighter side to life. 'Studies show that children in
the UK and the US are the least happy children in the
developed world,' Stuart told us. 'It's no coincidence that
we also spend less parental time with our children than

most other nations. Time spent with family is essential to children's well-being.'

After lunch we discussed the ways in which each of us were parented. Most of us in the room had been smacked as children, although a few of the younger attendees had lost privileges as punishment instead. Stuart then asked us to explain our own techniques for managing difficult behaviour. The *Supernanny* technique of placing children in time out was universal amongst us, the admission drawing a loud intake of breath from Stuart. 'So in order to teach our children to behave well we withdraw from them until they agree to do what we say, is that right?'

There were a few mutterings amongst our group, but nobody openly disagreed. 'Withdrawal of attention brings me nicely onto the A in PLACE,' Stuart said. 'Acceptance. Now, is there anyone here who will admit to not loving their children unconditionally?'

We all shook our heads. 'No, of course not. Most of us were loved unconditionally by our parents, and we love our children, whether birth or adopted, unconditionally as well. So why is it we pretend we don't?'

He looked around the room again, but didn't wait for an answer. 'We love our children unconditionally, but we attach conditions to our love and appear to withdraw it when they displease us, probably because that's the way we were parented ourselves. What therapeutic parenting is all about is *accepting* your child's inner life, whether you agree with it or not. That means it's as important to acknowledge the feelings of a two-year-old who is sobbing because you won't buy her the soft toy she's fallen in love with as it is to accept the loud complaints of a sixteen-year-old who's infuriated by your refusal to allow her to stay out until after eleven on a Saturday night.

'Accepting a child's feelings doesn't mean we're removing boundaries or losing our influence over them. We can empathise with their anger at the same time as imposing discipline. The latest research into the way the brain functions shows us that humans are designed for cooperation, but at the same time, each and every one of us is unique. We all have different hopes and dreams. Accepting that your child doesn't agree with everything you say is crucial to building a lasting, genuine relationship with them. There will be people here who weren't ever allowed to openly disagree with their parents as they grew up, am I right?'

There was a furious nodding of heads amongst our group. 'Right, and what do most of us do when our thoughts and feelings aren't accepted? We bury them away, don't we? We become secretive to distance ourselves from disapproval. It's our ancient desire to cooperate at work. It's wired into our DNA.'

As Stuart continued to talk about accepting a person for who they are – their thoughts and feelings, intentions, interests and values – rather than trying to impose our own ideas of who we think they should be – I thought about Jamie and his decision not to go to university. I felt a stab of guilt. I had thought that I was helping him by steering him towards a future where he wouldn't be disadvantaged by a lack of opportunity. In reality I was refusing to accept the person he himself wanted to be. After twenty years of parenting and over twelve years of fostering, I was still making rookie mistakes. I couldn't wait to get home and put it right.

Other carers shared stories from their pasts and soon it felt as though we were taking part in a group therapy session. Fostering and adoption courses often bring out powerful emotions amongst the attendees, and I could tell by the slight tremor in her voice that the young woman next to me was struggling to talk about her past. Her voice cracked as she spoke about the verbal abuse she had suffered from her disapproving mother. 'I'm sorry,' she said tearfully, burying her face in a hanky.

'It's okay. Take a few minutes,' Stuart said softly. She hurriedly left the room. 'It's not my intention to upset anyone,' Stuart said, discreetly keeping his gaze averted when she came back in and quietly took her seat. 'But as Freud once said, so much more eloquently than I ever could, it's necessary to understand our past before we can effectively move forward. By gaining an insight into what drives us as people, we can build stronger, healthier relationships with everyone around us.'

Chapter Nineteen

I managed to make it back to Millfield Primary just as the littlies were leaving the playground with their parents and the older children were beginning to steam out. My chest tightened when I caught sight of Archie. The unpleasant task of letting children down often fell to foster carers and it was up to me to break the news that yet another contact with his mother was to be cancelled.

I wasn't too worried about telling Bobbi; as I was on a course my mum had picked her up after collecting Megan from nursery. Bobbi had been delighted at the prospect of being collected by 'Nanny' and I doubted that she would even remember that she was supposed to be seeing her mum. I knew the rejection would hit Archie hard though, however much he tried to shrug it off.

His face clouded with confusion when he saw me. 'How come you're here, Rosie?' he asked, surprised not to see the contact worker who would take him to see his mother.

'Contact's been cancelled, honey.'

'Oh, why? Have they mucked it up again?'

'Erm, no. Your mum couldn't make it today. Perhaps Danny can tell you more. He's coming over a bit later.'

He looked at me for a second then turned away, his eyes clouded with hurt. 'I expect they've double-booked the rooms or something,' he said as we walked back to the car. 'Jason says social workers don't know their arses from their elbows.'

What a charmer, I thought. 'Mmm,' I said in a non-committal tone. The children I looked after were often defensive of their parents. While I believed in being as open and truthful as possible, I also knew that trusting in his mother's love was crucial for Archie's self-esteem. I wasn't about to undermine that conviction by saying negative things about her. Foster carers up and down the country are usually well practised in the art of biting their tongues.

Bobbi was waiting by the window at my mum's house, looking out for me. She greeted me with a hug and a part-pleased, part-relieved expression. 'She was a bit worried you wouldn't come back,' Mum whispered to me on our way out. I felt a little tug at my heart at the thought of her growing attachment to me and the inevitable separation that would, at some point in the near future, follow.

As we drove towards home, Archie told Bobbi all about social services and how useless they were, presumably using his mother's or Jason's words. There was a lack of energy in his voice as he spoke though. I could tell he was unconvinced and my heart ached for him.

'Mummy misses us so much, Rosie,' Bobbi said, after being indoctrinated by her brother. 'She misses us so much that she's working all day and all night to save up enough money for a big huge house where we can all be together and never be without her ever again.'

Children often try to replace their tragic thoughts, feelings and memories with fantasy. 'It's wonderful to imagine lots of lovely things in our minds,' I said, gently offering the suggestion that what she was saying might not be what was happening in real life. 'It can cheer us up when we're feeling sad.'

Archie was back on form by the time we got home, telling me jovially about a video someone had posted onto YouTube of a dog and cat bouncing together on a trampoline. 'I bet you'd like to have a go at that, wouldn't you, Mungo?' he said as we stepped in the house. Mungo's tail thumped excitedly on the floor and Archie leaned down, stroking his head.

'I think he's bouncy enough, don't you?' I laughed. 'He doesn't need a trampoline.'

As soon as they got their coats off the girls sat together in front of the dolls' house I'd bought Megan for Christmas. Bobbi still employed the toddler tactics of bash, smash and grab in her play, but lately I'd noticed a pause between her declaring an interest in whatever Megan was holding in her hand and snatching it, one where she barked 'PLEASE!' before taking possession. Megan regularly reminded Bobbi of the necessary etiquette when they were playing and it seemed to be slowly sinking in.

It was as I went through to the kitchen and poured everyone a glass of milk that a thought occurred to me. I gave the girls their drinks and walked over to Archie, who was sitting at the dining table and pulling books out of his school bag. 'Where did you see that video, Arch?' I asked lightly, lowering his drink to a coaster.

There was a pause. He glanced up slowly. 'What?'

'The video of the bouncing dog. Where did you watch it?' I was happy for the children to spend time on the family computer but, knowing how easy it was to unwittingly unearth disturbing material on video-sharing sites, YouTube was one of those I had blocked using parental controls.

'Erm.' He made a show of rifling through his bag, frowning as if he couldn't locate something. I folded my arms and waited. He dropped his rucksack and looked at me. 'What?'

'I asked you a question.'

Another pause. 'I saw it on YouTube.'

'Yes, I know, you said. But you can't get YouTube on our computer.'

'No, not here,' he said nonchalantly. 'Someone at school showed me.' He patted the books already spread out on the table. 'I can't find my maths set. Have you seen it?'

'Showed you on what?' I wasn't going to let this go.

'Their phone.'

'You're not allowed phones in school.'

'Yeah, but some kids have them. They get them out at break.'

I stared at him, not entirely convinced. 'And the teachers allow that?'

He shrugged. 'They're not that bothered as long as they don't get them out in class.'

I waited but he didn't say any more. 'Your maths set was in your room last time I looked. On the desk.'

He ran upstairs. I waited in the hall for him. 'Archie? You don't have a mobile phone, do you?' I asked as he came down. He stopped on the third stair, eyes wide with innocence. 'No, course not. I'd like one though.'

I laughed. 'Yes, I expect you would.'

'Tempted to get me one?'

I gave him a mock stern look. 'As my mum would say, you've got the cheek of the devil, Archie Brady.'

He grinned mischievously and gave a small shrug. 'Ah, well, worth a try.'

He managed to finish all his homework by the time the doorbell rang at five o'clock (on the dot) and was watching television with the girls when I showed Danny into the living area. 'Jason says social workers are never on time,' Archie said, after shaking Danny's hand. 'But you're never late.'

'Mate, it's true,' Danny said as he chucked Bobbi under the chin. 'Nice glasses, sweetheart.' She gave him a half-smile without glancing away from the telly. 'I'm up for the prize for the most reliable social worker in my office. None of the others come close.'

Danny and I shared some of the tamer social worker jokes we knew as the three of us sat at the table, but in all honesty it really was encouraging to know that an efficient social worker had been assigned to the children's case. Care proceedings could be resolved within a few months when the circumstances were straightforward and an efficient social worker was propelling the case along. Sadly, there were social workers that allowed cases to drift, and two of my placements – Tess and Harry, who came to me as babies – didn't move into permanence until they were almost ready for school.

'So, Archie,' Danny said softly, 'I spoke to your mum this morning, and I wanted to explain to you about contact and what's going to happen in the coming weeks.' Archie nodded quietly. 'As you know, your mum couldn't make it to contact again today, and we have a rule that says that if a parent misses several contacts in a row, they have to come in for a meeting before we can book any more dates at the family centre. So I'm afraid that means it might be a little while before you see your mum again.'

Archie looked at him. 'How long?'

Danny took a breath. 'That's difficult to say, son. I've given your mum some times and dates to come into the office to talk to me about it, but she' – Danny's eyes flicked over to me and then back again – 'wasn't sure whether she was free on any of them.' As far as I knew, Tanya didn't work, which made her inability to commit to an appointment with Danny all the more galling. 'If she manages to come in soon we can get a session set up very quickly afterwards,' Danny went on, 'but I need some assurances from her that she'll make every effort to turn up.'

'But that's not fair,' Archie complained earnestly. 'It wasn't Mum's fault she missed the contacts. The receptionist double-booked and cancelled her.'

'I don't think so, mate.'

Archie sat up straight in his chair. 'She did, honestly. Mum said she's a useless bitch.'

Danny frowned and looked at me. 'That's the first I've heard of it. Rosie, has Tanya said anything about this to you?'

I shook my head, my mind still stuck on Archie's words. 'I'll have a word with the centre and check,' Danny said, writing a note on his pad. 'But I'm pretty sure it's been your mum that's cancelled each time.'

'Archie,' I said. 'When did Mum tell you this?'

'When I spoke to her on the phone.'

'But you haven't spoken to her for ages.' Tanya had only answered her phone on one occasion since telephone contact had been agreed, and I had passed the handset straight to Archie as soon as I heard her voice.

I noticed a flicker of uncertainty in Archie's eyes. 'No, but she told me when we rang that time.'

I nodded doubtfully. I couldn't remember anything about cancelled contacts being spoken about, but then Archie had been wandering around when he spoke to her, so the conversation over the loudspeaker had been disjointed.

'Anyway,' Danny said, smiling at Archie kindly. 'You leave the worrying to me, okay? That's what I'm here for. You can call me if ever you have any questions that Rosie can't answer.' He inclined his head towards me. 'Rosie has my mobile number. You can ask her to call me whenever you like and we can have a chat, okay?'

Archie nodded, a glimmer of amusement back in his eyes. 'Rosie said she's going to get me my own mobile soon anyway.'

I patted his hand. 'He's a dreamer, this one.'

Danny laughed. 'So, Archie, is there anything else you wanna ask me before I go?'

'Will we be going home soon?'

Danny's expression grew serious. 'Do you remember what I told you when I came to Joan's house? We have to write some reports and do some assessments on your mum

Broken

and dad, then the judge will make a decision about who is the best person to take care of you and your sister.'

'But what happens if the judge decides that we can't live with either of them?'

'Well, we're a long way off making any big decisions yet,' Danny said evasively. 'We'll cross that bridge if we come to it.'

Archie wasn't going to let him off that easily. 'But you don't even like my mum. And she says you hate Jason. You're not going to let us go back to them, are you?'

Danny scratched his nose. 'It's not up to me, son, it's up to the judge. He's a wise man who's made lots of important decisions before.'

'But the judge makes his decision after reading your reports. So really it's you making the decision.' Archie stared penetratingly at the social worker.

Danny fell silent and drew a hand across his forehead. Archie continued with the probing questions, one after the other until the social worker, whom until that moment I had considered unflappable, looked thoroughly flustered. 'Archie,' I interjected. 'The court will appoint someone called a guardian ad litem for you and Bobbi; a person who will speak to the judge on your behalf. They'll meet with you, here probably, and ask you what you think should happen. You can tell him or her exactly how you feel. They represent children like you in court every day. It's their job to listen to you and report back to the judge so that he, or she, knows what your thoughts and wishes are.'

Archie's frown faded. 'That's okay then. I'll tell them I want to live with my dad.'

'Oh, o-kay,' Danny said, blinking in surprise. 'You sound very sure about that.'

'I am,' Archie said firmly. 'And Dad said I can, just as soon as he and Tracy sort their house out.'

Danny looked at me and then back to Archie. 'We'll have to see about that. Nothing's definite yet. Now, Rosie, is it okay if me and Archie have a little chat on our own for a minute?'

'Yes, of course,' I said, pushing my chair out. Social workers are supposed to build some one-to-one time into their visits to give children the opportunity to talk about any concerns or issues they may have with their carer. I often feel a bit uncomfortable as I busy myself somewhere in the house out of earshot, as if waiting to find out whether I've passed some sort of test. The worst complaint I'd ever had from a child was that I didn't have the television on enough, but, still, it wasn't the most enjoyable aspect of fostering. 'I'll get our things in from the car.'

Archie put a hand on my wrist. 'Don't go, Rosie.'

'I'll be back in a minute, love.'

'I just wanna know how you like it here, stuff like that,' Danny said lightly. 'It won't take a minute.'

'It's good. I like it,' Archie said flatly, as if that was all he was prepared to say on the matter. His brow furrowed again. 'If I can't go to Dad I can stay here, right?' He looked from me to Danny.

Danny's expression wavered. A look passed between us. We both knew that staying with me couldn't possibly be a long-term option; the children were getting older and were already at the upper age limit of sharing a room. 'We'll have to see,' Danny said. 'That's all a long time in the future and –'

'Anyway,' Archie cut in quickly, refusing to dwell on negatives or uncertainties for too long, 'I'll tell that person you're talking about …' He dipped his head towards me.

'The guardian.'

'Yep, I'll tell him where we want to go and that will be that.'

'Whatever happens, Archie,' I said, 'you and Bobbi will be safe.' I looked at Danny.

'Rosie's right, mate. We'll find the right place for you, don't you worry about that.'

Emily had kindly offered to prepare dinner for us since I'd been out of the house all day, and just before six o'clock she brought her speciality dish – spaghetti Bolognese with garlic bread and salad – to the table. 'That looks yummy,' Archie said, helping himself to a large portion. The compliments had been oozing out of him since Danny left. In the last twenty minutes he had manically complimented my hair (and I wasn't having a good hair day), the sound of my laugh and even the old baggy jumper I was wearing. I was growing increasingly uncomfortable with his ever more personal comments, but however much I tried to reassure him that they were unnecessary, they just kept on flowing out of him.

'You smell really nice, Rosie,' he said as I reached over the table for the serving spoon. 'I like your perfume.'

'Urgh, quit the smoozing,' Jamie said light-heartedly as he came into the room. He sat across the table from Archie. 'Not cool, dude, not cool at all.'

Archie flushed instantly. I busied myself with the cheese, sprinkling some over my pasta. 'D'you know what happened today?' Jamie said, artfully diverting everyone's attention away from Archie. 'There's this kid at school, right, he's so annoying, always bigging himself up and taking the pee out of everyone else. Anyway, he comes into assembly doing his usual thing, jabbing one of the younger kids in the back and generally being a pain and then –' Jamie broke off, chuckling to himself. Archie watched him, his face breaking into a smile. Soon we were all laughing as we waited for Jamie's punchline. '– then he – he slips over, right onto his podgy butt.'

Archie dropped his fork and held his stomach, rolling over with laughter.

'You're welcome,' Jamie said a bit later, as I rinsed the plates under the tap. Megan and Bobbi were watching the rest of their cartoon and Archie was up in his room.

'Oh, what for? Distracting Archie?'

He nodded.

'Yes, thanks for that,' I said. 'But it was *you* that upset him in the first place.'

'I'm doing him a favour, Mum. He'll get crucified when he gets to high school if he grovels round the teachers like he does to you.'

'You're probably right. Well, thanks – I think.'

'Thanks for what?' Emily asked, coming into the kitchen.

'Oh, nothing much,' Jamie said, throwing a peanut into the air and catching it on his tongue. 'I just rescued Mum's whole evening, that's all.'

Emily pulled a face. 'Drop-outs are useful for something then.'

Broken

'Emily!' I chided, but the pair of them were laughing.

'I'm so sorry I didn't respect your decision, Jamie,' I said later, as he joined me on the sofa. It was half past eight and Archie had just gone up to bed after our ritual game of cards.

'What?' Jamie reached for the remote and switched on the television.

I grabbed the handset and lowered the volume. 'I *said*, I'm sorry I didn't accept your inner life, or seemed not to. Because I do accept it. And you. And your decisions, unconditionally.'

'Ri-ght,' he said slowly, leaning away from me as if I'd suddenly lost my marbles. 'And what's this about exactly?'

'Your decision not to go to university, of course.'

'Oh yeah, course,' he said, still eyeing me warily. 'Don't worry about it.' He took back the remote and began flicking through the channels. 'Anyway,' he said, his eyes fixed on the screen. 'You'll be pleased to know that I decided to put in an application for prefect.'

'What? Really?'

'Yep.'

'But you must have missed the deadline.'

'Nope, I didn't. I put it in on the last day.'

'Great,' I said. 'Well, that'll be something positive for your CV if you're chosen.'

'Yeah,' he said absently, already absorbed in the match of American football playing out on screen.

'Jamie's applied for prefect,' I told Emily later, as we stood side by side in the bathroom brushing our teeth.

'Yes, I know, he wanted the parking space.'

'What?'

Emily rinsed her mouth with water and looked at me. 'Prefects get a space of their own in the school car park. Jamie reckons he's going to borrow your car if he passes his test and drive himself to school.'

I couldn't stop smiling to myself as I pulled my dressing gown on. I had been played, but I didn't mind all that much. However strange he'd considered our earlier conversation, Jamie knew that I accepted him unconditionally, whether I agreed with the choices he'd made or not. I just wished that Archie and Bobbi could be as certain of their own parents' love for them.

Chapter Twenty

The next few days passed, if not without incident, then with only a few hiccups here and there. Archie's offers to help whenever I so much as lifted a finger still came thick and fast, but since Jamie's comment at the dinner table he had toned down the intensity of his personal comments and stuck to heaping copious praise on my cooking skills.

Bobbi was making progress as well. Her meltdowns still came daily, but rather than throwing herself around as if trying to injure herself, she came straight to me whenever she lost control, responding quickly when I wrapped her up in a weighted blanket and held her close.

When I arrived to pick the children up from school on Friday 13 February though, I suspected that the improvements in their behaviour were confined to home. As soon as I parked the car in the road outside Millfield Primary I noticed Clare Barnard standing just inside the gates. She seemed to be watching the road and when she saw me on the pavement, she slipped out to see me. My heart sank.

'Don't look so queasy,' she said with a grin, smiling fondly at Megan when I picked her up. 'I just wanted a quick chat with you before the weekend.'

'Oh, nothing's wrong then?'

Clare adjusted her glasses and shook her head. 'Absolutely not. Quite the opposite. Miss Granville has put a note in Bobbi's home school diary, but I wanted to tell you in person. Bobbi's had a super week. Only a single incident of – well, no need to go into it – it was quickly dealt with. We've made real progress.'

'That's great news,' I said, thrilled.

Megan bobbed a little jig in my arms and clapped. 'Yay, Bobbi's a clever girl, Mummy.'

Clare laughed and leaned in so that her face was close to Megan's. 'She certainly is, and do you know why that is? I think it's down to the care you and your Mummy are giving her.'

Megan beamed. I lowered her to her feet and smiled gratefully at Clare. 'I appreciate you telling me. It's lovely to hear some good news, especially after the week they've had.' I had emailed Clare a few days earlier to inform her that contact with Tanya had been suspended. I had found over the years that most teachers were overwhelmingly sympathetic towards looked-after children. I tried to keep them updated on the inevitable twists and turns as their case progressed, ones that might upset the children and affect their behaviour at school.

'Yes, that must have been a blow for them.' Clare paused. 'Rosie,' she said after a time, 'I know it sounds weird, but in a funny way, I think the children are kind of relieved. Archie's teacher tells me that he's participated in some of his lessons this week, instead of spending most of his time staring out the window. And Bobbi's taken part in her phonics sessions for the first time ever.'

I smiled. 'That's amazing.'

'Now, whether that's got anything to do with the master-piece we created at the weekend or the spinning egg chair,' she said with a grin, 'or something else, I don't know. She's certainly been making use of the book corner, but only going after seeking permission, and Miss Granville was so pleased with her progress that she's made her Star of the Week.'

Bobbi charged out of her classroom a few minutes later, waving her Star of the Week certificate high in the air. 'Look, Rosie, look!' she shouted, her face a picture of delight.

I knelt down in front of her. 'What a super clever girl you are,' I said, kissing her cheek.

Bobbi couldn't wait to tell her dad the news. I dialled Jimmy's number as soon as we got home, set it to loud-speaker mode and rested the handset up against a book-shelf. 'My clever little princess,' Jimmy said, delight evident in his voice. 'I'm so proud of you.'

Bobbi, standing in front of the handset, gave a little wiggle. 'I got a certificate, look.' She waved the coveted paper in front of the phone.

Jimmy laughed. 'I can't see it, darlin',' he said softly. 'You can show me tomorrow. I can't wait.'

Bobbi tickled her own tummy in excitement. Mungo stared up at her, his tail thumping against her legs. There was a pause and then came the inevitable question all young children seemed to ask when having a telephone conversation. 'What you doing, Daddy?'

'I'm having a coffee with Tracy. I've got to be getting ready for work soon, sweetheart.'

There was another pause while Bobbi absorbed this information. Archie gave her a little shove and knelt down in front of the phone. 'Hi, Dad.'

'Oh, Archie, hi, son,' Jimmy said, but Bobbi began to wail.

'Rosie, it's my turn to speak to Daddy and Archie just pushed me!'

'Archie, let your sister finish what she was saying,' I said softly.

'But she's not saying anything! She's just standing there!'

'She's thinking. You can have your go in a minute.'

There was a soft, disembodied laugh, and then Jimmy's voice came over the loudspeaker. 'Thanks, Rosie. What else did you want to say to Daddy, Bobbi, darlin'?'

'Erm,' Bobbi said, her brow furrowed with concentration. She picked up the hem of her dress and screwed it up in a ball, her fingers twirling the material over and over as she tried to think of something to say. 'Erm ... Daddy, can I speak to Tracy?'

There was a pause, a rustle, and then Jimmy spoke again, his voice slightly strained. 'Sorry, darlin', she's just gone into the other room.'

'We're going to Pizza Hut!' Archie said a few minutes later, as he handed my phone back to me. His eyes were shining with excitement. 'And Dad says if there's time we might go to that new splash park that just opened.'

I smiled. 'That's wonderful!' I said, thrilled to see him so genuinely happy.

His expression grew thoughtful. 'What do you think I

might need to take, apart from my shorts and a towel? Will I need goggles?' I opened my mouth to speak but he raced to the stairs breathlessly, his voice quivering with excitement. 'I think I might, you know, Rosie, cos there's that big slide that ends in a plunge pool and you go right down under the water. I'll pack my bag now. There won't be much time in the morning. Dad says he's coming early so we get the whole day together!'

I waited until he disappeared upstairs and then switched the computer on and overrode the parental controls to pull up some promotional videos posted by the splash park. 'Shall we take a look?' I asked Archie when he came down.

'Oh, cool! Thanks, Rosie!' He sat Bobbi on his lap and watched the videos over and over again, his face flushed pink.

I woke to the sound of thunder on Saturday 14 February 2015, but by 7 a.m. the storm had cleared, leaving a bright blue sky in its wake. I sat on the sofa sipping my coffee, the only sounds a solitary bird call coming down the chimney and Archie tapping at the screen of the iPad next to me.

'How do you think they got those massive slides inside the dome?' He scrolled through the photos on the splash park website. 'They probably transported them in small pieces and fixed them together inside,' he added, answering his own question. I smiled at him. He'd already had the exact same conversation with Jamie when he'd got in from band practice last night. 'What's the time now, Rosie?'

'About three minutes after the last time you asked,' I said, laughing. 'Why don't you go and get washed and dressed? That will pass some time.'

I followed him into the hall. 'Here we are, Arch,' I said, reaching into my handbag. I handed him fifteen pounds. 'That's this week's pocket money plus a bit extra, in case you spot something special while you're out.'

Foster carers are paid a weekly wage for each child they look after, usually between £120 and £170 per week, depending on the local authority responsible for the child. We're also provided with an allowance on top of this amount, to cover the cost of clothes, shoes and other expenses, as well as pocket money (between five and ten pounds a week) and savings for the child. Archie hadn't shown much interest in the money I'd given him in the last few weeks, but now his face lit up. 'Wow, thanks, Rosie!'

I smiled. 'You're welcome, honey. I'm going to give Bobbi's money to Daddy for safekeeping. Remind her she can choose something if you visit a shop.'

The girls woke as Archie pounded up the stairs. I went to climb the stairs, but by the time I'd reached the bottom step they were already halfway down. 'Meggie wants to come with us to the splash park,' Bobbi announced, leading Megan down by the hand. 'I told her she can.'

Megan grinned and reached out her arms. Bobbi copied her. Bracing myself, I picked both of them up. 'That's very sweet of you, Bobbi, but I'm afraid Megan can't go with you.' There was a chorus of groans as I carried them, one on each hip, to the sofa. They giggled when I dropped them onto the cushions.

'Daddy won't mind!' Bobbi insisted. 'I'll call him and ask.'

I nursed them through the next couple of hours by working my way through the entire contents of the toy cupboard. By ten o'clock I felt as though I never wanted to set eyes on another board game for the rest of my life. 'Oh, where is he?' Bobbi groaned, teetering on the edge of a meltdown.

'Can you call him again, Rosie, please?' Archie asked politely, though there was an edge to his tone, and he was looking at me as if he held me responsible for his dad's failure to appear.

'I can't call again, Arch.' I had already tried Jimmy's number twice in the last hour. 'Are you sure he said nine o'clock?' It was now nearly half past ten.

'No!' he snapped uncharacteristically. And then, with more patience: 'I've already told you, he said before nine, so we'd have the whole day together.'

Bobbi threw herself onto her tummy and howled. Beside her, Megan's lip wobbled. I was just about to go to them when the doorbell rang. Mungo barked and skipped around my feet.

'Hooray!' Archie cheered. He grabbed the rucksack he had packed and kept at his side since yesterday and ran into the hall. Bobbi stopped mid-sob and leapt to her feet. She joined hands with Megan and the pair of them jumped up and down on the spot, grinning at each other.

'There you are, you see,' I said at the sound of a man's voice. As a safeguard against the possibility of abduction by a parent who has managed to discover my address, I don't usually allow fostered children to open the front door. Since we were expecting Jimmy, however, I was happy to let Archie do the honours today. 'Daddy must have been caught up in some traffic on the motorway. Now, get your bag, Bobbi, love. You'll –'

'Rosie?' Archie said, coming back into the room. His face had paled. 'There's a man asking to speak to you.'

I frowned and walked into the hall. 'Hello?' I said to the man in stained blue overalls standing on the doorstep. Mungo scooted to the door. I eased him back with my leg to stop him running out.

'Rosie?'

'Yes, can I help?'

'Sorry, love, I'm just bringing a message from Jimmy. He can't get here to see the kids today. He's lost his phone and didn't have your number. He's been wracking his brains trying to think how to get in touch with you, like, and I offered to give you a knock and let you know.' He looked down at his overalls. 'Breakdown cover, I was out this way this morning.'

I looked out onto the road, where a large tow truck was parked. 'Ah, that's very good of you, thank you.'

'Well, no one wants to see kids let down, do they?'

I shook my head. 'Is Jimmy not well?'

'Oh no, he's alright. It's Tracy. She's feeling a bit "delicate", so she says.' He hooked the air and gave me a look. 'Know what I mean? She says she can't do without him today.'

'I see,' I said, resisting the urge to join in and complain about Tracy. I gave him a slow eye roll instead. 'Ah well, I shall have to go and break the news to the children.'

'Poor kids,' he said, wrinkling his nose at me. 'I have to say, I don't know how you people do it. Got a lot of respect for foster carers, I have.' I thanked him and closed the door. Archie was standing by the sofa and chewing his bottom lip when I turned around. He still had hold of his rucksack but his shoulders were slumped, his expression forlorn.

Broken

'You heard the man then, Arch?' I said softly.

He nodded. 'Tracy's not well so Dad can't come.'

From the living room came a loud howl. Next thing I knew, Bobbi was hurtling up the hall towards me. I crouched down and she launched herself into my arms, her body trembling as she sobbed into my neck.

I stroked her back and gave Archie a sympathetic glance over her shoulder. He met my gaze and gave a little shrug, lowering his rucksack gently to the floor. 'I know how disappointed you must be,' I said. I stroked Bobbi's hair, admonishing myself for adding to their excitement by showing them the videos of the splash park online. I had been fostering long enough to know that there was every chance that the children would be let down by their father. I had allowed Jimmy's kindly roadside assistance to cloud my judgement, as well as his warmth towards the children. His affection had seemed so genuine that it was difficult to imagine him letting them down. Then again, I had known others capable of putting on an impressive act, managing to fool everyone into thinking they were loving parents.

I once looked after a nine-year-old girl, Phoebe, whose parents were well educated, well heeled and well spoken. Effectively blinded by her family's eloquence and their ability to 'talk the talk', Phoebe came close to returning to their care. It was only once she found the courage to disclose to me that her father had sexually abused her in the presence of her mother that the depth of her parents' deception was discovered.

'Tell you what, how about we all go to the splash park together this afternoon?' I said as Bobbi's sobs began to subside. 'I'll ask Emily and Jamie if they want to come and we could order a takeaway pizza for this evening as well.'

'That would be good, thanks, Rosie,' Archie said, giving me a brave smile. His tone was sombre though and his face was red from hairline to neck. There was also a shut-down, lifeless quality to his eyes that filled me with unease.

Chapter Twenty-One

Archie looked a fright the next morning; his eyes puffy, cheeks flushed. In manic tidying mode from the minute he came downstairs, he began piling up the breakfast bowls and sweeping the spoons away before any of us had even eaten. 'Archie, love,' I said, laughing, 'give us a chance. I've only just put those there.'

He grinned and set them out again, but there was a distant quality to his smile. Physically, he was with us, but it seemed that his mind was somewhere else. Hearing about the children's disappointment, Emily and Jamie had agreed to come with us to the splash park the previous day. Archie had been cheered by the news and seemed to enjoy charging down the slides after Jamie, but even that failed to erase the dull sadness in his eyes. I got the sense that he was struggling to contain himself as he walked around the table. He straightened the placemats and centralised the bowls with the studied caution of someone who was about ready to explode.

It was Sunday 15 February and though the children had only been living with us for just over six weeks, I felt I already had Bobbi sussed. Her favourite game was animal hospital, although as a rule of thumb, any game that incorporated bandages and plasters tickled her interest, as well as those Megan closely guarded as her own. She loved painting and colouring but refused to have anything to do with mouldable dough, which she described as 'disgusting'. I was also getting to know some of her triggers. I could tell when she was tired – her manic spins fading to drunken, endearing lollops – and when she was upping the ante for no other reason than because she needed a hug.

Archie, though, was still a mystery. I knew the image he liked to project well enough, and conversing with him was easy, but part of him was still more or less closed off. 'Who's going to be there today, Rosie?' he asked as he rearranged the cutlery so that it was perpendicular to the mats.

It wasn't the first time he'd asked and I could hear the reluctance in his voice. My friend Naomi had called the previous night and tearfully invited us to meet her at a stately home owned by the National Trust. I had first met Naomi on an Understanding Attachment course a year earlier, soon after she had adopted a sibling group of three. Overwhelmed and exhausted by the sudden change in her life, she had opened up to me over lunch one day and told me all about her struggles to build a family – her miscarriages and failed attempts at IVF.

When she and her husband had finally decided to adopt, social workers told her that they needed to mourn the losses they'd experienced before they could progress to being assessed, and it was another two years before they were finally matched with the siblings. The couple fell in love with the children on sight but the eldest child, who had been four at the time of placement, struggled to accept the loss of his old family and the imposition of a new one.

Aiden, now five, still insisted on using wet wipes whenever Naomi touched him, a daily rejection that broke her heart, and seemed intent on doing all he could to disrupt the growing bond between his new parents and younger siblings. Naomi and her husband understood that his behaviour was rooted in fear, but sometimes it was difficult for them not to take it personally.

I think being out of the house alleviated some of the pressure on the family, and Naomi often asked us to meet up, whatever the weather.

I had shown Archie, Bobbi and Megan pictures of the maze and natural play area we were planning to visit and they had all been excited, but as soon as I mentioned that we were meeting others there, Archie's face fell. He tried his hardest to project a confident image to the world but his fingers trembled at the prospect of being introduced to new people and I suspected that, on the inside, he was spinning as rapidly as his sister.

'Only my friend Naomi and her children,' I said lightly. 'Don't worry, honey, I'll make sure you have fun.'

'I'm not worried,' he said in an equally light, if slightly strained tone. He nudged a stray chair in line with the table and moved one of the bowls an inch to the right.

It was unseasonably mild for February and when we arrived it was so sunny that we left our coats in the car. Naomi was waiting for us near the gatekeeper's house at the entrance to the grounds, her children running around on the neatly manicured grass nearby.

Toby, Aiden's four-year-old brother, ran through the gates as soon as he saw us. I leaned down to talk to him. 'Hello, Toby, how are you?'

He turned his wide blue eyes up to look at me. 'Aiden says she not our real mummy,' he blurted out loudly, pointing at Naomi with the unapologetic, unflinching honesty that only young children are capable of.

'That's cos she's not,' Aiden said when he caught up with his brother. He was a thin boy with short brown hair, pale skin and downturned, slightly sunken eyes.

'She looks real enough to me,' I said lightly, glancing at Naomi. She was walking towards us with a slow, defeated air.

Toby looked thoughtful. 'Aiden says the other mummy is our real mummy, not this one, cos we didn't grow in her tummy. We grew in old mummy's tummy but Mummy says we're not allowed to see old mummy any more cos she's dangerous.'

'I didn't say that!' Naomi said defensively. She strode over, knelt down in front of Toby and held one of his hands. She reached out her other hand towards Aiden but he screwed his face up in disgust and looked away. Naomi turned back to Toby, her expression tense. 'I said that Tummy Mummy can't keep you safe, honey. I didn't say she was dangerous.'

Toby frowned, looking uncertain. Beside me, Archie and Bobbi were both paying close attention to the conversation. A strange expression flitted across Archie's face, one I couldn't quite decipher. A few feet away, Aiden was staring at his adoptive mother with a look of longing that tugged at my heart.

Broken

I crouched next to Naomi and pulled Megan onto my knee. 'Do you know what, Toby? Megan didn't grow in my tummy either. She grew in my heart, just like her brother and sister. And look,' I jabbed a forefinger first into my chest and then into Megan's. 'I'm real, she's real. And Mummy is real too.' Megan giggled. I tried to be as open as possible about her adoption, using the word lightly in everyday conversation so that the news that we weren't biologically related wouldn't come as a shock one day. I think its meaning was slowly beginning to sink in.

Toby grinned and smiled at Naomi. She gave him a hug and the tension in his face melted away. I eased Megan off my lap and was about to stand up when Archie leaned down, his face level with Toby's. 'Just because you grow in someone's tummy don't mean they love you better than someone else,' he said. His voice was laced with bitterness, but he was trying to make the little boy feel better. 'I grew in my mum's tummy, but Rosie's the one that cares about me.'

Naomi and I exchanged glances. It was a telling comment, one I wanted to record accurately once I got home. I smiled at Archie sadly, feeling ever so slightly choked.

'It tears me apart,' Naomi said later, as we sat side by side on a wooden bench near the exit of the maze. I pulled a flask out of my bag and poured us both a cup of tea, listening to the shouts and giggles from the children as they chased each other around on the other side of the tall hedge. 'I just don't know what I have to do to get through to him. I love him so much, but he doesn't even want to be in the same room as me.' She threw her eyes skyward.

'That's probably why I lost all those babies. *Him* up there knew I'd be a rubbish mum.' Naomi was a long-time member of the Salvation Army who had managed to cling onto her faith despite all she'd been through. Her lips trembled as she took a shaky sip of tea.

'Oh, Naz, you mustn't think that, really you mustn't. You were *meant* to be mummy to these children, and they were meant to be with you. All of that awful stuff you all went through helped you to find each other.' I squeezed her arm. 'You should have more faith in yourself. You're not doing anything wrong. Aiden is a very frightened little boy. He's petrified of getting too close in case he loses everything again, you know that. You've done the courses, got the T-shirts. But I tell you what. He wants you desperately; I can see it in his eyes.'

'Really?' She lowered her cup to her knee. 'I don't see that. You really think so?'

I told her about the way Aiden had looked at her earlier. 'You're getting closer than you think,' I said. She gave me a teary nod.

Not long afterwards, the children came charging out of the maze in a spray of woodchips and soil. 'Can we see the house now, Mummy?' Megan asked, giggling as Toby began to chase her around my legs. Megan loved the outdoors but old buildings held a special fascination for her and she'd been asking to look around the house ever since we arrived.

I glanced at Naomi. 'I'm up for it if you are,' she said.

All of the children surprised us with their enthusiasm, staring around the corniced ceilings and wood-panelled walls with awe. There was a chest of Victorian clothes in one of the bedrooms and they pulled the outfits on with glee, admiring themselves in the ornate free-standing mirror beside a four-poster bed.

Things only started to go pear-shaped once Bobbi caught sight of the dining room. Before I could catch hold of her hand she ran over to the polished table and tried to clamber onto one of the chairs. 'Not on there, dear!' cried one of the volunteers standing nearby.

'I'm *so* sorry,' I told the elderly gentleman as I jogged over to Bobbi and lifted her down. 'You mustn't climb on the furniture, Bobbi,' I said in a hushed voice. 'It's very old and precious. We have to take care of it.'

'But I want lunch,' she insisted, grabbing one of the sparkling silver forks and putting the prongs into her mouth. The volunteer's eyes widened, his mouth flapping silently up and down.

'No, Bobbi, put it back,' I said, wrestling the fork away from her. I handed it to the volunteer with profuse apologies. He took it silently, still staring at Bobbi with disbelief. Aiden, Toby and Skye, Naomi's youngest, lost no time in joining in the fun. Darting to the other end of the table, they grabbed whatever they could lay their small hands on. Placemats, utensils and serviettes clattered to the floor. The noise drew volunteers from all directions, abject horror on their faces.

'I'm so sorry,' I said, mortified. I slipped my arms around Bobbi's middle and pulled her away before she could upset anything else, aware that Naomi was now chasing her three children around the room. 'Come here, pickle,' I said, catching three-year-old Skye with my free hand. Deciding that divide and conquer was the best way to go I handed her to Archie, who was standing beside Megan at the door, the pair of them watching the carry-on with almost as much horror as the volunteers.

Naomi emerged from the dining room a minute or so later, two screaming children in tow and a sheen of perspiration on her forehead. Aiden kicked out at the furniture as Naomi pulled him along, nearly toppling a suit of armour as he rattled its arm.

We whizzed through the rest of the house, Archie calmly bringing up the rear with Skye in his arms and Megan at his side. By the time we reached the long dark passageway leading to the back exit we were practically running. 'No, Mummy, no!' Megan cried, when she realised that the heavy oak door in front of us led outside. 'We didn't see the kitchen!'

'I don't think the kitchens are open, darling,' I lied. Bobbi was making a determined effort to bite my cheek and I had a nasty feeling that that was just the warm-up. I wasn't sure I had the strength to keep her at bay for much longer.

Megan stopped. 'It *is*, Mummy. We passed it. It's down some stairs, I saw!'

'Okay, well, let's get some lunch and maybe we'll come back later.'

'No!' Megan roared as Archie ushered her out the door and onto the shingled drive. I lowered Bobbi to her feet and knelt in front of Megan, aware that we were beginning to gain the attention of other visitors.

'We'll go back in after lunch, Meggie, okay?' Next to me, Bobbi was spinning manically; human hoopla without the hoop.

Megan gave a reluctant nod. Bobbi pushed her out of the way and stamped her feet in front of me. 'I want food!'

she screamed, preparing to roar off into orbit. Megan burst into tears. Behind us, Naomi was emerging, the boys kicking at her shins and turning the air blue.

'Bobbi, you mustn't push Megan. Now, we'll go and get some lunch, but only when you've calmed down.'

'I am calm!' Bobbi hollered, spraying my cheeks with saliva.

I brushed my sleeve over my face and blinked. 'Good. That's good,' I said softly, trying to soothe her. A grey-haired gentleman gave us a wide berth as he exited the house after Naomi, eager not to be tarnished by association. Two well-dressed women strolled by, their faces agog. They turned their heads as they passed, indiscreetly keeping us in sight. When they reached a bench they sat down at an angle that allowed them an unimpeded view.

It was easy to guess what they were thinking – *fancy kowtowing to a child like that, what a slummy mummy, no wonder the girl's out of control*. If Jenny, one of my fostering friends had been with us, she probably would have engaged the women in conversation and told them that the children were new to the family and still undergoing training. Most people soften instantly when they find out that children are fostered, but it's something I rarely reveal unless it comes up in conversation, clinging as I do to the belief that it is wrong for anyone to judge. Sometimes I even felt tempted to offer horrified bystanders a hook to hang their condemnation on by slumping onto a nearby bench and cracking open a can of Strongbow.

I remembered the looks I used to get when I took nine-year-old Phoebe out. She was an easily revolted girl with a sharp tongue and if ever anyone showed an interest in her, she either insulted them with colourful profanities or heaved her lunch all over their feet.

Bobbi sucked in a lungful of air and released it in little breaths, doing her best to bring her temper under control. 'Good work, Bobbi,' I said, aware of the exchange of glances from the two women across the way. 'You're doing really well.'

'I'm going to lose it in a minute, I swear,' Naomi said behind me, the boys continuing their assault on her shins.

The two women continued to stare as we ushered six tired, angry children over the lawns towards the tea shop, no doubt wondering how the china teapots would fare once our motley crew arrived.

I read *The Velveteen Rabbit* by Margery Williams to Megan that evening and after the day we'd had, the words took on such a special significance that I emailed a short passage from the book to Naomi when I got downstairs.

'What is Real?' asked the velveteen rabbit one day.

'Real isn't how you are made,' said Horse. 'It's a thing that happens to you. When a child loves you for a long, long time, not just to play with, but REALLY loves you, then you become real.'

'Does it hurt?' asked the Rabbit.

'Sometimes,' said the Horse, '[but] when you are Real you don't mind being hurt … it takes a long time … by the time you are Real, most of your hair has been loved off and your eyes drop out and you get loose in all the joints and very shabby. But these things don't matter at all because once you are Real you can't be ugly …'

Chapter Twenty-Two

Jimmy called at nine thirty the next morning, just as I was letting myself back into the house after the nursery and school-run. It was Monday 16 February and we seemed to have turned a corner with the weather. The sun was shining brightly through the patio doors, the house warm even though the thermostat was turned low. 'How are the kids, Rosie?' he asked without preamble. 'I feel really bad letting them down like that.'

'Oh, hello, Jimmy. They were upset, to be honest, but we went to the splash park anyway so at least they got to do that.'

'Ahh, you're a bloody decent woman, so you are. I'm really grateful.'

'It wasn't a problem. I think they enjoyed themselves.'

'Good, that's good.' A few seconds of silence followed and then Jimmy added: 'Yeah, I mislaid my phone. I don't know how it happened cos when I woke up this morning, there it was, on the floor just under the bed. I swear I should've seen it, had it been there on Saturday.' His voice had softened, as if he were thinking aloud. For a second I wondered whether he had considered the possibility that Tracy might have hidden the phone and then engineered its reappearance, but I quickly admonished myself for such an uncharitable thought. I knew that jealousy of a partner's children was an issue for some people, but it wasn't fair to jump to conclusions. And, I reminded myself, it was none of my business either.

I made a non-committal sound and then he said: 'Can I call them tonight, love? I won't make it near bedtime just in case it upsets them, like. I just want them to know I'm thinking of them –'

'Of course, it's not a problem at all.'

'Six o'clock then, just before I set off for work.'

True to his word, Jimmy called on the dot of six o'clock. I hadn't told the children to expect his call in case he let them down again, so Archie was taken aback when I held the phone out to him. 'It's Dad? What, *my* dad?'

I laughed. 'Yes. Come on, he wants to talk to you.'

There was a big grin on Archie's face as he strolled around with the phone aloft, his sister clinging to his leg and stretching out her arms to hurry him along. Bobbi stilled when it was her turn to speak, twisting shyly from side to side.

'I'm going to call Danny and see if I can spend some time with them in half-term, if that's okay with you, Rosie?' Jimmy said, once he'd wished the children good-night. 'I don't want to go stepping on your toes if you've something planned but I want to see as much of them as I can.'

I suddenly felt a little more optimistic about the children's future. Jimmy sounded sincere about his plans; a good sign if they were ever to return to his care. 'We'll work around you,' I told him, my thoughts flashing to Tracy's sudden illness on Saturday and the mystery of his vanishing phone.

Jimmy would have to demonstrate his reliability and total commitment if he wanted social services to give serious consideration to his application as a full-time parent. Given that he had to work, he would also presumably have to prove that Tracy was in full support of the idea, so that there was someone to take care of the children while he wasn't around. I couldn't help wondering whether Tracy was quite as sold on the idea of becoming a ready-made family of four as Jimmy seemed to be.

The week passed quickly and before we knew it half-term was upon us. After checking with Danny, I agreed a few times during the week for Jimmy to take the children out. The first date we'd arranged was Tuesday 24 February. Jimmy was to pick the children up at ten o'clock and take them back to his house for the day. I wondered how Tracy felt about the arrangement. Worried that she might somehow talk Jimmy into cancelling again, by Monday I found myself tensing every time my mobile pinged. Archie and Bobbi had been thrilled at the prospect of spending so much time with their father and I dreaded having to witness disappointment on their faces all over again.

Bobbi was the first to wake on Tuesday morning. She came downstairs with a fluffy pink bag I'd bought her already packed, her glasses a little skew-whiff on her face.

She sat on my lap on the sofa and took out each item one by one. 'This is my glasses case,' she said, holding it up reverentially, 'because I might play with Daddy in Tracy's garden and I don't want them to get squished. And this is my lip cream in case it's windy.' There was a look of such excitement on her face that I found myself praying that Jimmy would turn up.

When the doorbell rang at just after half past nine, Archie and Bobbi dashed into the hall with their bags clutched to their chests. Their faces fell at the sight of Gary, my ex-husband, who had popped over to take Emily and Jamie out for a cooked breakfast. Bobbi quickly recovered from her disappointment. She ran over to Gary and wrapped her arms around his leg. 'Bobbi, this is Gary, but you don't know him,' I said gently, repeating the mantra I'd grown used to over the weeks. Gary and I exchanged looks as I pulled her away. 'We only hug people we know very well, sweetie.'

'You must be Bobbi,' Gary said, crouching down to say hello. 'I like your glasses, they're cool.' Bobbi grinned and turned her head from side to side to show them off.

'That's Archie,' Bobbi said with a shy half-turn towards her brother.

'Hello, Gary,' Archie said politely.

'Hi, Archie. You're a Mancunian, I hear.' Gary and I had separated years earlier after he'd had an affair, but he had remained very involved in Emily and Jamie's lives. In recent years we had managed to salvage a friendship of sorts and, to his credit, he had welcomed Megan with open arms when she joined our family. He never left her out if ever he brought gifts for Emily and Jamie, and she often tagged along if they went somewhere child-friendly.

Broken

Megan interrupted the football banter that followed when she skidded into the hall and leapt onto Gary for a hug. 'Can I come to breakfast?'

Gary looked at me. 'That okay?' I nodded and smiled. 'Well, then, yes, you can, little one. As a matter of fact I was hoping you would. I need someone to keep Emily and Jamie in line now, don't I?'

Megan beamed and ran off to round up her brother and sister. Archie and Bobbi sat side by side on the sofa after Gary and the children left, forlorn expressions on their faces. I kept them occupied with a game of I-spy but when ten o'clock came and went their interest waned and melancholy took over.

When I called Jimmy's mobile number and got an unobtainable tone, my heart sank. I was about to suggest that we all go outside and bounce on the trampoline, when the doorbell rang again. Much to my relief, it was Jimmy I saw when I opened the door, Tracy standing on the path behind him. 'Dad!' Archie shouted, charging into the hall. I stepped aside and he threw himself at his father. I was so pleased to see him that I could have hugged him myself. Bobbi trotted into the hall after us. Overwhelmed with the anxiety of waiting, she burst into tears.

'Ahh, come here, darlin',' Jimmy said, squatting down and giving her a hug. He looked up at me. 'Sorry, Rosie. I mislaid my car keys.'

'Oh,' was all I could summon. I found myself beginning to doubt anything Jimmy said. My gaze strayed to Tracy, who was standing with her arms folded. She gave me a tight smile and then looked down at her feet.

It was raining by the time the children got their coats and shoes on. They ran outside to join their father and giggled as he took their hands and ran across the drive. Tracy followed them, frowning up at the sky.

While the house was empty I took the opportunity to write to Megan's birth mother. Christina had been granted letterbox contact twice yearly, which meant that, unless I felt that it was damaging in some way, I was obliged to update her on how Megan was doing. I sat at the computer and stared at the blank screen with a familiar feeling of resentment. It wasn't that I harboured any bad feeling towards Christina; quite the opposite in fact – Megan existed because of her, and we had built a positive relationship during the time I had fostered Megan.

What irritated me was that I wasn't allowed to be honest about Megan and the everyday difficulties she battled with as a result of Christina's drug and alcohol abuse while pregnant. In one of the first contact letters I wrote, I spoke of Megan's love of the outdoors, her enthusiasm for life and her gift for bringing people together. I also made reference to her abdominal discomfort and her struggles at nursery because of her hearing difficulties and developmental delay. I sent the letter via the local authority offices for forwarding on to Christina and the social worker that checked the contents had a fit of the vapours. 'You can't say that!' she had said over the telephone. When I asked why not she said that birth parents tended to blame the local authority if their children were ill. 'Besides,' she said, 'Christina might find it emotionally upsetting.'

While I usually went out of my way not to cause upset to anyone, I felt it was negligent to censor the truth in this case – Christina was a young woman who, in all likelihood, would go on to have more children, perhaps many of them. If being honest about the consequences of her actions was to go some way in keeping any future unborn children healthy, I was of the opinion that exposing her to a little guilt was a small price to pay.

I made myself a cup of tea and shook any lingering resentment away, and once I got started on the letter, the words came easily. Megan was such a joy that it wasn't difficult to find wonderful things to say about her.

The rain grew heavier throughout the morning and Megan, Jamie and Emily were drenched when Gary dropped them back home. Megan 'helped' me make some jam tarts after lunch, and the doorbell rang just as I was getting them out of the oven. I couldn't help but express my surprise. 'Oh, you're early!'

Archie and Bobbi trudged into the hall, their faces glum. They cheered a little at the sight of Megan, and Bobbi willingly submitted to a full-throttle hug. 'Sorry, Rosie,' Jimmy said, sounding thoroughly fed up himself. 'Tracy's got a cold coming so she couldn't trudge around in the rain.'

I looked at her. 'Oh, but I thought you were going back to your house for the day?' I couldn't imagine what difference wet weather made if they were tucked up indoors.

'We decided not to spend too much time in the car,' Jimmy explained a little sheepishly. 'It's at least an hour each way. We went to the park instead, but Tracy started to feel a bit shaky.'

'Oh dear. I've got a Lemsip in the cupboard if you'd like one?'

'I've already taken something,' she said with a loud sniff. She folded her arms over her fur coat with a theatrical little shiver.

'Rosie?' Archie tapped me on the arm. 'Can Dad stay and play on the Wii?'

'We-ell, I'm not sure,' I said slowly, with an uncertain glance towards Jimmy. Birth parents sometimes felt uncomfortable under what might be perceived to be a critical gaze from their child's foster carer. Jimmy raised his eyebrows though, looking hopeful.

Bobbi and Megan jumped up and down on my feet, their hands pressed together in prayer-like poses. 'Oh please, Rosie, please can he?'

'Yes,' I smiled. 'Yes, of course.' Archie and Bobbi cheered and pulled their father into the living room. Megan skipped after them. 'Meggie, you come with me, sweetheart.'

She looked crestfallen.

'She can join in,' Jimmy said. 'The more the merrier.'

I hesitated for only a second before agreeing. Usually I would have kept Megan away from contact sessions, but the children had been removed from Tanya's care, not Jimmy's. Besides, Danny had assured me that there were no safety issues and I planned to stay just a few feet away, in the kitchen.

'Jaysus, will you give me a minute,' Jimmy said as the children pulled on his hands. Tracy closed her eyes and let out a small sigh. When she opened her eyes and saw me looking at her she reset her expression and gave me a stiff smile.

'Shall we leave them to it?' I said, with a tilt of my head. 'Come to the kitchen and I'll make you a nice hot drink.'

* * *

Tracy took a cautious sip of her steaming coffee and lowered it to the breakfast bar, a trace of red lipstick clinging to the rim. She had been telling me about her sister's recent move to the Welsh coast as I made the drinks, and the plans she and Jimmy were making to visit the site where her brother-in-law was self-building a house.

I sat on the high stool beside her, a hot cup of tea in my hand, and began to wonder whether I'd misjudged her. With the short skirt she was wearing barely covering her knickers and her cleavage peeping through her low-cut top, she was what my mother might have labelled 'a bit brassy', but she was friendly enough. It was a pleasant conversation and with loud bellows of laughter reaching us from the living area, I found I was even enjoying myself. It was almost as if we were two mums catching up after picking the children up from school.

I could tell that Tracy was relaxing as well. The excessively affected tone she had adopted on arrival to prove she was unwell, one that sounded as if she were auditioning for a voiceover part in a flu remedy ad, had vanished, and she had finally removed her fur coat. It lay discarded like roadkill on the worktop behind us.

'I love the idea of building my own house,' I told her as she flicked through the travel brochure she'd pulled from her bag. 'I've always fancied a bit of *The Good Life*, you know?'

She looked up, her expression blank.

'Oh, you're too young to remember. It was a comedy about a couple who gave up their jobs and became self-sufficient; grew all their own vegetables, kept pigs and chickens. I used to dream about living like that; a garden full of animals and a house full of kids.' Tracy shuddered theatrically. I laughed. 'Horses for courses, I guess.' She grinned and went back to thumbing through the shiny pages. 'Going somewhere nice?' I asked, when she'd reached the last page.

She leaned back in her chair. 'Hopefully, if I can convince Jim.'

'Is he not keen on travelling?'

She pulled a face. 'His idea of a good time is a week at Butlins with the kids.'

I laughed. 'Not really your scene?'

She shuddered again and shook her head. 'It's hard to find the money though, cos we're saving up to move. We really need a bigger place.' So, plans were in motion for the children to move in, I thought, feeling more encouraged. 'My sister showed me the plans for her house; there'll be a games room, two shower rooms, a master bedroom with an en-suite. It looks perfect.'

'Sounds fabulous.'

She nodded wistfully. 'Somewhere similar isn't completely out of our reach. Jim earns alright and you can get *so* much more for your money in parts of Wales, can't you? We're in a pokey three-bed terrace at the moment, one tiny reception room, no downstairs lav. Out there we could get a detached with three bedrooms, two receptions, two bathrooms and a massive garden. Me and Jim were looking on the Internet last night.'

'Sounds gorgeous,' I said, smiling.

She nodded enthusiastically, her eyes shining at the thought. 'I said to Jimmy, if we tart our place up a bit and get it on the market in time for spring, there's nothing to stop us finding a place and moving in before the summer.'

'Oh, imagine that! The kids would love it.'

Her dreamy expression vanished. 'Oh yes, maybe,' she said, her eyes dropping to her cup. There was a pause while we both sipped our drinks. 'Course, it wouldn't be right to move them away from their school and everything,' she said sweetly, her eyes not quite meeting mine. 'They're so happy there.'

I looked at her. 'They're not actually. I don't think they like it at all.' She looked away again, took another sip of her coffee. I waited. 'Are you finding the children a bit of a handful, Tracy?' I asked after a time. She gave a stiff little shrug and folded her arms. I adopted a sympathetic tone to try and get her to lower her guard. 'It takes a bit of adjusting to, I should think, especially if you're not used to children.'

'I'm not,' she said, in immediate agreement. 'I mean, my sister's got a couple of kids and I absolutely love them, but they're family, aren't they?' She must have noticed a change in my expression because she faltered then. 'I – I mean, Archie and Bobbi are as well, Jimmy's family, that is. That's why I thought it best to let them down gently, you know, give them a dry run by missing a contact every now and again, so they don't get too used to seeing him. It'll be too far for them to visit much once we move.'

It wasn't up to me to challenge her, but it was so transparently obvious that she didn't want to build a family with the children, or even support Jimmy in maintaining a distant relationship with them. I couldn't sit silently while she pretended that she was doing everyone a favour. 'But I thought the plan was for them to come and live with you and Jimmy full-time? That's why you're being assessed, isn't it?' I worked hard to keep my tone mild so that she wouldn't sense my irritation.

'Well, yeah, it's been suggested, but Jimmy has enough on his plate, to be honest with you, and I can't be around when he's not, like the social are expecting. I'm too young to get tied down with two kids that are nothing to do with me, and all because his slag of an ex-wife can't get her shit together.'

I stared at her in disbelief. 'Does Jimmy know this is how you feel?'

She sniffed. 'He'll come around to seeing things my way. All it is is he feels bad saying no to having them when he knows they'll be stuck in care.' She examined her nails and then tapped them on the breakfast bar. 'But it's only guilt, isn't it? And you can't live your life like that.'

There was a pause, and then I said: 'I think it's best to be open about the way you feel. It'll be unsettling for the children otherwise.'

She rubbed a hand up and down her tanned arm. 'Hmm, but kids are resilient, aren't they? And I'm not sure Jimmy's quite ready to hear it yet, if you know what I mean. S'easy to get men to come round to our way of thinking though, isn't it?' she said with a wink. 'All we have to do is withhold certain privileges, then let them collect their winnings when they do things our way.' She performed a little shimmy that made her breasts jiggle, then huffed a laugh.

I stared at her. 'You do realise that I'll need to let the children's social worker know what you've just said.'

Her smile faded as she met my gaze. 'Sorry,' I said. 'I'm obliged to report anything that's likely to have an effect on the children. It's not something I can keep to myself.'

Broken

She coughed, her intermittent cold making a sudden reappearance, then gave a little shrug. I slipped off the stool and pulled on my yellow rubber gloves. I felt so irritated that it took all my resolve not to slam the cups and plates down on the draining board as I stood at the sink washing up.

From the living area came jumbled sounds of excitement, the voices of the children and Jimmy's all mingling joyously together.

Chapter Twenty-Three

I switched the computer on and signed into my email account later that evening, as soon as the children had gone to bed. I typed Danny's details into the address bar and then stared at the screen, my fingers curled motionless over the keyboard. It was important for me to stick to the facts and record any information I held accurately, but somehow it felt disloyal to report details of the conversation I'd shared with Tracy earlier that afternoon, one that, until I'd informed her otherwise, she had likely assumed to be private.

Come on, Rosie, get a grip, I told myself. It was never easy to report negative observations against birth parents or their wider family, but it was something that foster carers were sometimes required to do. Foster carers' diaries are occasionally summoned by the family court and used as evidence, most often in respect of mother and baby placements, where information on how a mother is coping with the day-to-day care of her infant is crucial in aiding social workers' decisions about their future.

I reminded myself that my priority was the children. I pushed away what I told myself was misguided loyalty towards someone who actually didn't seem to care all that much and tapped away at the keyboard. I took care to emphasise the positive relationship between Jimmy and the children, as well as summarising my conversation with Tracy.

Emily and Jamie, out with friends, weren't due back until after midnight, so after sending the email I switched the television on with the intention of watching a couple of back-to-back episodes of *House of Cards*. I found it difficult to concentrate though. I couldn't stop wondering how Jimmy really felt about living with Archie and Bobbi full-time. Lots of birth parents claimed to adore their children, in fact most screamed their undying love from the rooftops. It often turned out that their words were empty, the instinct to put the needs of their children above their own sadly lacking.

As social services' investigation progressed, both Tanya and Jimmy would be asked to nominate any friends or family members who would like to be assessed as long-term carers for the children, in the event that the judgment of the court went against them. As far as I knew, though, there were no grandparents, or at least none that were involved in the children's lives, and no aunts or uncles either.

My mind wandered, so much so that I gave up on the TV show and went up to have a shower instead. I stood under the hot spray and thought about the limited possibilities the social workers had to consider. If the children were unable to return to their own family, long-term foster carers would be sought. Long-term foster carers are expected to commit to caring for any children placed with them until they reach adulthood, but disruptions are commonplace. My chest ached at the thought of the children being moved around the system, or perhaps even being separated.

What little chance some children stood of having a settled life, I thought as I wrapped my dressing gown around me. I went downstairs and made some cocoa, a feeling of melancholy settling over me.

I woke early the next morning, Wednesday 25 February, excited to reveal to the children my plans for the day. When they got up I asked them to sit on the sofa, and then I presented them each with a ticket I'd printed online. 'Huh? What is it?' Bobbi asked, staring blankly at the thin piece of paper. Megan, clueless as to what is was, looked thrilled with it anyway and gave it a kiss. Archie looked up at me, his eyes wide with disbelief. 'Is this real, Rosie?'

I nodded, unable to take my eyes from his face. His chest was heaving rapidly up and down. He looked close to tears. 'I don't believe it!' He leapt from the sofa, threw his arms around me and jumped us both up and down. I hugged him back, laughing.

'What is it?' Bobbi asked. She was clutching Megan's hand.

Archie spun around. 'We're going to see Harry Potter!' he said breathlessly. 'We're actually going to see HARRY POTTER!' I had booked tickets for the Warner Bros. Studio Tour after Archie had shown such an interest in the books. The girls screeched with excitement and hugged him, though I wasn't sure they had any idea what was in store. Still, my heart swelled to see them all so happy.

Broken

'Make sure you bring your pocket money, Arch. There's a gift shop there and something's bound to catch your eye.'

He stiffened. 'Okay.' His reaction puzzled me, but there was so much to do before we left that I didn't ask him any more about it.

Since Emily and Jamie had been keen to come along as well, my brother Chris lent me his seven-seater for the day. We dropped Mungo at my mum's and then set off. Already in upbeat moods after spending the day with their father, spirits were high as we made the journey down to London, the children only starting to bicker when we were about twenty miles away from the studio.

The weather had turned again. It was dry but cold and we wrapped ourselves up when we arrived in the car park. Emily held the girls' gloved hands and walked towards the shuttle bus stop. Archie chattered animatedly to Jamie, who actually seemed enthused by the idea of the visit himself.

The soundtrack from the *Harry Potter* films was playing as we entered the foyer. Enthralled, Archie was trembling visibly as we waited for our allocated time slot. He chewed his nails as we joined the queue to go into the studios, his fingers white where he was gripping his ticket so tightly. I took a photo of him standing beside the iconic 'bed under the stairs' set, realising as I did so that his attraction to the story was perhaps so strong, not only because its central theme is one of loss and grief, but also because he identified so easily with the main character; a boy who had lots of different places to stay, but nowhere he could truly call home.

When we walked through the ornate oak doors leading to the Great Hall, Archie paled, so much so that I thought he might faint. We made our way around the hall slowly, the girls staring around at the twinkling lights, chandeliers and ghostly portraits with almost as much awe as Archie. The children posed for photos on Privet Drive, 'flew' on a broomstick in front of a green screen and then we went to one of the cafes and drank butterbeer from tankards. It was lovely to spend some time together that wasn't dictated by school runs and homework and for the first time since the children had arrived, I felt as if they were really part of the family.

After the tour we visited the gift shop, where I bought everyone a packet of Bertie Bott's Every Flavour Beans. Archie stared around the shelves with a look of longing. 'Seen anything you like, Archie?'

'Not really.' He shrugged as if he wasn't really interested, but I knew that was unlikely to be the case. I wondered whether he'd perhaps forgotten to bring his wallet, and was too polite to say so.

'I can lend you some if you don't have it on you.'

'I do have it,' he said, with a slight edge to his tone. 'I just don't want anything.'

I puzzled over it. I knew he must have at least fifty pounds saved up from the money I'd given him each week. I couldn't work out why he was reluctant to spend it.

Bobbi skipped along towards the bus stop at the end of the tour, more relaxed than I'd ever seen her before. She spun in circles as we waited for the shuttle and threw herself into each of us in turn, but it was in fun rather than fury. I imagined myself at the local Accident & Emergency Department having to explain away all sorts of hideous injuries when she tossed herself close to the brick wall behind us, but somehow she escaped without a scratch. She was like a human rubber ball.

Archie was noticeably more relaxed as well. When we got home he flopped between the girls on the sofa, stretching out until he was lying behind them. I pottered around on the other side of the room, setting the table and folding clothes, and for the first time ever, he didn't offer to help.

When I told them that dinner was ready the girls ran over but Archie just lifted one eye. 'I don't want to move,' he said with a yawn. 'I really can't be bothered.' I couldn't help but smile. He hauled himself up and sauntered over, flopping onto the dining chair with a loud groan.

I had noticed that his compliments were less fervent when they came, something that led me to believe that he felt more confidence in my dependability. His trust meant a lot to me. He also seemed happier to let me do the caring so that he could get on with the business of being a child.

My subconscious still whispered away at me however, telling me there was something I was missing.

Danny replied to my email late the next evening, on Thursday 26 February:

Hi Rosie

I appreciate you bringing this to my attention.
Having visited Jimmy and Tracy a few days ago I came to more or less the same conclusion myself.

I called Jimmy yesterday after reading your email, and he admitted that Tracy is making life difficult.

She hasn't told him outright that she's against the plan, but she's evasive whenever he mentions the kids and he even suspects that she hid his car keys to avoid spending a day with them!

He assures me that he'll bring her round to the idea, but I'm not sure that living with a reluctant step-parent is the ideal situation for the kids, especially in light of the environment they've just been removed from. Anyway, on top of all that, I heard from Tanya this afternoon, who's made some very serious allegations against Jimmy.

It could be that this is in response to the news that her contact has been reduced, but the allegations will have to be investigated. They'll be no contact between Jimmy and the kids until it's been resolved. I've explained the situation to him, and I'd be grateful if you could break the news to the kids; I'm up to my neck in it here.

We're back in court at the end of March, but I think it's safe to say that things aren't looking at all hopeful for a return to either Tanya or Jimmy. I'll tell you more when we next meet.

Regards, Danny

I went to bed with a heavy heart that night, dreading the thought of breaking the news to the children in the morning.

* * *

Broken

Archie was the first to wake. When he came downstairs he was already dressed, his rucksack packed and in place on his back. I was standing in the hall as he came down the stairs, a beaming smile on his face. 'Have you texted Dad yet, Rosie? I think he's coming early but I don't know for definite.'

'I haven't, no,' I said, my chest tightening. His smile faded. 'I'm afraid Dad can't see you today, Arch. He's got to meet with Danny first and discuss a few things.' I decided not to break the news about reduced contact with his mum. There was no urgency in telling him, and one bit of bad news was enough for him to absorb for now.

He dropped his rucksack and stared at me. His cheeks coloured, the flush deepening and spreading down his chin and across his neck. 'Okay,' was all he said, though his features had hardened, his eyes blazing with quiet, unsettling fury. 'S'cuse please,' he said tightly, moving slowly past me.

Bobbi's forehead puckered when I told her the news about twenty minutes later. Sitting on the sofa, she held her breath and looked at her brother, as if checking to see what sort of reaction might be appropriate. 'It's alright, Bobs, it doesn't matter,' he said calmly, the shutters back in place over his eyes. 'Can we still go somewhere good though, Rosie, please?'

Bobbi fixed her gaze on me, still looking as if she might cry. I chucked her under the chin with my forefinger. 'Of course we can. We'll have a lovely time.' The tension left her face immediately. When Megan got up she ran to her and the pair of them sat in front of the dolls' house, playing and giggling together.

'Are we still playing Rummy later?' Archie asked in a strained voice as we watched them. Our card games seemed to have become his lifeline, an anchor for him to cling to through all the turbulence of each day.

'I'm looking forward to it,' I said, patting his shoulder.

We sat down together just after eight o'clock that evening. I could feel him watching me as I shuffled the cards. I guessed there was something on his mind. 'Rosie, when we've finished our game can I call Dad and tell him about the Harry Potter trip?'

I hesitated, rehearsing the words in my mind before saying them. 'I'm afraid you can't at the moment, Arch.' A flicker of pain crossed his eyes, but a moment later it was gone. I dealt the hand and fanned my own cards out. He studied me carefully.

'When am I seeing Mum next? We haven't seen her for ages. They must have sorted things out at the contact centre by now.'

I sighed, lowering my cards to my lap. I dearly wanted to protect him from any more upset, but he had to find out sooner or later. It seemed wrong to withhold information from him when he'd directly asked about something. I took a breath. 'I think you'll be seeing her next month sometime.'

He frowned. 'But that's ages away. I'm supposed to see her before then.'

I licked my lips. 'Danny says that you'll be seeing her once a month from now on.'

'Why?'

'The judge has made the decision.'

Broken

'But that's not fair! Why?'

It was so difficult to find words gentle enough to explain to him that his mother was slowly withdrawing from his life of her own accord. How could I possibly frame the brutal reality in a way that wouldn't cause him lasting psychological damage? My stomach pulsed with sympathy. 'Erm, well, I think the judge feels that once a month is enough for now, love. All any of us want is to keep you safe.'

'But what about Mum?' he said, his face creased with concern. 'I need to make sure she's safe too.' All along I had sensed that his feelings for his mother were muddled and complex. Whenever contact was due he had withdrawn into himself, but despite the personal cost he wanted to see her nevertheless, mostly, it seemed, because he felt duty-bound to make sure she was okay. It was heartbreaking. 'Archie, love, I'm sure your mum is fine.'

He gave a stiff nod and lowered his gaze, staring silently at his cards.

Chapter Twenty-Four

It was a few days later, on Monday 3 March 2015, that I gained my first real glimpse of the pain Archie had battled so hard to keep hidden away.

I had gone to the supermarket straight after dropping the children at school, and it was just as I'd carried all the bags through to the kitchen that the telephone rang. It was Clare Barnard, the SENCO. 'Rosie, sorry, I need you to come into school. Right now, if you can.'

My chest tightened. 'What's happened? Are the children okay?'

'They're fine. I mean, they're well, but there's been an incident with Archie. We need to speak to you urgently.'

I quickly stowed the cold items in the fridge and grabbed my keys. I made it to the school within fifteen minutes, nerves churning in my stomach. Clare met me in reception, her expression grim, and showed me through to her office. 'Archie has been giving money to some of the Year Six boys,' she said, as soon as I sat down. 'It's been going on for weeks apparently, but it's only just come to the attention of the staff.'

'Poor Archie,' I said, my chest tightening with pity. The expression on Clare's face told me that she didn't share my feelings. Her lips were set hard, her eyes uncompromisingly clear. I felt a flare of irritation towards her. 'You know who they are, then? The boys involved?'

She nodded. 'One of them came to me this morning to report it.'

I raised my eyebrows, surprised. 'They're nice boys, Rosie,' Clare continued. 'They've been taking Archie's money, but not in the way you probably think. Archie has been plying them with cash so that they'll let him join in when they play football. They're reluctant to let the younger ones play; you know what children are like. But it seems that Archie has been bribing his way onto the team.'

My heart lurched. Abandoned by his family and ostracised by his peers, Archie was a boy so desperate for friendship that he'd resorted to paying other children to spend time with him. I didn't know about Clare, but the thought of a child being *that* lonely made my heart bleed.

I couldn't understand, then, why Clare's expression remained so impassive. I was also bemused as to why I had been summoned so urgently. My heart ached for Archie, but surely giving his pocket money away wasn't really a matter deserving of such gravity? 'Poor Archie. He's all over the place at the moment.'

Clare nodded, softening a little, but then she pressed her lips together. 'That's not the worst of it, Rosie, I'm afraid. The boy who came to me didn't want to get Archie into trouble, but he was very upset by something Archie had showed him on his phone.'

I looked up sharply. 'On whose phone?'

'Archie's phone.'

'Archie doesn't have a –'

My words trailed off as Clare reached into one of the trays on her desk. She pulled out a mobile phone and held it up. 'Do you recognise this?'

I shook my head, incredulous. 'I've never seen it before. That's an iPhone, isn't it? It can't be Archie's.'

'Archie has admitted that it is. You didn't know he had one?' She turned the handset this way and that, as if I might suddenly remember seeing it around.

'No! I wouldn't allow a child of his age to take a phone into school.' With a slow stomach roll, I remembered Archie's disinterest in telephone contact with his mother. Could it be that he'd been calling her while out of earshot, up in his room? My thoughts tumbled over themselves, and then rewound to what Clare had just said. 'What was it that upset this boy?'

Clare grimaced and lowered the phone to her desk. 'Oh no,' I said, covering my face with my hands. Anticipating her answer, I was beginning to feel quite sick.

'I'm afraid so. It was very explicit material.'

My stomach contracted. 'Where has he found stuff like that? YouTube? Or one of the other sites?'

'I don't think you're quite grasping the stuff I'm talking about, Rosie. This sort of thing isn't new to us. Most of the Year Sixes bring phones to school; even some of the Year Fours and Fives have them. We know they circulate videos between themselves, things I personally wouldn't want children to watch, but what Archie had on his phone is another level entirely. We're not talking topless ladies in skimpy underwear. This is seriously nasty material. The sort of thing I've never seen in my life, and I've been around the block a few times, I can tell you.'

I groaned, my stomach flipping somersaults. 'So what happens now?'

Clare tapped her fingers on the phone. 'I've confiscated it, obviously. Mrs Cullum-Coggan is off today, so I've had to make a decision myself, and I'm going to send him home. He was in quite a state when I confronted him over it, so I think it's best all round if he stays off for a couple of days. He's waiting with one of the TAs at the moment. I'll take you to him now.'

It was almost half past eleven when we reached reception and not long until I needed to pick the girls up. Archie hung back as the TA walked towards me, his head dipped to his chest, school shirt hanging below his school jumper and wavy hair sticking out in all directions. 'Hello, Arch,' I said softly. He mumbled something but kept his eyes averted. Usually an expert at deadpan, there was something alarming about the discomfort so evident on his face.

'Bye, Archie, love,' the TA said when she reached me. She was a plump woman, not much taller than him. I was relieved to hear kindliness in her tone. She gave me a grim smile and patted him on the shoulder before turning and walking away.

'Thank you, Rosie,' Clare said beside me. She looked at Archie over the top of her glasses. 'We'll see you on Thursday, young man.'

He said goodbye politely, his eyes flicking towards her and then quickly away. I gave Clare one last look over my shoulder before we left and she raised her eyes at me.

'You've had quite a morning, love, haven't you?' I said as we crossed the playground towards the road. He gave a small nod but didn't say anything. 'It's not worth going home. We have to pick the girls up soon. How about a walk beside the river?' He gave a little shrug and followed me silently to the car.

It may have been winter outside, but the car had a microclimate all of its own with Archie in it. I looked in the rear-view mirror as I drove towards the river. His inscrutable expression had reappeared, but hot fury simmered underneath; I could feel it radiating from him. I knew that getting him to talk about what he'd done was likely to be an uphill battle.

We walked wordlessly through the woods leading to the river. The ground was hard, though not icy, the air having lost its bitter edge. It was windy on the riverbank though, and quite nippy. Archie sat with his head tucked into his coat and his hands deep inside his pockets while I ordered drinks from the tea hut. I handed him a hot chocolate and sat beside him, so that we were both facing the river. I blew across the steaming surface of my takeaway tea. 'Do you want to tell me what happened, Arch?'

He looked down at his lap. 'Not really.'

I was about to say something when I caught sight of a toddler running along the towpath behind the hut. There was no sign of anyone with him and he seemed to be heading directly for the water. When he got dangerously close I jumped out of my seat ready to grab him. A woman pushing a buggy ran in front of me and whipped him back. She carried him under her arm like a roll of carpet and as she passed she gave me a grateful smile. It was only then, as she strapped the little boy in the buggy and tucked a blanket around him, that my thoughts turned suddenly to Bobbi. A sensation of momentary weightlessness hit me. At the same time, I felt a cold chill run across the back of my neck.

The thought of a boy of Archie's age watching pornographic content was deeply concerning, but if Bobbi had been exposed to it as well … the idea made my stomach churn. I looked at Archie, filled with sadness for his loss of innocence. It was as if his childhood had been taken away from him. I wondered whether there was a way of getting it back. But then, you couldn't ever 'unsee' something, could you?

Never had I been so grateful for the Safer Caring guidelines issued by my fostering agency than I had at that moment. At least, I told myself, there was no way that Megan could have seen the content on Archie's phone, since she'd never been left alone with him. My rules wouldn't have helped Bobbi though, since she had shared a room with Archie, both in my house and in their own.

I didn't want to cause Archie any further humiliation, but I needed to get the conversation going somehow. Feeling that his pocket money was the issue that might embarrass him the least, I said: 'Miss Barnard tells me that you've been giving money to some of the boys.'

He looked up across the river. His hot chocolate stood untouched on the table in front of him. 'You can talk to me, Archie. I'm not cross. I just want you to help me understand.' One of his knees began to wobble. The metal chair he was sitting on rattled against the hard ground in synchrony with his vibrating knee. And then another thought occurred to me. 'Was that what you intended to do with my bracelet? Give it to someone at school?'

He turned sharply. 'That wasn't me! Bobbi took it.' His cheeks coloured. 'She didn't mean anything bad by it. She didn't know what she was doing.'

I held up a hand. 'This isn't about blame.' He looked relieved and turned away again. 'I wondered what had happened to the pocket money I'd given you,' I persisted, making an effort to lighten my tone. 'I thought there was something odd going on when we came out of the Harry Potter shop empty-handed.'

He blinked, his lips curving ever so slightly upwards. 'There was me asking why you weren't treating yourself to one of the wands, and all the time you had no money left to spend in there.' My tone grew serious again. 'I wish I'd known, Arch.'

'Sorry,' he said quietly, a clipped edge to his voice.

'You don't have to apologise, honey. But I would like to know why you've been giving your money away.'

'They all hate me!' he said, his eyes suddenly flashing with anger. 'All of them.' He dropped his head and stared into his lap again.

'The children at school?'

'Yes,' he snapped. 'Everyone else has got someone to go round with. I'm always on my own.' When he looked at me his eyes were brimming with tears.

'And you thought giving them money would make them include you?'

He nodded. 'It backfired though, didn't it, cos they went and told on me.'

'It's good that they did though, love, in a way. Because now we know how you feel we can try to help you.'

'No one can help! I'm weird and everyone hates me, even my own mum and dad.' He leapt from his seat and stamped away to the water's edge, where he picked up some stones and tossed them in the water. I dearly wanted to help him, but it was time to pick Megan up. I left him alone for another minute or so and then grabbed our drinks.

'We have to go and get the girls now. We'll talk more later.' He ignored me, but when I walked away I sensed him behind me. It was like being shadowed by a black cloud; so visceral was his misery.

Megan was delighted when she saw him, but for once, he didn't respond when she spoke to him. She stared at him in puzzlement and then looked up at me. 'Archie's a bit tired, love,' I said, steering her away from him.

He wanted to wait outside the school reception while I went in to collect Bobbi. The receptionist threw me a sympathetic glance – clearly word had already got around amongst the staff. Bobbi threw her arms around Megan when she saw her and didn't seem to notice the change in routine when she saw Archie waiting outside.

'Got any chocolate?' she asked with the merest glance at her brother. She handed her book bag to me and looked up hopefully. She may have lost the urgency over mealtimes at home but, like most children when they came out of school, she was ravenously hungry and she needed a snack. 'NOW, Rosie!'

I pulled some Milky Way bars out of my pocket and gave one to her and another to Megan. 'There you go. We've got lunch when we get home.' Bobbi opened the wrapper with her teeth and wolfed it down in one. The girls' happy chatter mercifully lightened the tension in the car as we drove towards home.

'I'm really tired,' Archie said when we got in. 'Can I go to bed?'

I wanted to encourage him to confide in me but knew it was probably best not to push him to talk. 'Of course you can. Shall I bring you some lunch?' He shook his head and walked away with the gait of an elderly man. His shoulders were slumped and his movements lethargic, as if life's troubles had knocked all the energy out of him.

After preparing lunch for the girls I sent an email to Danny, telling him what had happened at school. I also completed my log then played a board game called Tummy Ache with the girls. At just after half past three I went up to Archie. He was sitting on his top bunk, reading his book. 'You must be hungry, Arch. Do you want to come down for lunch?'

'I'm at a really exciting bit,' he said in an even tone. Somehow, he'd managed to fix his mask back in place. 'Can I stay here and read? I'm not hungry yet.'

'Okay, I'll call you at dinner time if you're not down by then.' About half an hour later I poured some orange juice into a glass in the kitchen, picked it up, put it down again then stared at it. I couldn't decide whether to leave him alone or remind him I was around if he needed me. In the end I took it up. 'Thank you,' he said before I'd taken a few steps into the room.

Broken

On my way out I glanced under the bed, wondering whether their bounty of food had been refreshed. I couldn't see anything and hadn't noticed food going missing from the kitchen, but, then again, I hadn't noticed that he'd had a mobile phone, so there was every chance he'd managed to smuggle enough for a siege.

The events of the day spooled through my mind on a loop as I prepared dinner. I kept thinking about the allegations made by Tanya against Jimmy. I had no idea of the exact nature of her accusations, but could it be that she was somehow trying to protect the children from him? And perhaps that was why both Tanya and Jason had objected so strongly to contact between the children and their father at the LAC Review.

I called Archie down for dinner at half past five. He joined Megan, Bobbi and me at the table and although it was his favourite – chicken fajitas – he hardly ate a thing. I found my own appetite lacking too. Neither of us, it seemed, relished the prospect of playing cards together this evening.

Chapter Twenty-Five

'But I'm really tired, Rosie,' Archie insisted, after I'd settled the girls in bed. He was standing in the doorway of the living area, one foot edging back into the hall.

'Let's not play cards then, love.' Grasping the nettle, I sat on the sofa and patted the cushion beside me. 'We'll have a quick chat, then you can go up to bed.'

He walked forward warily, dropping down on the edge of the cushion at the opposite end of the sofa with a loud huff. 'I don't know why you have to keep going on about it.'

'I asked you about your pocket money,' I said gently. 'But we didn't speak about your phone.'

He stiffened. 'So, I had a phone and didn't tell you. Sorry, okay.'

I angled myself so that I was facing him, though he remained perched on the edge, staring straight ahead. 'You should have told me about the phone, but that's not what I'm most concerned about, Archie. What worries me is what you've been watching on it, and what you've been showing your friends at school.'

Broken

'They're not my friends!' he snapped, spinning around to face me. 'I told you, they hate me.'

'I'm sure they don't –'

'It's not fair!' he shouted. 'The other kids show gross stuff on their phones all the time! Ambrose in Year Four showed a clip of a snake eating a cow once. It made Chloe puke all over the playground but she still never sneaked on him. Everyone thought it was hilarious. It's only when I do it they freak.'

I paused. 'I didn't see what was on your phone, Archie, and I don't want to either, but from what Clare was saying, it was pretty nasty stuff. Not just something you could have downloaded from an ordinary website.'

A flush of shame flew across his cheeks, quickly followed by a flash of fury. 'What would you know about it?' he screamed. He began slapping the back of his head repeatedly, and hard. 'You can't even work the telly remote!'

I gave him a long steady look.

'Well, you can't! And your phone is as old as you are. You haven't got a clue.'

'Archie …'

He stared at me in fury but then his shoulders slumped, as if he realised it was useless to protest. He covered his face with his hands. 'I'm sorry,' he said, his voice cracking.

I shuffled along the sofa until I was about a foot away from him. 'It's not actually your fault, love. None of this is. It's the fault of whoever gave you the phone. Was it your mum?'

His hands dropped from his face. He sniffed, keeping his face angled away. 'No.'

269

'Who gave it to you then? Your dad?' Had the provider of the phone – and as far as I was concerned it was bound to be either his mother or father – also sent Archie the content on it, I wondered. Or was that something he had managed to download himself? I felt entirely out of my depth and hoped that Danny would contact me soon.

Archie stayed silent. 'Listen, love. Someone pays the bill for the phone. It won't be difficult to find out who it is.'

He turned around. 'Find out?'

'Well, I'm going to have to tell Danny about this, and he'll –'

'No, please don't tell anyone! Please, Rosie!'

His voice cracked again and I felt a wave of pity roll over me. 'I have to, honey, and Danny will want to find out where the videos came from, as well as the phone.' I wasn't sure whether that was even possible, what with data protection and privacy rules in place. No doubt the police could find out what they needed to know, but I had already heard that CEOP, the Child Exploitation and Online Protection Centre, was operating beyond capacity. I doubted that precious resources could be spared for an investigation such as this. Still, Archie didn't know that.

He lifted his knee and rested it on the cushion, turning slightly towards me. 'No one will find out,' he said quietly.

'Sorry?'

'There's no way you can find out. It's an iPhone. Unless I tell someone the code, it's impossible to get into it.'

'I don't think so,' I said, though I only had one of those old Nokia handsets. When it came to mobile phone technology, I only had a sketchy understanding. As for downloading videos, I was absolutely clueless.

'Yes it is! Jason says –' He stopped suddenly, realising that he'd said more than intended.

'So Jason gave you the phone?' He shook his head, turned away.

I stared at the back of his head. 'Archie,' I said slowly. 'Have you ever shown those videos to Bobbi?'

He spun around, his eyes wide with horror. 'No!'

I levelled my gaze, my mind returning to the pictures she had drawn when she first arrived in placement, the strange, inappropriate comments to the other girls at school, and the excrement smeared over my mother's rug. 'Never? Not any of them?'

'I wouldn't do that!' he said, and then he burst into tears. 'I would never do that, honestly, Rosie. She doesn't even know I've got a phone. I knew she'd say something if she saw it so I kept it secret.'

He held my gaze as tears spilled from his eyes. It wasn't one of his halfway looks, where he couldn't quite meet my eye. It was a direct stare, searing and honest, and I believed that he was telling the truth. 'I believe you, Arch.' I put my arm around him, noticing his thinness as I held him. 'I'm sorry. I had to ask.' He rested his head on my shoulder, his body trembling as he cried and cried. I held him for a long time, rocking him and telling him that everything was going to be okay. When he went up to bed I recorded everything he had said as accurately as I could, a ball of anger snarling in the pit of my stomach as I typed.

The telephone rang at half past nine, just after I'd sat down with Emily to watch a new episode of *House of Cards*. It was Danny, still at work, despite the lateness of the hour. 'Sorry,

Rosie. I tried to get round to calling you earlier but we had an emergency come up. How is he?'

'He's upset. Defensive. Protecting someone.'

'Ah, he's not coughed up to anything yet then?'

'He's admitted showing stuff to the children at school. I think he's just so desperate to make friends, Danny. He thought that was the way to do it. They all show each other hideous stuff apparently, though I think what Archie had on his phone truly shocked them all.'

'And you had no idea he had a phone?' There was no reproof in Danny's tone, but I felt the sting of guilt anyway.

'Absolutely no idea. He must have had it in his rucksack when he arrived. I did suspect. I asked him once if he had one, but he denied it and I took him at his word.' I knew that the use of mobile phones was the source of much conflict in fostering families. Disagreements about who was responsible for topping up credit and keeping handsets under pillows when sleeping regularly cropped up, but some foster carers had even been filmed when in the middle of a rant, the footage posted up on social media for birth families to access. The more I thought about it, the more foolish I felt. I resolved to make more of an effort to check in future when new children arrived in placement.

'I'm not blaming you, Rosie. There's no way you could have known unless you'd searched his bag, and we obviously don't expect you to do that. Where is the phone now?'

'I've confiscated it.'

'Good. We'll pick it up soon, though I'm not sure what can be done about it yet. They'll be a strategy meeting in the next few days.' There was a pause, and then he said:

'I'm pretty certain that the children will be removed and placed separately after that.'

'Oh no, Danny, don't say that.'

He sighed. 'It's pretty inevitable. It's not that what Archie has done is that unusual. Believe me, it isn't. Most kids are exposed to explicit images before their teenage years these days. But when the fact that the kids are sharing a room is brought to everyone's attention, it's unlikely they'll allow it to continue. Just think of the risks. When you think about the way Bobbi's been behaving at school, it suggests she's been acting out what she's seen as a way of trying to understand it. Whether that's what went on in the past, or what Archie's exposed her to is anyone's guess.'

'But he'd never hurt Bobbi,' I insisted, a band tightening around my chest. 'He loves her to pieces. He's so protective of her.'

'I'm sure he is, Rosie. I'm not saying it's deliberate on his part, poor kid. But I suspect my manager will be thinking trauma bond, and if that is the case, it's not good for either of them.' Traumatic bonding is the term used to describe the powerful attachment that often exists between a destructive person and their victim. Siblings that share a trauma bond are usually placed separately to avoid the risk of continuing abuse. As far as I could tell, Archie was Bobbi's protector, not her abuser, but I also appreciated the difficulty for social workers who had to make snap decisions from afar, sometimes without much personal experience of the children involved.

'I could separate their room,' I pressed on. I knew that some agency foster carers who provided placements for asylum seekers had separated spare bedrooms into two, sometimes even three separate sleeping pods using four by twos and some MDF. It wasn't an ideal scenario, but the usual rules had been relaxed through desperate need.

'Rosie, let's see what happens. I'll say my piece at the meeting, but I'm not hopeful. Not hopeful at all.'

Chapter Twenty-Six

Archie spent the next day, Tuesday 4 March, in his room, emerging reluctantly for meals and the school run. Bobbi lashed out at me that afternoon, the first violent episode from her in weeks. While she seemed generally unaware and absorbed in her own little world, I think she sensed there was something amiss. I noticed her watching Archie during dinner that evening, an unusual sharpness in her gaze.

I spent a bit of extra time playing with her after Megan had gone to bed, and then invited her to join me on the sofa so that I could read *My Underpants Rule* to her while no one else was around. It was the book that Danny had recommended after I'd told him about Bobbi's inappropriate language at school. It had been delivered by Amazon that morning.

Bobbi wasn't a bookworm like her brother, but she scrambled onto the sofa eagerly – pleased, I think, to have been singled out for individual attention. The book was colourful and she gave the story her full attention while snuggling beside me. 'What's under my pants belongs only to me,' I read, 'And others can't touch there or ask me to see ...' I turned each page slowly, willing her to confide in me while at the same time praying there wasn't anything for her to disclose.

There were scenarios that children might find themselves in described at the end of the book. Bobbi looked thoughtful but not upset as we discussed how she might react if she found herself in a situation that made her uncomfortable. I watched her as she looked at the lively illustrations, resisting the urge to question her. I wondered what was going through her mind. Did she even possess the words to tell me what she might have endured, I wondered. I let her flick through the book for a while, and when she'd finished I asked her whether she liked it.

She nodded and looked at me. 'It's good. I've had it before though.'

'Have you? At school?' I knew that stay safe lessons had been introduced in some schools for children as young as four, to encourage them to reach out for help if they were suffering abuse.

'Daddy read it to me when I see'd him ages ago,' she said, plonking the book at her side and climbing onto my lap. I felt a quickening in my chest; an invisible high five. I gave her a hug and carried her upstairs to brush her teeth, thrilled to think that Jimmy was innocent of any allegations thrown at him by Tanya and Jason.

If Jimmy had ever harmed Bobbi or Archie, there was no way he would have read a book like that to them. It was a simple yet incontrovertible truth as far as I was concerned, and I couldn't wait to call Danny and tell him.

* * *

'Even if that is the case,' Danny said over the telephone on the Wednesday morning, 'Tracy has made it clear she doesn't want the children. Their house is on the market and they'll be moving out of the area as soon as it's sold.'

'And what about Jimmy?'

'I can't even get hold of him. His phone's switched off and he hasn't responded to any of my messages.'

My heart sank. It was hard to believe that a man who had seemed so fond of his children could abandon them on the say-so of a woman. I hated the thought of the children moving on when we were on the verge of finding out what really happened to them. Archie was close to confiding in me, I was sure of it. I was also certain that moving him on to another foster carer so soon after the mobile-phone episode would feel like a punishment; yet another rejection to increase his shame.

'We're holding a strategy meeting in the morning,' Danny said flatly. 'I'll give you a ring when I know more.'

Archie spent much of the rest of the day in his room. Whenever I spoke to him he answered with good manners, his seething anger having been replaced with a lethargic, quiet depression.

Archie hovered close to me when we went to Millfield Primary the next day. It was Thursday 6 March and I knew that the strategy meeting would be taking place at some time during the morning. Anxiety swirled around my chest as I watched the older children crossing the playground towards their classrooms. Archie looked so tortured about spending the day at school that it was all I could do not to wrap my arms around him and take him back home. 'I'll see you this afternoon, honey,' I said, resisting the urge to tell him he could have one more day off. He dipped his head close to my shoulder and then joined the back of the disinterested throng. My heart ached for him.

I went on a cleaning mission as soon as I got home. I turned the radio on and stripped every bed in the house of its sheets in an attempt to occupy my mind. I kept the volume low though, keen to hear the telephone if it went. Danny finally called my mobile around midday. 'Hello,' I said eagerly when I saw his name displayed, though I could tell by his tone that it wasn't good news.

'We're going to have to move them, Rosie. It was a unanimous decision, I'm afraid.'

I felt a tug at my heart. 'Oh no.'

'I know you were hoping for better news, but it looks like we might have found a placement for Archie already; an older couple with no children at home. There's nothing for Bobbi yet, but we're hopeful we'll find somewhere quickly for her too.'

I groaned, my heart breaking at the thought of the siblings being separated. 'I know how you feel,' Danny said, 'but they'll have supervised contact between them regularly, so it won't be as bad as you fear.' It was bad enough, and I could tell from Danny's tone that he thought so too. 'The carers have a holiday booked but it's only a week. They'll be ready for Archie from 17 March. Until then we'd be grateful if you could be extra vigilant at home.'

That was only ten or so days away. I swallowed hard, emotion tightening my throat. 'Don't say anything to the

Broken

kids yet. We'll break the news a few days before they move on. We don't want to cause them any more stress than we have to.'

279

Chapter Twenty-Seven

The girls sang in the car all the way home. It was a proper cats' chorus, but listening to them brought a lump to my throat. I thought back to the frenzied, agitated child I had collected from Joan's house on New Year's Day and my throat tightened still further; Bobbi had come such a long way in the last couple of months. But had she also been damaged during that time, by her own brother, I wondered. I looked at her in the rear-view mirror, her face bright and shiny as she beamed across at Megan, and I felt a clawing in my stomach; an urge to find out more.

I set some paints out on the table when we got home and as I watched them play I wracked my brains, trying to think of a way of finding out whether Archie was telling the truth. And then it occurred to me.

My handbag was hanging over the newel post in the hall. I opened it and pulled out the white iPhone – despite what Danny had said, no one from social services had materialised to collect it. I took it into the dining area and sat down next to Bobbi. 'What's that?' she asked, when I held it up.

'It's a phone. Can I see, Mummy?' Megan asked.

I turned it over in my hand and showed them. Megan reached out for it. Bobbi ran her eyes over it with a blank expression and then went back to dabbing her brush in some red paint. I pulled it back out of Megan's reach. 'Just a minute, Meggie. Bobbi? Hey, Bobbi, look at me.'

Engrossed in what she was doing, she lifted her head reluctantly. 'What?'

'Do you know whose phone this is?'

'Huh?'

'Who does this phone belong to?'

She shrugged. 'Dunno.'

'Is it Archie's?'

The glaze over her eyes cleared. 'Archie don't have a phone,' she said in a tone that suggested she considered me slightly daft. It was a simple test, but one that left no doubt in my mind that Archie had been telling the truth. I scribbled a quick note on my log, reminding myself to email Danny as soon as I got a chance.

I wasn't sure if I was imagining it, but Archie seemed a little lighter on his feet when we picked him up that afternoon. 'So your first day back wasn't too bad then?' I said as we walked back to the car.

He shrugged. 'It was alright actually. We've been put into groups to do a book project and Miss Barnard says me and Charlie can help her organise a Harry Potter display since we're experts.' I smiled, pleased to hear that Clare was making efforts to draw him into the fold.

At dinnertime he told me about some ideas he'd already had for the project and I noticed as he spoke that he had less difficultly maintaining eye contact. It was as if he felt more at ease with himself after being found out. He hovered around me as I cleared away the dishes after dinner, though, and I sensed he had more to say. It came out later that evening, when I came back down after putting the girls to bed.

'Has anyone heard from my dad?' he asked, as soon as I stepped into the room. He was standing between the sofa and the bookshelf, the TV remote in his hand.

'I'm afraid not, honey. Not yet.'

'What will happen if we never hear from him again?' He set the handset on one of the shelves and ran his fingers over the spines of the books, his face angled away.

'Well, there are lots of lovely foster carers who would love to take care of children as wonderful as you and Bobbi. Long-term carers who will look after you until you're grown-up.'

He looked at me and opened his mouth to speak. All that came out was a croak. I took a step closer. 'It's okay to feel a bit anxious about it, love, that's normal.'

He shook his head. 'It's not that.' He sounded bunged up.

'What is it then?'

'It won't be you?' He risked a glance at me. His face crumpled; his voice breaking. 'It won't be here, with you?'

I took a breath. 'Not with me, no,' I said hoarsely. I was beginning to feel choked myself.

His lower lip wobbled and he burst into tears. I was across the room then, taking him into my arms. He rested his head onto my shoulder and wept, his hands clutching fast at my jumper. I held him for several minutes until his sobs began to subside, and then he pulled away, his head level with my shoulder. 'You don't want us then,' he managed shakily, his eyes filled with the pain of rejection. Suddenly he seemed very small and my heart broke for him.

I rested my hands firmly on his shoulders, battling to keep my own emotions in check. 'Archie, sweetie, that isn't it at all, honestly it isn't.' I dropped my hands and grabbed his, gripping them tightly in my own. 'I would love you to be able to stay here,' I said, surprised to find that I truly meant it. For the first few weeks of their stay with us I had been mentally crossing off each difficult day in my mind. Now, I felt like they belonged, as if they were part of the family. 'But you're both getting older and you'll soon need a room of your own. I'm afraid that just isn't possible here.'

'I don't mind sharing. Or Bobbi could have the bedroom and I'll sleep downstairs.'

'Oh, Arch, it wouldn't be allowed, honey.'

He took a deep shuddery breath and nodded. I pulled him close and he started to cry again, softly, onto my shoulder. I thought back to Tracy's words about children being resilient. I don't share that view. I think that we're born with powerful coping strategies to help us survive, but that isn't the same thing at all. I had little doubt that both Archie and Bobbi would somehow get through – powerless to do anything about the circumstances they found themselves in, they had little choice but to soldier on.

After a minute or so he pulled away, took a breath and then looked at me: 'Is it cos of what I did at school? With the phone?'

'Absolutely not,' I said firmly. I grabbed his hand and led him to the sofa. He sat down next to me.

'Is it because you think I showed Bobbi that stuff then?' His eyes, already swollen and puffy, filled with tears again. 'Because I honestly didn't. I wouldn't. I tried to stop –' He slapped a hand over his mouth and looked away.

I slipped a finger under his chin and steered his face back to mine. 'Archie, listen to me. I know you didn't show those videos to Bobbi. I absolutely believe you. But it's very important that you tell me where they came from. No one should show a child something like that. It was very wrong. You do know that, don't you? There's nothing for you to feel ashamed of.'

He looked at me thoughtfully, as if taking what I'd said on board. 'I didn't want to watch them,' he said in a small voice. 'I hate it all. The noises and the things they do. It makes me sick. I thought the kids would be amazed that I had something like that though. I thought they'd talk to me if I showed them.'

I nodded. I remembered what the tutor had said on the therapeutic parenting course about humans being social beings with a desperate need to belong. It was easy to understand that a child who felt so alone might use anything in his power to reach out to his peers. 'I get that, Arch. You wanted to make friends. It wasn't the right way to go about it, but I can understand why you did it.'

We were silent for a moment. 'Where did you get that stuff, Arch? The videos and the phone?'

'I can't tell you.'

'Why not?'

'Because of Mum.'

'What about your mum? You're afraid of getting her into trouble?'

He twisted his lips. 'Sort of.'

As I looked at him I suddenly thought of Taylor again; the ten-year-old girl who had lived in an environment of severe domestic abuse before coming to stay with me. Taylor had desperately wanted to confide in me but, fearful of what her father might do to her mother if she did, she kept her pain buried away. 'You're worried about what might happen to her if you tell me?'

He took a shaky breath and nodded. 'There are things that can be done to protect your mum, Archie, but only if we know what's really going on at home.'

He gave me a long searching look. Sensing that he was about to speak out, my pulse began to quicken. 'Jason gave me the phone,' he blurted out suddenly. 'He put the stuff on there and told me to watch it. I told him I didn't like it but he made me. I was sick and he thought it was funny.'

'That was very wrong of him,' I said, trying to keep an even expression. I wondered whether Tanya knew anything about it, but it would have been wrong of me to ask leading questions. Instead I said: 'That must have been very difficult for you.'

He nodded. 'It was horrible, but I didn't care as long as he left Bobbi out of it.'

My stomach tightened. 'And did he?' It was a leading question of sorts, but it came out before I could suppress it.

He nodded. 'I tried so hard to keep her away, especially when the others came. The trouble was she wouldn't go to bed. She used to creep down to see what the noise was.'

'Others? What others?'

'The people that came to see Mum and Jason.' It was a scenario I had heard about before; children settling themselves and their younger siblings in bed while drug- and alcohol-fuelled parties raged on below. Another mystery solved, I thought. That was why Archie had been so desperate to keep Bobbi awake during the day; so that he could get her safely tucked up in bed before Jason and his mates came round. My heart broke a little bit more.

'I hated it when they came round,' Archie continued. 'They wouldn't leave Mum alone, all rolling on top of her. It made me so sick.' His face contorted and he slammed his fist into the sofa cushion. 'I used to get so mad, especially if Bobbi wouldn't go to bed.'

I gave my head a shake. There was so much to take in. I couldn't quite process all that he was telling me. 'Wouldn't leave her alone? The people that came over, you mean?'

He nodded. 'Yeah, you know, kissing and all that other gross stuff.'

I tried to rein in my shock but it was an effort not to gape. 'You've been very brave, Arch. Really very brave.'

'What will happen now?' He looked at me anxiously, but there was a softness in his features that I'd never seen before. It was as if he'd been unburdened, the heavy weight of his secrets lifted.

'I'll have to tell Danny what you've said. And he'll do his best to look after your mum, I promise you. Whatever help she needs will be offered to her.' Having seen the efforts made by social workers to help women (and sometimes men) living with abusive partners, I spoke with full confidence. There was help out there, I knew that. What I wasn't at all certain about was whether Tanya would be willing to accept it.

* * *

It wasn't until Archie went to bed that the full horror of his disclosures hit me; the brutal, repulsive reality of them. It was hard to believe that the children had been treated so badly by people who should have known better, should have done better. After saying goodnight to Archie I came downstairs and lifted the telephone on impulse. It was after nine but I dialled Danny's office number anyway, just in case he was still there. He answered on the third ring, sounding tired. 'Tell me if you're about to go home,' I said. 'I can fire off an email instead.'

'Na,' he yawned. 'The missus isn't expecting me back till the early hours. Go for it.'

I told him that it was Jason who had given Archie the phone and also about Archie's efforts to keep Bobbi safe. I then told him about the 'people' coming to the house and what had sounded very much like group-sex sessions. Danny groaned. 'Fuck!' he said angrily. 'Those poor bloody kids.'

'And Archie's so worried about his mum. He thinks Jason will hurt her if he finds out that he's told us. I promised him that you'd offer Tanya all the help she needs.'

'That's a given, but you know as well as I do that she'll probably throw it back in my face.'

We were silent for a moment. 'So what happens now?'

I heard Danny take a breath. 'We'll involve the police and see if there's a case to answer. There's the phone as evidence, but to be honest it isn't much to go on. Jason could easily deny giving it to Archie. He'll probably claim it was stolen from him. As for the rest, that's down to the police. They won't ever be returning to Tanya's care, though, I can tell you that pretty much for certain.'

We were silent for a moment. 'Why would they do it, Danny? Why take the chance of letting Archie keep the phone when there was all that stuff on it, when they knew he was coming into care?'

He gave a mirthless laugh. 'The same reason people join chat rooms and arrange to meet young teenage girls, knowing there's a chance they'll be caught by paedo hunters. P'raps Jason thought he'd done enough, said enough, to scare Archie into keeping quiet. These people love holding power over others, Rosie. They get so much sick pleasure out of it that they don't care about the damage they're doing or the lives they're ruining. It's like that Shakespeare quote my old drill sergeant used to come out with – "Hell is empty, and all the devils are here!" – and you know what, Rosie? I think it's just as fitting to the world of social services as it was on the battlefield.'

Chapter Twenty-Eight

Expert at burying the unpalatable, Archie seemed to put the idea of moving on out of his mind over the next few days. He was still as polite as ever and as keen on keeping everything shipshape, but his simmering anger had subsided, leaving a quietly thoughtful boy behind.

Armed with more information about what had gone on at home, I hoped that Danny and his team would decide to leave the siblings with me until a final decision had been made on their case, so that there was some distance between his disclosure and yet another move.

I hadn't heard back from Danny and I told myself that that was good news, but I also knew that foster carers were often the last to find out when plans were being made. I had heard through the grapevine that social workers had turned up at a foster carer's house without warning and removed the young child in her care after they discovered that she had arranged a baptism for the forthcoming week-end. Alarmed by the possibility of the child being baptised without prior consent of social workers or birth family, the local authority had swooped before the ceremony could be carried out.

On Sunday 9 March, after a relatively peaceful morning at home, Emily offered to take Archie, Bobbi and Megan to the park to give me a chance to catch up on some house-work. With Jamie quarantined in his room after a stomach upset and Mungo chasing birds in the garden, I decided to make the most of the peace by making myself a cheeky cup of tea and logging onto one of the news sites before making a start on the chores.

My plan was scuppered by a knock at the door about two minutes after Emily and the children left. 'What have you forgotten now?' I called out as I walked up the hall. Emily was one of those people who rarely left the house without returning for some forgotten item. I pulled open the door, stunned to see Jimmy standing on the doorstep. He looked tired and sweaty, and his shoelaces were undone. I didn't know what to do. For a second I just stood there staring at him.

'Rosie, sorry to drop this on you, but I have to see the kids.'

'They're not here, Jimmy. And anyway, I can't let you see them without Danny's agreement.' I had no idea if the investigation into Tanya's allegations had progressed, or whether Archie's disclosure had helped to expose them as unfounded, but I knew that granting him access to the chil-dren wasn't something I was authorised to do.

He looked alarmed. 'They've not been moved, have they?'

'No, they're out with their social worker,' I lied, begin-ning to close the door. I didn't want him driving around looking for them. 'Sorry, Jimmy.'

'Wait!' He lifted his hand, pressing his palm against the door. 'Please, Rosie, can I talk to you?' He took a step back and I opened the door wider. 'I don't mean to cause any trouble, love. I just need to know how they are. Please.'

I looked at him for a second and then grabbed my keys from a hook on the wall. I wasn't comfortable letting him into the house, especially as the children might return at any minute, so I unlocked my car and invited him to join me. 'I've only got a few minutes,' I said, as he climbed into the passenger seat next to me.

He rubbed his hands over his unshaven jaw and turned, with difficulty in the cramped space, towards me. 'Thanks, Rosie. I really appreciate it, God knows I do.'

I nodded. There were deep circles around his eyes and his skin was flaky. He looked like he hadn't slept for a week. 'They're doing okay, Jimmy,' I said, softening. 'They're missing you of course, but they're coping.'

He let out a groan. 'After all they've been through, now this. I was so relieved when I heard they'd been taken into care. How bloody awful is that? To know that your kids are better off with strangers than with their own mother.'

I didn't say anything. I just let him talk. 'She weren't cut out for motherhood; I knew that the second she gave birth to Archie. It was me what changed his nappies and did the bottles. She just weren't interested.' In full flow, he didn't wait for an answer. 'I didn't mind though. I loved looking after him, but then after Bobbi came along she threw me out. I knew it would all go downhill after that but there weren't nothing I could do. She moved some fella in. Not Jason, some other bell-end, and poor Bobbi got ignored. I tried to see them as much as I could, but when Jason came on the scene he stopped her letting me. I told the social something weren't right, but they never bloody listened to me.

'When they finally took them off her I thought, this is it, I'm in with a chance of keeping them, and then this happens. It's so fucking frustrating!' He slammed his hand down on the dashboard. Alarmed, I reached for the door handle and made to get out. 'God, sorry, love. I'm so sorry. I don't want to frighten you.' Emotional, he covered his face with his hands. I closed the car door softly.

'It's really tough, Jimmy. I know they mean a lot to you.'

'They're the world to me,' he said, dropping his hands to his lap. 'Honest to God, I love the bones of them. I've left her, you know. Tracy. If she doesn't want my kids, there's no future for us.'

'Really?' I looked at him. 'That's wonderful, Jimmy! I mean, not wonderful that you've split up, but for the children, I mean. They'll be overjoyed.'

'It was all for nothing if I can't have them. I'm under investigation after what Tanya and that bloke,' he said, spitting the word out as if it was a nasty taste, 'that cave dweller, after all the fucking awful things they said.' He looked at me. 'Did you know they've accused me of being a nonce? As if I'd hurt my own fucking kids.'

I sat and listened to him in silence. It was clear from the way he was talking that he had absolutely no idea what Archie had told me about life at home. I dreaded to think what Jimmy might do when he found out. 'That bloke, Jason, he could start a fight in an empty room, so he could. I never trusted him from the moment I set eyes on him. A bottom feeder, that's what he is. D'you know what it's like to have someone move in with your little girl when you wouldn't trust him to take care of a dog?' His jaw hardened. 'I tell you what, though. If I find out that bastard's hurt my kids I'll tear him limb from fucking limb.'

I didn't doubt it for a second. 'I understand how you feel, Jimmy, but I still can't let you see the children until we've spoken to Danny.'

He turned to me. My heart hammered in my chest. 'Fair enough. I know you're looking out for them. I'll call Danny first thing in the morning.'

Chapter Twenty-Nine

'I can't find my book, Rosie!' came Archie's anguished call from his bedroom. 'Where's my book?'

'Which one, love?' I called up the stairs. Bobbi, who hadn't left my side since she had woken that morning, wrapped her arms around my middle and tried to hoist me single-handedly back to the dining table, where we'd spent the best part of an hour gluing material onto loo rolls and transforming them into dolls.

'You know,' he said with the exasperated tone he used when he was trying hard to hold himself together. 'The one Emily gave me yesterday. *Harry Potter and the Goblet of Fire.*'

It was almost lunchtime on the last Saturday in March and I had already packed up all of Archie and Bobbi's clothes, leaving Archie to round up all the other bits and bobs they'd amassed over the last twelve or so weeks, as well as the farewell presents we had bought for them – a mobile vet clinic for Bobbi and, to his teary delight, Dumbledore's wand for Archie. Danny, who had not long left after making a farewell visit, had brought gifts of his own. Touchingly, he'd even thought of Megan and brought her a set of colouring pens.

'Just a minute, Bobbi, love,' I said, holding onto the newel post for balance. Up the stairs I shouted: 'It's down here on the coffee table. You left it there last night.' We had played an extra-long session of Rummy yesterday evening, though every so often, when remembering that it was to be our last card playing session together, Archie had grown tearful. Too upset to go up to bed after our final game, I had agreed that he could stay downstairs with Emily, Jamie and me, to read his book.

He ran straight upstairs to fetch his duvet, but there was still no sign of him ten minutes later. I found him sitting on the floor beneath the window in his room, weeping. I squatted beside him and clutched his hand. He had fallen asleep on the sofa downstairs not long after that, exhausted by the emotional upheaval of his forthcoming move.

'Okay,' came a wobbly reply.

'That's not fair!' Bobbi squawked when we walked over to the dining table. Megan had been productive in our absence; a great pile of feathers, fluffy balls, glue sticks and glitter in front of her. The rest of the table was bare.

'Meggie,' I said warningly, taking the chair opposite hers. She pouted and conceded an almost-empty pot of glitter. Bobbi, unsure how to feel over the last few days, climbed onto my lap and began to cry. She hadn't reacted immediately when I had broken the news a week ago that they were leaving us, but since then she had taken to shadowing me through each day and calling out again at night. 'More than that, Meggie, please.'

A few seconds later she swept roughly half the booty back to our side of the table, frowning and grumbling ungraciously under her breath. She wasn't best pleased about losing her playmates, but I also suspected that the transition was reminding her of her own shaky past.

When several 'dollies' were 'dressed', I cut some ribbon to use as hair. Megan grabbed the first strip and reached for a glue stick. A struggle ensued, Megan reluctant to relinquish her grip and Bobbi 'absolutely needing it right this minute NOW!'. I scrabbled around and found another stick, but neither of them wanted it, despite it being identical to the one they were fighting over.

I tried to lighten the mood, but I felt sad myself. It pressed on me as I umpired their battle; the thought of all the upheaval Archie and Bobbi had been through in their short lives, the missing years of childhood, the trauma and loss. I could only hope that this coming move would be their last until they came of age, and hopefully even beyond, through the uncertain years of early adulthood and, finally, independence.

Archie came down in the middle of another power struggle, this one over a pot of purple glitter and an under-inflated red balloon. Red-nosed and silent, he sat on the dining chair next to mine, replacing the lids on the pens and generally restoring order to proceedings.

When the doorbell rang, my heart fluttered. Mungo skidded ahead of me into the hall, his tail wagging frantically. He leapt in circles around my legs as I opened the door, and when Jimmy walked into the hall he jumped between us, yapping at the air.

'Jimmy, what happened?' I exclaimed. There were purple bruises across his neck and chin, and one of his eyes was swollen, with a cut across the lid.

At that moment Bobbi hared up the hall. 'Daddy!'

Darling!' he cried, sweeping her up and cuddling her close. After a moment she leaned back and examined his face, then prodded the cut above his eye. 'Why you got blood, Daddy?'

He winced and gently pulled her hand away. 'T'was a crocodile,' he said, snapping his teeth close to her nose and making her giggle. I gave him a long steady look. I might have assumed that, being a doorman, he'd had a run-in with a difficult client, but something about the way he raised his eyebrows at me said different. I suddenly pictured a shocked Jason opening his front door to find Jimmy on his doorstep. I hate violence of any kind, but it was difficult to summon any regret over the meting out of this particular rough justice.

Despite the cuts and bruises, Jimmy was clean-shaven and bright-eyed, a different man to the defeated one who had turned up unannounced on that day back in early March. Since then he had dedicated every waking moment to finding a home for himself and the children and, after getting the all-clear from Danny, had finally paid the deposit on a three-bedroom flat, close to Millfield Primary. Their regular attendance, extra support in the form of a TA especially for Bobbi and the SENCO's interventions were beginning to pay dividends, the children finally making friends and even bringing classmates back for tea in the last couple of weeks. Staying at the same school gave them the opportunity to build on the social progress they'd made and, still adjusting to the loss of their mother from their lives, it was one less upheaval for them to cope with.

At Jimmy's invitation, I had taken Archie and Bobbi for a tour of their new home. They had charged delightedly through the empty, echoey rooms while Jimmy explained his predicament – Tracy had changed the locks on the house they'd shared, and was refusing to even allow him access to retrieve his personal belongings. As soon as the court approved the move, the children were supposed to move in with Jimmy, but there wasn't a stick of furniture in the place. The children and I met up with Naomi that afternoon, and Archie told her all about it.

'What, nothing? Absolutely nothing?'

I shook my head. 'I've been collecting a few things here and there – some utensils, plates and saucepans – so at least they can eat,' I told her with a rueful smile, 'though they'll have to sit on the floor to do it.' In reality, I suspected that Danny wouldn't release the children to Jimmy's care until the flat was habitable, but I held off voicing my doubts to the children until I heard otherwise.

Naomi spent the next forty-eight hours mobilising the congregation at the Sally Army. Within a few days they had collected enough household goods to furnish the entire flat – beds for Bobbi and Archie and a double for Jimmy, a sofa and two armchairs, a fridge, and even a small television.

Their willingness to help put me in mind of an article I had read about innate goodness and the longing most people have to express the loving kindness that is so often crowded out by modern life. It was reassuring to know that society had a safety net, and that humanity won out in the end.

Broken

'Have you remembered your rucksack, honey?' I asked Archie, who was hovering beside me in the hall. The suitcases stood upright between us, along with two large holdalls and a colourful plastic box full of books.

He nodded and pointed to the gap between the suitcases. 'It's there,' he said quietly. His chest was puffed out with emotion, his arms glued to his sides in that buttoned-up way of his. I gave his hand a reassuring squeeze.

'Archie,' Jimmy said, noticing him for the first time. 'This is it, son,' he said, opening his arms. 'A new start.'

I watched father and son hugging each other, swallowing down the lump in my throat. 'Rosie,' Jimmy said when they pulled apart. He gave my hand a powerful shake. 'I can't thank you enough, darling.'

'Pleased to help,' I said, trying hard not to cry myself. I hated goodbyes, especially when I knew it was more than likely that we would never see each other again.

'We'll stay in touch,' Jimmy promised, before carrying the children's belongings to his car.

Emily and Jamie, home for the day, joined us on the drive. We all took turns to hug each other, Jimmy watching and, I have to say, looking a bit teary-eyed himself. Instead of a hug, Jamie gave Archie a playful shove in the chest and clapped him on the back, a grinning Archie meeting his hand in a high five. When it came to Megan and Bobbi's turn, they almost fell over sideways, so enthusiastic was their embrace. We all laughed, and then Jimmy lifted Bobbi onto his shoulders. 'Right, come on then.'

'Bye bye, Rosie. Rosie, bye!' Bobbi called out as they crossed the drive. I gave Archie's shoulder one last squeeze and then he followed his father and sister across the road.

He paused before getting into the car, then turned and waved. I smiled and waved back, hoping with all my heart that the family would find happiness together. What Archie and Bobbi had seen could never be undone, but I hoped that their father's love would restore their faith in the world, redressing the balance and showing them that many more good things happen in life than bad.

Emily smiled and sniffed and dabbed her eyes on her sleeve. Jamie picked Megan up and the three of them walked back into the house, Mungo following closely at their heels. I stood on the drive for a few moments longer, waiting until Jimmy's car had disappeared around the corner of the road.

'Mummy?' came Megan's voice from the hall. 'Mummy, come and play!' I smiled to myself and turned back to the house.

Epilogue

Just over a week after the children had moved on, Naomi called and asked us to join her at the beach for the day.

'Guess who turned up at church yesterday,' she said, as we stretched our picnic blankets over the sand. It was Monday 6 April, and, unusually for a bank holiday, there wasn't a drop of rain in sight.

'Who?'

'Jimmy and the children,' she said with a smile. She slipped off her shoes and we sat together on the blanket. At the shore, Megan, Toby and Skye were holding hands and jumping barefoot over the surf. A few feet away, looking a little lost, stood Aiden.

'Really?' My heart lifted at the news. Danny had called a few days earlier after paying a visit to Jimmy, and told me that all seemed well, but most people worked hard to put on a show if they were within fifty yards of a social worker. The fact that Jimmy was up to socialising with the children spoke volumes about how they were really doing.

Naomi nodded. 'Archie and Bobbi brought Easter eggs for your three. Jimmy asked me to pass them on, but I left them at home in the fridge.'

Jimmy struck me as an unlikely churchgoer, but I think he and the children probably found comfort in the strong sense of belonging provided by the Sally Army's close-knit community. He became a regular visitor to Naomi's church and I still hear news of the family that way. Up to the time of writing, the three of them were doing amazingly well.

Helpful Reading

Inside I'm Hurting by Louise Bomber
The Explosive Child by Ross W. Greene
*Creating Loving Attachments: Parenting with PACE to
    Nurture Confidence and Security in the Troubled Child*
    by Kim S. Golding and Daniel A. Hughes
The Primal Wound by Nancy Verrier
From Fear to Love: Parenting Difficult Adopted Children
    by B. Bryan Post
*Bubble Wrapped Children: How Social Networking is
    Transforming the Face of 21st Century Adoption* by
    Helen Oakwater
Trying Differently Rather than Harder by Diane Malbin
The Boy Who Was Raised as a Dog by Bruce D. Perry
My Underpants Rule by Kate and Rod Power

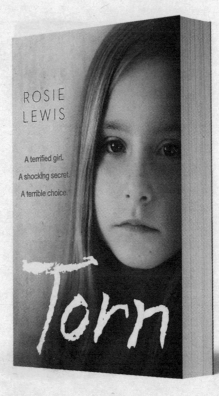

Rosie struggles when she agrees to take in
Taylor and her younger brother, Reece

She finds herself battling an unknown monster in
their past, as social media and the internet become a means
to control and manipulate the siblings while in her care.
And then a more sinister turn of events causes Rosie to dig
into their past, desperate to discover the truth before
her time with them is over and they must be
returned to their family.

TORN

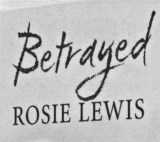

The struggle to escape a life defined
by family honour

With Rosie's support, thirteen-year-old Zadie gradually
begins to settle into her new surroundings. But loyalty
to her relatives and fear of bringing shame on her
family keeps preventing Zadie from confessing
the horrifying truth about her past. Will Rosie be
able to persuade her to open up in time?

BETRAYED

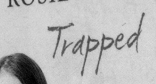

The terrifying true story of a secret world of abuse

Phoebe, an autistic nine-year-old girl, is taken into care when a chance comment to one of her teachers alerts the authorities. After several shocking incidents of self-harming and threats to kill, experienced foster carer Rosie Lewis begins to suspect that there is much more to Phoebe's horrific past than she could ever have imagined.

TRAPPED

AVAILABLE AS E-BOOK ONLY

ROSIE LEWIS
Helpless
A true story

An abandoned baby girl

Rosie is called to look after a new baby, born to an addict mother on a freezing-cold December night, and to care for her until she can meet her forever family.

HELPLESS

ROSIE LEWIS
A Small Boy's Cry
A true story

Toddler Charlie is found after falling from a second-floor window

Once he is taken into care, Rosie helps terrified Charlie open up and uncovers his traumatic past.

A SMALL BOY'S CRY

ROSIE LEWIS

Two More Sleeps

A true short story

Found beneath a bench, seemingly alone

Angell comes into the home and heart of foster carer Rosie Lewis. Will Angell be destined to spend the rest of her childhood in care or will her mother return for her?

TWO MORE SLEEPS

ROSIE LEWIS

Unexpected

A True Short Story

Ellen is so shocked by the sudden birth of her baby girl that she abandons the newborn in hospital

Rosie struggles to understand how anyone can treat a baby in this way, but with time she begins to see the dark secret Ellen is hiding.

UNEXPECTED

Moving Memoirs

Stories of hope, courage and the power of love…

If you loved this book, then you will love our Moving Memoirs eNewsletter

Sign up to…

- Be the first to hear about new books

- Get sneak previews from your favourite authors

- Read exclusive interviews

- Be entered into our monthly prize draw to win one of our latest releases before it's even hit the shops!

Sign up at

www.moving-memoirs.com